STOCKPORT

KT-231-238

THE STUDENT
VEGETARIAN
COOKBOOK

150 QUICK AND EASY VEGETARIAN RECIPES TO SUIT ALL BUDGETS

Beverly LeBlanc

Virgin BOOKS

Heaton Moor

123087

To PMOB, my collaborator.

The nutritional information in this book
is for reference only. The recipes and any
suggestions are to be used at the reader's
sole discretion and risk. Always consult
a doctor if you are in any doubt about
nutritional or medical conditions.

ACKNOWLEDGEMENTS
Again, I am indebted to my husband, Philip
Back, who shopped, tested and tasted with
good spirit, as well as Sally-Anne Hinchcliffe,
Henry Johnston, Norma MacMillan, Ricki Ostrov
and Susanna Tee, all of whom helped in one way
or another. I would also like to thank Judy
Chilcote, my agent, and Carolyn Thorne at Virgin
Books for commissioning this book.

First published in Great Britain in 2005 by
Virgin Books Ltd
Thames Wharf Studios
Rainville Road
London
W6 9HA

Copyright © Beverly LeBlanc 2005

The right of Beverly LeBlanc to be identified as the Author
of this Work has been asserted by her in accordance with
the Copyright, Designs and Patents Act, 1988.

This book is sold subject to the condition that it shall
not, by way of trade or otherwise, be lent, resold, hired
out or otherwise circulated without the publisher's prior
written consent in any form of binding or cover other
than that in which it is published and without a similar
condition including this condition being imposed on
the subsequent purchaser.

A catalogue record for this book is available from the
British Library.

ISBN 0 7535 1051 0

Designed by Smith & Gilmour
Printed and bound in Spain

STOCKPORT COLLEGE
LEAF   CENTRE
34 6006209   9/8/06
LRS 1101
4WK   641.563
123087   LEB

CONTENTS

INTRODUCTION

It's great to be a student and it's great to be a vegetarian. But getting the combination right can be tricky, especially when you are new to shopping and cooking for yourself. It's well worth the effort though.

Beer, beans and brown rice might technically be a vegetarian diet, but it isn't a healthy option. In fact, when you team it with more booze, fags and late nights, it's downright bad for you. If you were a beansprout you really would be wilting. Ready-meals and take-aways are the easiest options for meat-free mealtimes, but they are a fast way to go broke. Your money will run out before the end of term.

But, even if you've never peeled a potato, let alone cooked a meal, don't panic. If you can read, you can cook. This book won't turn you into a TV chef, but it will teach you how to feed yourself without a lot of hassle or expense. And it might make you particularly popular with your friends and flatmates. Variety is the spice of life, and this book contains enough easy recipes and ideas to keep you going all year.

When you have chosen a vegetarian lifestyle, it is important that your diet contains a wide combination of vegetables, fruit, grains, pulses and dairy products throughout the day everyday, and hopefully this book will give you enough inspiration to ensure that cooking and mealtimes are always enjoyable. One of the plus points of a meat-free diet is that you can draw on cuisines from around the world. You won't be stuck with a steady diet of beans on toast or lentil burgers. In fact, you'll be spoilt for choice.

And, of course, when you cook for yourself, rather than relying on 'ping' cuisine, you can use fresh, natural ingredients. You'll taste the difference.

Cooking can also boost your social life. There is more than a grain of truth in the belief that the way to someone's heart is through his (or her) stomach!

The collection of international recipes in this book will feed you 24/7. You'll find plenty of ideas for quick breakfasts, snacks, meals, midnight munchies and revision refuels. Not to mention hangover busters, soothing smoothies and tantalising teas for when you need to give yourself a hug. When it's time to stop studying and start partying, there are plenty of cocktail recipes to get the party started, too. If making time to cook each day is difficult, the recipes in 'Weekend Cooking' will help you stock the fridge so you have a supply of food that can be reheated throughout the week.

You'll soon be a confident vegetarian cook. And – who knows? – cooking might become a hobby for life. So get into the kitchen and get cooking.

I hope you enjoy trying these recipes as much as I have enjoyed compiling and testing them.

BEING A VEGETARIAN

Vegetarians are as diverse as the selection of fruit and vegetables you'll find at the greengrocer's or the supermarket. The most basic definition of a vegetarian is someone who doesn't eat meat, poultry, game, fish, shellfish or crustacea, or slaughter by-products, such as gelatine or animal fats. Instead, vegetarians choose to live on a diet of grains, pulses, nuts, seeds, vegetables and fruits, with or without the inclusion of dairy products and eggs.

Some vegetarians make this choice for ethical and moral reasons, others for religious reasons and many simply because of the appeal of eating lots of flavourful fruit and vegetables. But whatever the reasons, the popularity of vegetarianism is increasing around the world.

These are the most common types of vegetarian diets:
▸ **Lacto-ovo-vegetarian:** This type of vegetarian includes dairy products and eggs in their diet. This is the most common type of vegetarian and this book caters specifically for those of you who have chosen this diet, although many recipes are also suitable for other vegetarians.
▸ **Lacto-vegetarian:** Eats dairy products, but no eggs. If this is your choice you will still find many suitable recipes in this book.
▸ **Vegan:** This is a loosely defined term that usually means a vegetarian who doesn't include any dairy products or eggs in their diet. This book also includes many recipes suitable for this diet and you will find those highlighted with an easy-to-spot symbol at the top of each recipe. Look also for Vegan Notes at the bottom of many recipes, which make simple suggestions for adapting the recipe.
▸ **Fruitarian:** These vegetarians eat mostly raw fruit, grains and nuts in the belief that only plant foods that can be harvested without killing a plant should be eaten.
▸ **Macrobiotic:** A diet that is followed for spiritual and philosophical reasons, which aims to maintain a balance between foods seen as ying (positive) and yang (negative).
▸ **Demi-veg:** A popular term for a diet that includes fish, but no meat.

IS BEING GREEN HEALTHY?

The answer has to be overwhelmingly yes. Just cutting meat from your diet, however, doesn't automatically mean you eat a healthy diet, but with very little effort there are big health benefits to be gained from a vegetarian diet. Health experts agree that eating at least five portions of fruit and veg a day is the most basic step towards good health – and what could be easier on a vegetarian diet?

GOING GREEN

When you decide to stop eating meat and seafood and become a vegetarian, you'll be joining a growing global tradition. If you're new to vegetarianism it might be a comforting thought to realise that the everyday green diet includes so many familiar favourite dishes. Beans on toast, spaghetti with tomato sauce, scrambled eggs, toasted cheese sandwiches and take-away favourites such as aloo gobi, for example, are all vegetarian dishes.

Top Tips for Going Green:
▶ Cook for yourself and you'll clear the first hurdle. It's always difficult for family cooks to prepare balanced vegetarian meals if only one person is a veggie. That's no longer a problem when you're in charge of meal planning.
▶ Make a list of your favourite food and see how many vegetarian dishes you've included. Eat one of these every day – you'll be on your way.
▶ Go gradual. It's difficult to change a lifetime's worth of eating habits in one hit, so take your time. Start by cutting out red meat for a couple of weeks, then cut out poultry and finally fish and shellfish.
▶ Expand your horizons – try the vegetarian options the next time you order Chinese or Indian.
▶ Cook something new two or three times a week. Go through this book and highlight recipes you've never had before. They might become firm favourites.

EAT WELL TO LIVE WELL

There is more to being a vegetarian than just eating tofu, alfalfa, brown rice and peanut butter sandwiches.

Just as the vegetables you eat need tending before they land on your plate, so your body needs careful attention, too. And that means eating a varied diet every day so you get plenty of vitamins, minerals and other nutrients, such as protein, carbohydrates, fat and fibre. When you eat a varied diet you'll be on top form all term.

Eating well isn't complicated and it isn't time consuming. You don't need a Masters degree in nutrition to look after yourself, but a little basic information will make healthy eating, well, a piece of carrot cake.

When you're old enough to legally drink, you're old enough to take responsibility for your eating habits.

HEALTHY EATING ISN'T A HARD NUT TO CRACK – TOP TIPS IN A NUTSHELL

▸ Eat wholegrain starchy foods, such as bread, cereal, rice and potatoes.
▸ Eat at least 5 portions of fruit and veg every day. These can be fresh, canned, dried or frozen.
▸ Eat moderate amounts of protein, including vegetarian soya and pulse alternatives, and low-fat dairy products. Commercial textured vegetable protein (TVP) is another option.
▸ Eat foods that are low in fat and contain little sugar. This probably means cutting back on sweets, savoury snacks and pastries.
▸ Eat fresh foods – after several weeks of feasting on fresh fruits and vegetables you'll appreciate how much better they taste.

VARIETY IS THE KEY FOR VEGGIES

Only by eating a wide variety of foods every day will you be certain of consuming the right combination of nutrients that keep you healthy. It isn't difficult. But until it becomes second nature, it can help to plan your week's eating in advance. Advance planning will also streamline your shopping trips (page 22).

The Vegetarian Society of Great Britain recommends the following food choices for daily diets:

- 4–5 servings of fruit and veg
- 3–4 servings of cereals/grains or potatoes
- 2–3 servings of pulses, nuts and seeds
- 2 servings of milk, cheese, eggs or soya products
- A small amount of vegetable oil and margarine or butter
- Some yeast extract, such as Marmite, fortified with vitamin B12

Does that look overwhelming? It isn't! It might look like you'll do nothing but eat from the time you get up until you go to bed again, but that isn't the case. Beans on toast, a peanut butter sandwich on wholemeal bread, a vegetable and noodle stir-fry, pasta with a vegetable sauce and a jacket potato with beans and cheese are all familiar everyday favourites that give you one or two servings from at least two food groups.

BE GREEN THE COLOURFUL WAY – EAT A RAINBOW

One way to ensure a wide mix of foods at mealtimes is to arrange the colours of the rainbow on your plate. If you regularly eat a selection of red, green, yellow and orange fruit and vegetables you'll be on your way to being a healthy vegetarian. There will be a pot of good healthy life at the end of the rainbow.

WHAT YOU NEED TO KNOW

All the food you eat will contain a combination of proteins, carbohydrates and fats. Here's the lowdown on what you need to know to keep yourself healthy.

POSITIVE PROTEINS

Proteins are made up of amino acids, which are called the body's building blocks. There are two types of protein: 'complete' and 'incomplete'. Animal products, such as meat, chicken and fish, are complete proteins and contain all the amino acids the human body needs to function efficiently. The protein in non-animal foods, such as vegetables, fruit, grains, nuts and seeds, however, is called incomplete because none of them contain *all* essential amino acids. (The exception is soya.) When you eat a wide variety of non-meat foods throughout the day, however, you will get the benefits. Golden Lentils & Rice (page 134), for example, is an Indian dish that combines the amino acids found in rice with the complementary amino acids provided by lentils, so in that single dish your body is getting all the essential amino acids it needs.

You don't need a lot of protein – it should only make up about 15 per cent of your daily calorie intake – but without it you won't feel good and you won't look good.

Cheese and other dairy products are complete proteins, but they are also high in saturated fat, which is linked to many health problems, such as heart disease. Just eating cheese or full-fat yoghurt as a replacement for meat will outweigh the benefits of a balanced vegetarian diet – remember, it's called 'vegetarianism' not 'cheeseism'. A cheese omelette for breakfast, a cheese sandwich for lunch and baked macaroni and cheese for supper won't be good for you.

GOOD SOURCES:
- Soya products such as tofu, soya milk and commercial textured vegetable protein (TVP)
- Pulses – beans, peas and lentils
- Whole grains and cereals
- Nuts and seeds
- Dairy products – butter, cheese and cow's milk
- Free-range eggs

GET YOUR CARBS

Carbohydrates have had bad press over the past couple of years with the popularity of the low-carb Atkins Diet. But everyone needs carbs. These are the nutrients that give you energy. You can't party without carbohydrates.

Carbohydrates can be 'simple' or 'complex', and it is the complex carbohydrates that form the backbone of a healthy diet, be it vegetarian or otherwise.

Simple carbohydrates are easily digested sugars – you know, the quick boost from a chocolate bar – but they have very little going for them nutritionally. Complex carbohydrates, on the other hand, are what you want. You get these from fruits, vegetables and whole grains, which provide vitamins and minerals along with starch. Complex carbohydrates are digested more slowly than simple ones. This means that when you eat a jacket potato with beans you'll have a more even level of energy than if you snack on a biscuit. The chocolate choice will give you a quick fix, but you'll come crashing down.

Another benefit of a diet rich in complex carbohydrates is that it contains fibre, which keeps your digestive tract functioning.

GOOD SOURCES:
- Virtually all fruit and veg, especially root vegetables, potatoes and bananas
- Pulses – beans, peas and lentils
- Whole grains, cereals and rice
- Pasta

FATS

You'd have to be oblivious to the world around you not to have heard that fatty food is bad for you. You do, however, need small amounts of fat every day, so it's worth appreciating that there are both 'good' and 'bad' fats, depending on how 'saturated' they are.

- **Saturated fats** come from animal products and are called 'the bad' fat. This is because they are linked to serious health problems such as heart disease. Saturated fats are solid at room temperature, which should tell you instantly that butter should only be used occasionally.
- **Polyunsaturated fats**, which are soft or liquid at room temperature, are considered less harmful from a health perspective, but should still not be consumed in excess. They are linked with the reduction of heart disease and some types of cancer. Vegetable oils, such as sunflower and rapeseed, and nut oils, such as walnut, as well as sesame oil, are all polyunsaturated. You want to use these for everyday cooking and salad dressings.

Polyunsaturated fats can be divided into two types: omega-3 fatty acids and omega-6 fatty acids. Ideally you want to consume more of the omega-3 fatty acids, which come from rapeseed and soya oils and some spreads.
- **Trans fats** start out as polyunsaturated, but their chemical components change during processing, so they literally transform and become more like saturated fats. Many margarines contain trans fat.
- **Monounsaturated fats** are considered the least harmful but, again, they should still only be consumed in moderation. These are contained in avocados, olives and olive oils, and many nuts. One of the reasons the so-called Mediterranean Diet is considered so healthy is because it features olive oil as the fat of choice for cooking.

One of the big bonuses of a vegetarian diet, however, is that most fruit and veg are very low in saturated fat. And even the fatty plant foods, such as avocados, olives, nuts and seeds, contain the 'good' fats. That doesn't mean it is OK for you to go overboard and eat these with every meal. Both good and bad fats are high in calories. If you overindulge you'll soon see the result on the scales even if you only eat 'good' fats.

And don't forget, full-fat dairy products such as butter, cheese, cream and yoghurt contain saturated fats, so you want to keep these to a minimum. Ice cream is fine for an occasional treat, but you shouldn't eat it every day.

One of the main sources of fats in vegetarian diets is cooking oil. The recipes in this book recommend using olive, sunflower, canola and occasionally groundnut oils for cooking. These vegetable oils are monounsaturated or polyunsaturated.

But even if you make the effort to cook with monounsaturated or polyunsaturated fats, you can still end up eating large amounts of saturated fat if you rely on processed foods and dairy products. That's one good reason for taking up cooking – as well as the pleasure it can give you, you have better control over your saturated-fat consumption. That might pay big dividends later in your life.

Most of the fat in your daily diet doesn't come from the actual ingredients. It gets added in the kitchen. A jacket potato, for example, comes out of the oven without any saturated fat, but if you smother it with butter and grated cheese you might as well have deep-fried chips. Instead, try spicy beans or mixed-vegetable ratatouille for the topping.

The reason fatty foods are so popular is because fat makes food taste good and feel good in the mouth. Use fat sparingly and compensate with lots of delicious flavours from herbs and spices. Let the flavours of the ingredients shine through.

GOOD SOURCES OF 'GOOD' FATS:

▸ Vegetable oils – rapeseed, groundnut, olive, sesame, sunflower
▸ Nuts and nut oils
▸ Some margarines – read the label to make sure they do not contain trans fats
▸ Olives
▸ Avocados

ESSENTIAL VITAMINS & MINERALS

You can't see them. You can't taste them. But vitamins and minerals are essential substances in food your body needs to function. Fortunately, fruits and vegetables are loaded with a range of these essential nutrients. It can't be overstated: eating a variety of foods ensures you get all you need.

Most vitamins come from your food, although some are manufactured by your body. Your body can store vitamins A, D, E, K and B12, but you need to get a good supply of all others from your diet.

Vitamins are either water-soluble (B-complex and C) or fat-soluble (A, D, E and K). Water-soluble vitamins are easily destroyed during food storage and the preparation and cooking processes; fat-soluble vitamins are less likely to be destroyed during the cooking processes. Preparing fruit and vegetables just before cooking helps preserve the vitamins. And when you incorporate the cooking liquid in your dish, such as when you make soups and vegetable stews, you conserve the water-soluble vitamins, rather than throwing them down the drain.

Minerals, inorganic substances, are necessary for your body to carry out many vital functions, from maintaining your nervous system and metabolic processes to strengthening your skeleton.

VITAL VITAMINS

Vitamin A: This is essential for normal growth and development, and good vision, especially night vision. It is also necessary for cell maintenance and immune functions.
GOOD SOURCES:
▶ Dairy products – butter, cheese, egg yolks, whole cow's milk, fortified margarine
▶ Dark leafy green vegetables, such as broccoli, sprouting broccoli and spinach
▶ Orange-coloured fruit – melons, mangoes, peppers, sweet potatoes, winter squash
▶ Dried apricots

Vitamin B1 (thiamine): Your body needs this vitamin to convert carbohydrates into energy, and to nourish your brain and nervous system.
GOOD SOURCES:
▶ Dairy products – butter, cow's milk, yoghurt
▶ Wholegrain bread, cereals and fortified breakfast cereals
▶ Leafy green vegetables
▶ Porridge
▶ Nuts

Vitamin B2 (riboflavin): This vitamin helps cells release energy from fat and protein, and keeps your immune system running smoothly. It is also essential for growth and healthy eyes and hair.

GOOD SOURCES:
- Dairy products – cheese, cow's milk, yoghurt
- Wholegrain breads and cereals, and fortified breakfast cereals
- Leafy green vegetables
- Marmite

Vitamin B3 (niacin): You need this vitamin to enable your body to release energy from food.

GOOD SOURCES:
- Eggs
- Cow's milk
- Jacket potatoes
- Nuts, including peanut butter
- Whole grains, including brown rice

Vitamin B5 (pantothenic acid): Small amounts of this vitamin aid many metabolic reactions, including energy production.

GOOD SOURCES:
- Egg yolks
- Nuts
- Pulses
- Whole grains

Vitamin B6 (pyridoxine): This vitamin helps your body use protein, keeps your immune system healthy and helps form red blood cells.

GOOD SOURCE:
- Fortified breakfast cereals

Vitamin B12 (cyanocobalamin): This is essential for overall growth and the formation of red blood cells. It also keeps the nervous system healthy.

GOOD SOURCES:
- Fortified dairy products, including milk, cheese and eggs
- Fortified breakfast cereals
- Marmite
- Seaweeds and alfalfa sprouts

Folate/folic acid: This vitamin aids the production of red blood cells and may protect against heart disease. It is especially important if you are planning to become pregnant.

GOOD SOURCES:
- Green vegetables – asparagus, Brussels sprouts, peas and especially leafy green vegetables, such as broccoli, cabbage and spinach

- Beans – fresh and dried
- Nuts, especially peanuts
- Fortified breakfast cereals
- Marmite
- Wholemeal bread
- Yeast extract

Vitamin C (ascorbic acid): When vitamin-C rich foods are eaten with iron-rich foods, vitamin C increases the iron absorption. It is also used in the structure of connective tissue and helps heal wounds and fractures. Vitamin C may also prevent some types of cancer.

GOOD SOURCES:
- All fresh fruit, especially citrus fruit and berries; kiwifruit is a powerhouse of vitamin C
- Leafy green vegetables
- Potatoes
- Red peppers
- Tomatoes

Vitamin D (cholecalciferol): This vitamin promotes the absorption of calcium from food for healthy bones and teeth. Most vitamin D is made by the body when the skin is exposed to sunlight.

GOOD SOURCES:
- Egg yolks
- Fortified margarines, powdered milk and breakfast cereals

Vitamin E: Vitamin E protects cell membranes and has a key anti-inflammatory action. Its antioxidant actions may prevent heart disease and certain types of cancer.

GOOD SOURCES:
- Avocados
- Vegetable oils
- Leafy green vegetables
- Nuts and peanut butter
- Wholegrain cereals and wheatgerm

Vitamin K: Essential for blood clotting and bone formation.

GOOD SOURCES:
- Carrots
- Leafy green vegetables, such as Brussels sprouts, Savoy cabbage and spinach
- Seaweeds

MIGHTY MINERALS

Calcium: This is essential for the development of strong bones and teeth, blood clotting and nerve formation.
GOOD SOURCES:
➤ Bread
➤ Dairy products – cheese, cow's milk and yoghurt; semi-skimmed and skimmed versions have a higher concentration of calcium
➤ Dried fruit, especially apricots
➤ Fortified soya milk and tofu
➤ Leafy green vegetables, especially watercress
➤ Wholemeal and white flours

Chloride: Your body's fluid balance is maintained by this mineral.
GOOD SOURCES:
➤ Salt, but too much is not a good thing

Copper: This mineral helps your body absorb iron from food, and assists with bone growth and the formation of connective tissue.
GOOD SOURCES:
➤ Leafy green vegetables

➤ **Iodine:** The thyroid gland needs iodine to function properly.
GOOD SOURCES:
➤ Cow's milk
➤ Seaweed

Iron: This is essential for the formation of red blood cells.
GOOD SOURCES:
➤ Dark leafy green vegetables – but, of course, Popeye already told you that
➤ Fortified bread and breakfast cereals
➤ Pulses and beans
➤ Wholemeal cereals and wheatgerm

Magnesium: This mineral is involved in energy production and calcium formation.
GOOD SOURCES:
➤ Dried fruit
➤ Nuts and seeds
➤ Spinach
➤ Soya products
➤ Wholegrain cereals and wheatgerm

Phosphorus: This is essential for the release of energy from foods and other chemical reactions in the body. It is also essential for the formation of cells, bones and teeth.

GOOD SOURCES:
▸ Cheese and cow's milk
▸ Eggs

Potassium: This mineral exists in all foods, except fats, oils and sugar. It regulates blood pressure and maintains fluid balance, and helps keep cells functioning properly.

GOOD SOURCES:
▸ Bananas
▸ Kiwifruit

Selenium: Selenium helps protect cells against damage from oxidation.

GOOD SOURCES:
▸ Brazil nuts
▸ Cheese and eggs
▸ Cereals

Sodium: As well as helping to regulate your body's fluid balance, sodium is essential for nerve and muscle functions, and it is involved in energy use. It is also involved in taste perception.

GOOD SOURCE:
▸ Table salt is the main source

Zinc: This is essential for normal growth, as well as reproduction; it keeps the immune system healthy and is involved in taste perception.

GOOD SOURCES:
▸ Cheese and eggs
▸ Nuts and seeds, especially peanuts
▸ Pulses, especially lentils
▸ Sunflower seeds
▸ Wholegrain cereals

THE ROUGH STUFF

Fibre isn't a nutrient but you need some in your diet. It is the naturally occurring, non-digestive substances found in all plant cell walls that keeps your digestive tract functioning efficiently.

There are two types of dietary fibre. Soluble fibre, which you get from eating oats, pulses, fruit and vegetables, can help reduce the risk of

Supplements

It might be tempting to think that if you pop a multi-vitamin and mineral pill every morning, all the nutritional bases are covered and you won't have to give healthy eating a second thought. Wrong! It is possible to get too much of a single vitamin and the result can be toxic. It is best to consult your GP before taking supplements. (Vegans, however, should consider taking a B12 supplement and including soya products fortified with B12 in their diet, because this vitamin, responsible for the formation of red blood cells and keeping the nervous system healthy, isn't available from any other food on a vegan diet. Again, consult your GP.)

heart disease by lowering blood cholesterol levels. It also helps to control blood sugar levels, so you don't feel bursting with energy one minute and dying for a nap half an hour later. Insoluble fibre, found in wholegrain cereals and fruit and vegetables, especially leafy green vegetables, adds bulk to food passing through the gut and helps prevent constipation and haemorrhoids. It may also reduce the risk of bowel cancer.

DRINK UP – WATER THAT IS!

Ever notice how much the wilting spider plant in the corner of your room perks up when you give it a good drink of water? Well, just as that plant needs water, so do you. Your body is about 70 per cent water and you can't live without it. You could survive a couple of weeks without food, but you won't last for more than a couple of days without the miracle liquid.

In addition to the liquid you get from food, you should drink about 2 litres of water a day. Fruit juices, milk and other liquids that don't include alcohol or caffeine can count towards the goal.

BE PRO-ANTIOXIDANTS

Antioxidants are the nutritional good guys of healthy eating. They are naturally occurring substances in food that counter the long-term ageing and debilitating effects of toxins from the environment, smoking and bad eating. Bright-orange sweet potatoes, leafy greens, citrus fruit and nuts are great sources, so they are easy to fit into your diet. An antioxidant-rich diet today is like depositing good health in a bank for your later years.

KITTING OUT YOUR KITCHEN

You could get by with a corkscrew and a can opener but there wouldn't be much variety or freshness in your mealtimes. If you're cooking for yourself for the first time, you're going to need some decent equipment. Decent doesn't mean expensive – try supermarkets instead of specialist kitchen shops. But you don't want the cheapest either. Cheap kitchen kit makes cooking difficult – eggs burn in thin frying pans. And cheap kitchen equipment is a false economy because it doesn't last and you will have to replace everything next year.

Getting the basic essentials will save you time; other fancy bits of equipment are more of a luxury and can be bought as your interest in cooking and your cash flow increase. Have a look at the lists below to see what you need to start off with. It's also worth talking to housemates so there aren't more toasters than students, but no kettle.

One great way to get your kit is to raid friends and relatives – doting aunties are always a good source of kitchen basics!

> **Cheap Shopping**
> Try car-boot sales, jumble sales and charity shops for good-quality, second-hand kitchen equipment at bargain prices. It's also worth sending out an emergency SOS to all relations and neighbours before you leave home.

THE BAREST ESSENTIALS

Don't leave home without:
- *Can opener:* Canned baked beans and other beans, pulses and tomatoes make one of these essential.
- *Chopping board.*
- *Colander and/or large sieve:* Essential for draining pasta and rinsing canned beans and pulses. Make life easy for yourself and get a freestanding colander with handles on both sides.
- *Corkscrew and bottle opener:* Well, it's obvious, isn't it!
- *Knives:* Knives are the workhorses of the kitchen. A cheap knife with a flimsy or dull blade can turn the simplest task, like chopping an onion, into a chore. Buy the best you can afford. There are many knives for specific purposes, but if you only get one, buy a 20–25cm cook's knife.

Other useful knives include a serrated bread knife, a small paring knife and a small serrated knife for slicing tomatoes and oranges. Never buy a knife without holding it to make sure it feels comfortable in your hand.

▸ **Steamer:** Absolutely essential for tender-crisp veggies. If someone is funding your shopping, or you are the house cook, go for a deluxe, multi-tiered model, complete with a heavy-based saucepan and lid. That way you can steam lots of veggies at once. Otherwise an inexpensive collapsible metal or Chinese bamboo steamer will do just fine. Make sure you get one that fits your wok or saucepan.

▸ **Wok:** Nothing beats a Chinese wok for fast cooking – and at a pinch it can double as a frying pan or saucepan (buy one with a lid). Buy the largest one you have storage space for. Look for a long handle on one side and a grip handle on the other side. Traditional round-bottom woks with a stand only work over a gas flame, but flat-bottomed woks intended for electric hobs are also sold. A good non-stick surface is worth paying for because you'll be able to use less oil in your cooking.

WHAT YOU REALLY SHOULDN'T LEAVE HOME WITHOUT

Add these to the list above and you should be able to make every recipe in the book.

▸ **Baking sheet(s).**

▸ **Blender:** If you're going to splash out on one extravagance, this is it. It's not essential (you can duplicate most of its tasks by hand) but it makes kitchen time easy. With a blender you can start the day with smoothies and make large batches of creamy soups. Save your pennies to buy a blender.

▸ **Bowls.**

▸ **Cake tin(s):** These come in a variety of shapes and sizes, and baking is one time when size does matter. If you can't resist the Chocolate Slices, you'll need a 30 x 20cm roulade tin, and for Orange Flapjacks you'll need a 20cm round sandwich tin.

▸ **Fish slice or palette knife:** To save your fingers when you turn hot food.

▸ **Flameproof casserole:** An all-in-one cooking pot that saves on washing-up. Flameproof casseroles can be used on the hob and under the grill, as well as in the oven; ovenproof casseroles can only be used in the oven. Make sure the lid fits tightly.

▸ **Frying pan:** You can get by with a wok, but a good frying pan makes many dishes easier to cook. Pay extra for a non-stick surface and you'll have to shop less frequently for cooking oil – and you might save centimetres on your waist. Do not, however, even consider a cheap frying pan. Cooking will become an unpleasant experience when everything burns on the bottom.

▸ **Glass jars:** Air-tight containers are necessary for storing flours, rice, dried beans and grains, and jars are an ideal, cheap solution. Save a jar that will fit on a fridge door shelf for making vinaigrette dressing.

▸ **Grater:** A traditional box grater works fine for grating carrots and cheese.

▸ **Hand-held electric mixer:** Not essential, but very useful if you like making desserts, such as cookies and cakes. Also helps make the smoothest, creamiest mashed potatoes.

▸ **Kitchen scales.**

▸ **Measuring spoons:** You'll add less cooking oil to your food if you measure it, rather than just sloshing it into the pan.

▸ **Oven gloves/mitts:** Buy good thick ones. You'll regret it if you don't.

▸ **Ovenproof dishes:** Get a selection and save on washing-up because these go straight from the oven to table so you don't dirty serving dishes.

▸ **Potato masher.**

▸ **Roasting tin:** Buy the best you can afford, with a thick base.

▸ **Saucepan(s):** These come in many sizes, so think about what you will be using them for before you buy. If you like pasta, buy the biggest pan you can afford. You can get through the year with just a wok, but two saucepans will make life in the kitchen easier.

▸ **Tea towels.**

▸ **Vegetable peeler:** An old-fashioned peeler with a swivel blade works best.

▸ **Wooden spoons:** Get several – these are really cheap.

. . . and, of course, don't forget the washing-up liquid and the dish cloths. Somebody has to do it!

OPTIONAL EXTRAS

▸ **Garlic press:** This is optional – if you don't have one, you can use the side of a knife to crush garlic cloves.

▸ **Measuring jug:** If you have a pint beer mug it holds 600 ml and you can get by estimating liquids, but if you want to make large pots of soup, invest in a large measuring jug.

▸ **Pestle and mortar:** Helps you savour the flavour of freshly ground spices.

TIME FOR THE SUPERMARKET SWEEP

If you are truly a kitchen virgin, cooking for the very first time, you're going to have to start with a trip to the supermarket. When there's no food in the fridge, there won't be any on your plate. And nothing is worse than coming home late with the appetite of a bear to find an empty fridge.

You can do grocery shopping on an ad-hoc basis, running to the shops every time you decide to cook, but you will save time and money with a few simple shopping strategies.

Grocery shopping is as much about finances as it is about what you put in your trolley. At the start of term work out with your flatmates how much you want to spend on groceries each week – be realistic so you have a chance of sticking to it. If you don't, you'll eat like a king at the start of term, but like a pauper by the end. (If this does happen, turn to Cooking When U R Broke on page 207.)

BARGAIN HUNTING

Find out where and when your local market takes place. It will be a good source of fruit and veg that might be cheaper than the supermarket. Mind you, the old trick of visiting the supermarket at 3.30pm on a Sunday and getting marked-down food is worth knowing. Just be sure to take note of the 'use by' date.

▸ Don't shop hungry: This is when you are most vulnerable to impulse shopping and blowing the budget.
▸ Look for own brands: Supermarket own brands can represent real value. Keep your eye open for '3 for 2' offers, but remember it is only a bargain if you need it and will eat it.
▸ Make a list: A list helps you get what you need and not a lot of non-essentials.
▸ Shop around: Spend some time at the beginning of term comparing prices on your weekly staples, such as pasta, beans and oils, so you'll know where to shop. And keep a list of these prices so you know a bargain when you see one.

STOCKING HEALTHY STORE CUPBOARDS

If you don't have a good variety of staple ingredients in the cupboard all your intentions of good eating will be down the drain in the first week of term. Think about the recipes you will cook frequently and tailor your personal shopping list from the ingredients below.

The Cans
Buy as many of these non-perishables as you can carry, and you'll only have to shop for fresh fruit and veg and dairy products once or twice a week. With a good supply of canned goods, you'll always be able to knock up a meal.
- Baked beans: A meal on toast.
- Sweetcorn kernels.
- Tomatoes: Lots of recipes include a can. Stock up.
- Pulses: Borlotti, butter, flageolet and kidney beans, along with chickpeas and lentils, are the inexpensive foundation of many vegetarian meals.

The Jars
- Curry pastes and powders: Pick the degree of heat that suits you.
- Herbs and spices: The list will grow the more you cook, but start with salt and pepper, dried mixed herbs, dried thyme and bay leaves.
- Honey: Spread on toast for a quick breakfast.
- Oriental sauces: Keep jars of black bean and hoi sin sauce, Chinese rice wine and rice vinegar to add flavour to quick stir-fries.
- Pesto sauce: Toss with hot pasta or use in dips. Or make your own (page 117).
- Soy sauce: A condiment that adds a salty, slightly tart flavour to Oriental dishes; use sparingly. Dark soy is less salty than light; mushroom soy has extra depth of flavour. Sweet soy sauce is thick and used in stir-fries.
- Tahini paste: Sesame seed paste, an essential ingredient for making hummus (page 175).
- Vegetable and nut oils: Stock up on sunflower, rapeseed and olive oils for everyday cooking and groundnut oil for Indian dishes. Save extra-virgin olive oil for salads. Sesame oil is added to stir-fries, and walnut oil is good in vinaigrette dressing (page 172).
- Vinegars: Red- and white-wine vinegars are inexpensive and ideal for everyday use, but a jar of good balsamic vinegar is useful, too.

Too Cheap To Be Good
Do not buy oil simply labelled as 'blended vegetable oil', even if it looks like a bargain. It will contain palm oil, which is high in saturated fats, and other hydrogenated oils.

The Packets

Once you open bags of flours, rice and grains, transfer the contents to air-tight containers to prevent weevils forming. Wholemeal grains and flours and nuts and seeds have high oil contents that can become rancid, so don't forget about them at the back of the cupboard. Store in a cool, dark cupboard.

▸ Instant couscous.

▸ Dried fruit: Extend the shelf life by storing in a glass jar in the fridge.

▸ Flour: Choose wholemeal or white plain flour, as you like. Self-raising flour is useful if you do lots of baking. Flour is rancid when it tastes bitter.

▸ Grains: Stock up on pot barley, bulgar wheat, instant polenta and porridge oats. Plus whatever you like to add to breakfast cereals.

▸ Nuts and seeds: Stock up on a variety to use in cooking, sprinkle over salads and occasional snacks. Sesame seeds are popular in Oriental dishes. Avoid dry-roasted nuts that are covered with artificial flavourings. These are rancid when the texture becomes rubbery and hollow, and they taste mouldy. Do not eat.

▸ Pasta: You can never have too much pasta. Get a variety of Italian dried pasta, Asian rice sticks, Chinese egg noodles and cellophane noodles made from mung beans. Good-quality Italian pasta will include durum wheat in the ingredients. Avoid really cheap pasta because it will fall apart while cooking.

▸ Rice: The basis of many inexpensive meals. Stock a variety in long, medium and short grain to use in sweet and savoury dishes. Brown rice gives you more nutrients and fibre than refined white, as well as a nuttier flavour and chewier texture. Try it if you've never had it before.

▸ Stock cubes: Only as a last resort. Before you stock up, try home-made stock (page 164) to taste the difference.

READ THE LABELS – WHAT TO AVOID

Vegetarians have to be canny shoppers. Lots of animal products and by-products are hidden in processed foods. Even an innocent-looking broccoli and sweetcorn quiche, for example, will probably contain lard in the pastry. Beware!

Here are some of the ingredients the Vegetarian Society of Great Britain highlights:

► Aspic: A savoury jelly derived from meat or fish.
► Calf rennet: An enzyme taken from the stomach of a newly killed calf that is used in cheese making. Always look for vegetarian cheese that has been processed without animal rennet.
► Chitin: A stabiliser derived from arthropod exoskeletons. Used in whipped-cream desserts.
► Cochineal: A red food colouring made from crushed insects. Used in many processed Indian foods.
► Gelatine: A gelling agent made from animal ligaments, skins, tendons and bones; used in jellies, yoghurts and some sweets.
► Isinglass: Used in some alcohols, this is a fining agent from the bladders of some tropical fish.
► Pepsin: An enzyme from a pig's stomach, used like rennet (above).
► Suet: You'll see this labelled as 'animal fat' in biscuits, pastry and margarines.
► Whey: Often used in crisps, whey and whey powder are the by-products of cheese making, which might contain animal rennet.

FRESH FOODS

Bread: Sandwiches certainly don't have to be boring. Supermarkets, whole-food shops and ethnic-food shops offer great variety. Try pita bread and soft flour tortillas for portable sandwiches to go. Or try Italian ciabatta and focaccia for door-stoppers. (See more ideas on page 501.) Choose wholemeal bread for extra nutrients.

Better Bread
► Most bread stays fresh at room temperature in an air-tight bag or tin. Do not put it in the fridge, as it becomes stale quicker.
► If you find you and your flatmates tend to forget about bread and find it often becomes mouldy, put slices in freezer-proof bags and store in the freezer or ice-cube compartment of your fridge. Put pieces of greaseproof paper between the slices so you can peel off exactly what you want. The slices will thaw in 10–15 minutes at room temperature – take them out before you go to bed or when you first wake up before you get dressed.

Fresh fruit: Supermarkets provide year-round choice, but if you stick to natural seasons fruit tastes best and is cheapest. Even if it looks like a bargain, never buy fruit with damaged skins, mould or signs of spoilage. Also, as soon as you see a piece of fruit that is starting to spoil, throw it out – it will contaminate any other nearby fruit.

- Bananas, citrus fruit, melons and pineapples are best stored at cool room temperature.
- Apples, grapes, mangoes, nectarines, passion fruit, plums, pomegranates, quince and star fruit are best kept in the crisper drawer at the bottom of the fridge.
- Berries, cherries and figs should be eaten as soon as you get them home.
- Kiwifruit are best stored away from other fruit, because the ethylene emitted by the other fruit will make the kiwis oversoft.
- Tomatoes: Eat soon after buying as refrigeration kills the flavour; do not store in direct sunlight.

Garlic: Do not buy sprouting garlic. Store in a cool, dry, well-ventilated place – you'll find perforated earthenware jars for this purpose. Do not put in the fridge, or its flavour will taint other ingredients.

Herbs: Fresh herbs aren't a natural staple for cash-strapped students, but if you find you enjoy cooking you will appreciate the extra flavour they add. Dried herbs are fine, but they don't come close to the flavour of the fresh version. When you get them home, trim the stalks and put them in water, then place in the fridge and cover with a plastic bag and chop as required. There is a lot of flavour in parsley and coriander stalks; crush and add them to slow-cooking dishes, such as home-made stock.

Fresh vegetables: Most are best put in the drawer at the bottom of the fridge.

- Onions: Only buy if they feel firm and the inner skin is tight. These are best kept in a cool and well-ventilated place. If you don't use a whole onion at once, use the leftover soon, as it will start to lose its flavour.
- Do not buy sprouting potatoes. New potatoes are fine in the fridge, but older ones are best in a cool, dark place.

Nice & Ripe
If you buy under-ripe fruit, including tomatoes, put them in a paper bag at room temperature out of direct sunlight. This will speed the ripening process.

STOCKING THE FRIDGE

Dairy products are highly perishable because of the fat they contain, so put them straight into the fridge when you get home from the shops. You'll find it best to shop for these often in small quantities to avoid a fridge full of mouldy containers. Observe the 'use by' dates on the packaging.

Cheese: Not all cheese is suitable for vegetarians, as it contains animal rennet. Look for the cheeses specifically labelled as 'suitable for vegetarians', which will have been made without animal rennet. The good news is that many traditional British cheeses fit the bill.

Cream: Save for the occasional indulgence.

Eggs: Buy free-range.

Milk: Cow's milk comes with varying degrees of fat, and semi-skimmed milk was used for recipe testing. Soya milk can be substituted for cow's milk in any recipe.

Yoghurt: Greek-style and natural yoghurts are useful in cooking and for making smoothies.

FRIDGE HYGIENE

Your fridge can be a breeding ground for bacteria, which can make you ill. Make sure you clear out any rotting foods. Your nose will tell you instantly if there is anything that should be in the bin instead of the fridge. Wipe the base and sides at least once a term with a disinfectant and a damp kitchen cloth.

If the fridge is old, it's a good idea to buy an oven thermometer, which isn't expensive. Bacteria thrive on foods in temperatures above 10°C and below 65°C.

Follow these simple steps to keep food poisoning at bay:
- Follow all storage information on packaging.
- Don't leave the fridge door open longer than necessary. When the door is open, the internal temperature rises.
- Completely cool cooked foods before you put them in the fridge.

Hangovers are Hell

Yes, it is true that some medical studies suggest a modest amount of regular alcohol might offer health benefits. Unfortunately, this doesn't apply to the amount of drinking many students indulge in.

Being drunk is *not* good for you. And the not-so-subtle giveaway is the pounding headache, dizziness, the vomiting and retching that follow too much alcohol.

Too much booze is bad for your body, and the hangover is your body's way of letting you know. Have you ever noticed that as soon as you drink 'too much' you run to the loo all the time? That is the start of your body's payback time.

WHY YOU FEEL SO WRETCHED

When you are hung over it is because all the trips to the loo have left your body depleted in various vitamins and minerals. The pounding headaches and vomiting are caused by the loss of potassium and sodium. The alcohol has also depleted the vitamin C in your body; the imbalance of acid and alkaline in your gut is why you feel so queasy, even after the vomiting has stopped.

The weariness that makes you want to roll over and abandon all lectures for the day is not just because you came home as the sun was rising. It is because your body is working overtime to get you better. Also, no matter how long you sleep, the alcohol in your system will probably prevent your body from entering REM (Rapid Eye Movement), the stage of sleep that refreshes your body.

Another reason you don't want to move is because the sugars in the alcohol raise your blood sugar levels. When your blood sugar levels come back down again, the queasy feeling can be due to a fall in glucose, leaving you feeling like a damp dish rag. This typically occurs between 6 and 36 hours after an alcoholic binge, especially if you started drinking on an empty stomach.

BETTER SAFE THAN SORRY

Abstinence is the only 100 per cent effective 'remedy' for a hangover. Assuming you aren't going down that road, however, *never* drink on an empty stomach. Go for bulk and eat starchy foods that provide a slow, long-lasting release of energy. Opt for foods like wholemeal-bread sandwiches or jacket potatoes before you go out. While you are out, beware: traditional bar snacks such as nuts and crisps are salty and will only encourage you to drink more. Instead, it is better to alternate alcoholic and non-alcoholic drinks.

On the whole, it's a good idea to avoid high-fat foods, but if there is ever a time to justify a greasy fry-up or a big bowl of chips it might be before you go out drinking. Alcoholic absorption is much lower after you've eaten something fatty, such as oil or cream.

Don't Mix Your Drinks
Think carefully before you combine beer, wine and spirits in the same drinking session. Remember: 'Wine before beer will leave you feeling queer. Beer before wine and you'll feel just fine.' On the other hand, however: 'Beer before liquor and you'll never feel sicker.'

CLEAR THINKING

Clear drinks, such as gin, vodka and wine, are less likely to give you a hangover if you drink in moderation. Darker drinks, such as brandy, red wine and whisky, contain congeners, which are a by-product of alcohol metabolism. The congeners will leave you feeling worse for wear.

Also, never forget, the cheaper the booze is, the worse your hangover is likely to be!

HANGOVER BUSTERS – WHAT MIGHT HELP YOU RECOVER

▸ Get some decent sleep. Be sure to drink a glass of water before you hit the sack – it will help rehydrate you and might prevent a pounding head.

▸ Eat Something. You won't be able to face a feast, but your body needs nourishment and you need to restore your blood sugar levels. Fried eggs might be tempting, but your already precarious stomach doesn't need any grease. Milk Toast (page 37), Rice 'Soup' (page 33) and Overnight Porridge (page 34), if you had foresight, are all gentle starts. Or try a little honey on toast. The natural sugar in honey is easily absorbed and will raise your blood sugar levels.

▸ Unzip a banana. Bananas are like wonder drugs for hangover sufferers. The potassium they contain might help ease the aches and cramps, and their magnesium should help stop the pounding head. Try a sliced banana and peanut butter sandwich on wholemeal bread. If that seems like more than you can manage, whiz up a Tropical Smoothie (page 45).

▸ Down some OJ. It's good for replacing vitamin C and potassium. The natural sugars in any fruit juice help your body break down any alcohol that is left.

▸ Cut the caffeine. Drink water, rather than coffee or tea, because the caffeine in them will only make you go to the loo again and right now your body needs rehydration. Try a herbal tea, or see if you can talk a friend or flatmate into making a mug of Head Clearer (page 48) for you. Lime Tea (page 47) is gentle and soothing.

▸ Try a tomato. It's a powerhouse of vitamin C. Add a little diced tomato to scrambled eggs and spoon them over a slice of wholemeal toast. It will give you protein, vitamins and slow-release energy.

▸ Fresh ginger is excellent for settling upset stomachs. Try Spiced Tea (page 46) or Head Clearer (page 48).

▸ Many hangover sufferers swear by the 'hair of the dog', or having another alcoholic drink. This might mask unpleasant hangover symptoms, but it only delays the inevitable. And it can make the most horrid symptoms worse. If you insist on going down this road, try a Bloody Mary (page 216), because at least the tomato juice should boost your energy.

▸ When you finally crawl out of bed, go for simple, plain food. Try a jacket potato or scrambled eggs and toast. If there is a slice of Spanish Tortilla (page 210) in the fridge, it will hit the spot.

How To Use This Book

WHAT THE SYMBOLS MEAN

As you flip through the recipes, the easy-to-spot symbols give you a quick clue as to what each recipe is like.

 Vegan These are recipes suitable for anyone who follows a vegan diet. You might, however, have to make some of the regular substitutions, such as soya milk for cow's milk (or try the almond milk on page 45, or milk made from oats or rice). Vegan Notes give tips for adapting recipes, or vegan variations to main recipes.

Be sure to read the labels on packets of pasta, flour tortillas and pita breads, to be certain they do not contain eggs or butter.

 Quick When you are hungry and want to eat in a hurry, these are the recipes for you. All the prep work and cooking time should not take more than 20 minutes in total. This might not sound super speedy but remember, that is less time than it takes for you to heat the oven and cook most ready-meals! With these recipes, you should be sitting down to eat within 20 minutes of walking into the kitchen.

 Hangover busters These aren't claiming to leave you feeling as right as rain, but they might get you back on your feet and feeling better. They will replenish the vitamins and minerals in your body, and start raising your blood sugar levels. When you're feeling really awful, eat small amounts and sip liquids – and remember, the only real hangover buster is moderation while you are drinking.

ALL-DAY BREAKFASTS & COMFORTING DRINKS

When it comes to healthy eating, you should start as you mean to go on. Eating breakfast is the first step to a healthy lifestyle – even if you don't get up until after noon.

Not everyone is a morning person and you might be tempted to skip what is often called the most important meal of the day. But anyone can manage a slice of wholemeal bread and glass of orange juice or a handful of dried fruit. Your body needs the nourishment to wake up, and you'll kick-start your brain into action.

And if too much alcohol the night before has taken its toll, try one of the simple smoothies. They are easy to make and easy to drink, even when you can barely stand up.

Vegetarian breakfasts have endless easy options. Try DIY Muesli (page 35) or Overnight Porridge (page 34) for complex carbs that will get you going for hours and hours.

Less conventional starts to the day:
- Artichoke & Pepper Frittata (page 70)
- Bubble & Squeak (page 80)
- Red Lentil Dahl (page 148)
- Soda Bread (page 171)
- Spanish Tortilla (page 210)
- Tomato Bread (page 52)

Rice 'Soup'

MAKES **1 SERVING**
PREP TIME: **SECONDS (AS LONG AS YOU HAVE LEFTOVER RICE)**
COOKING TIME: **2–3 MINUTES**

MILLIONS OF CHINESE CAN'T BE WRONG. EVERY DAY MOST CHINESE START THEIR DAY WITH A BOWL OF CONGEE, WHICH IS LIKE A RICE SOUP. GET IN THE HABIT OF ALWAYS COOKING MORE RICE THAN YOU WILL NEED AND THIS SIMPLE START TO THE DAY WILL BE READY IN A MATTER OF MINUTES. EVEN IF THE ONLY THING YOU CAN FIND IN THE FRIDGE IS LEFTOVER RICE FROM A TAKE-AWAY, YOU'VE GOT THE MAKINGS OF A WARMING BREAKFAST.

IF YOU DON'T HAVE ANY LEFTOVER RICE, THE INSTRUCTIONS FOR COOKING RICE ARE ON PAGE 131.

About 200 ml pint milk
About 50 g cooked brown or white long-,
    medium- or short-grain rice
Brown sugar or honey to taste

OPTIONAL EXTRAS:
- Chopped ready-to-eat dried fruit
- Raisins or sultanas
- Pinch of ground mixed spice
- Whatever you fancy in the cupboard

1. Put the milk and rice in a saucepan over a medium heat and stir in any of the optional extras, if you like.

2. Heat the rice and milk, stirring until bubbles just start to break the surface, then turn down the heat and leave to simmer until the rice is hot, stirring occasionally.

3. Pour into a bowl and stir in brown sugar or honey to taste.

Cooking Hot Porridge

Porridge is the ultimate power breakfast. Porridge oats from the supermarket will come with cooking instructions, but if you buy in bulk from a whole-food shop, put 30–40 g rolled oats in a heatproof bowl with a pinch of salt. (Scottish tradition dictates that you add a pat of butter, but vegans can omit.) Pour over enough boiling water to cover, then stir until soft and blended. Add cold milk and any fruit you like. Or lightly sprinkle with dark muscovado sugar, which gives a rich caramel flavour.

Overnight Porridge

MAKES **1 SERVING**
PREP TIME: **ABOUT 1 MINUTE**
NO COOKING

A BIT HUNG OVER? NOT REALLY AWAKE? SLOW TO GET GOING IN THE MORNING? THIS
IS THE BREAKFAST FOR YOU! IT WILL KEEP YOU GOING UNTIL THE NEXT MEAL WITH VERY
LITTLE EFFORT. ALL YOU HAVE TO DO IS MIX THE PORRIDGE OATS AND MILK TOGETHER
BEFORE YOU HIT THE SACK AND BREAKFAST WILL BE WAITING. AND IF YOU GET BORED
WITH THIS VERSION, USE STIRRED YOGHURT INSTEAD OF THE MILK.

30–40 g rolled porridge oats
About 60 ml milk
Pinch of salt
Fruit to serve

1. Put the porridge oats in a bowl, add the milk and salt and stir together.
The amount of milk you use depends on how thick or runny you like
your porridge. At this stage you want at least a thin layer of milk on the
surface as the oats will absorb the milk overnight: if you don't add
enough milk now, you'll have gluelike porridge in the morning.

2. In the morning, give the porridge a good stir and add a little extra milk,
if you want. Top the porridge with a fruit of your choice – try raisins with
sunflower seeds; chopped ready-to-eat dried apricots with a pinch of
ground cinnamon; Fruit Spread (page 153); or whatever you are in the
mood for.

OTHER FLAVOUR IDEAS:
- Grated apple with toasted hazelnuts or almonds (page 35)
- Sliced banana and honey
- Ready-to-eat prunes
- Fresh strawberries, raspberries or blueberries with a dollop of yoghurt
- Soak the porridge overnight in orange juice, rather than milk

DIY Muesli

MAKES **ABOUT 20 SERVINGS**
PREP TIME: **ABOUT 5 MINUTES**
NO COOKING

IF ONLY LIFE WAS ALWAYS SO PREDICTABLE – THIS RECIPE LETS YOU HAVE WHAT YOU WANT WHEN YOU WANT! YOU CAN MIX AND MATCH THE INGREDIENTS FOR A FLAVOUR COMBINATION THAT PUTS A SMILE ON YOUR FACE IN THE MORNINGS.

A BOWL OF CRUNCHY GRAINS AND NUTS WITH LOTS OF DRIED AND FRESH FRUIT AND CHILLED MILK MIGHT NOT HAVE THE SAME INSTANT APPEAL AS A FRIED BREAKFAST, BUT THIS IS THE HEALTHIER OPTION ON A REGULAR BASIS AND SO MUCH QUICKER. AND THERE IS LESS WASHING-UP, TOO.

IF YOU WANT VARIETY TO YOUR MORNINGS – AND TO SAVE LOTS OF MONEY – GET TOGETHER WITH SEVERAL FRIENDS TO BUY THE BASIC INGREDIENTS IN BULK AT A WHOLE-FOOD SHOP.

STORE THE BASIC MIXTURE IN AN AIR-TIGHT CONTAINER AND ADD EXTRA FRUIT AND NUTS AS YOU LIKE TO EACH BOWL. TRY SOME OF THE FLAVOURING IDEAS LISTED FOR OVERNIGHT PORRIDGE (PAGE 34).

5 mugs jumbo rolled porridge oats
1 mug barley flakes
1 mug dried ready-to-eat apricots or dried cherries
1 mug raisins or sultanas
1 mug dried apples
$^1/_2$ mug toasted hazelnuts (below)
$^1/_2$ mug wheat germ
$^1/_4$ mug toasted almond flakes (below)
1 $^1/_2$ tablespoons ground cinnamon or mixed spice, or to taste
Any extra dried fruit, or seeds – try sunflower or flax seeds, if you like
Fresh fruit, such as sliced banana, to serve (optional)

1. Put all the ingredients in a large bowl and mix together. Transfer the muesli to an air-tight container, where it should stay fresh for at least a month if you remember to reseal the jar after using.

2. When you are ready to eat, tip the sealed jar upside down to redistribute any ingredients that have sunk to the bottom, then turn upright again. Put a handful of muesli in a bowl and add any fresh fruit, if you want, then pour over chilled milk. What could be easier?

Toasting Nuts
Lightly toasted nuts add extra flavour. You can either put them in an ungreased frying pan over a medium heat and stir frequently until they are golden brown, or toast them in a preheated 180°C/350°F/Gas 4 oven for 5–8 minutes, stirring occasionally. Whichever method you choose, be sure to watch them constantly because they burn quickly.

Tip toasted hazelnuts into a clean tea towel and rub them around to remove the thin brown skins.

Overnight Dried Fruit Salad

MAKES **6–8 SERVINGS**
PREP TIME: **ABOUT 15 MINUTES, PLUS AT LEAST 8 HOURS**
SOAKING / NO COOKING

THIS MIGHT SOUND OLD-FASHIONED BUT IT'S A GOOD BREAKFAST IN A HURRY. AND
WITH A BOWL OF THIS IN THE FRIDGE YOU'VE ALSO GOT A FRUITY DESSERT OR SNACK AT
ANY TIME OF THE DAY. EAT THIS PLAIN, SPOONED OVER OVERNIGHT PORRIDGE (PAGE 34)
OR WITH A SPOONFUL OF YOGHURT. JUST DON'T GET CAUGHT EATING IT STRAIGHT FROM
THE FRIDGE – YOUR FLATMATES MIGHT NOT BE PLEASED.

50 g dried apricots
50 g dried apple rings
50 g dried banana rings
50 g dried mangoes or figs
300 ml unsweetened orange juice
300 ml water

1. Cut the dried fruit into bite-sized pieces and put in a bowl. Pour over
the orange juice and water and stir together.

2. Cover tightly with clingfilm and place in the fridge overnight or for
at least 8 hours.

VARIATIONS
► The variations are literally limitless – use any dried fruit you like
in any combination. The selection above is only to give you an idea.
► Try different juice, too.
► For Spiced Dried Fruit Compote, put 1 cinnamon stick, 1 star anise,
1 lightly crushed green cardamom pod and 2 cloves in a saucepan with
the orange juice and water. Bring to the boil and boil for 1–2 minutes.
Remove the pan from the heat and leave to cool, then strain the liquid
over the fruit.

Cook's Tip
Dip the knife in caster sugar before you cut the dried fruit. The sugar
stops the fruit from sticking. Or you can rub the blade with a little
vegetable oil.

A Slice of Toast . . . or 2

MAKES **1 SERVING**
NO PREP TIME
COOKING TIME: **ABOUT 4 MINUTES**

ABOUT THE ONLY THING QUICKER OR EASIER THAN TOAST IN THE MORNING IS A PLAIN
SLICE OF BREAD – BUT EVEN THAT IS BETTER THAN SKIPPING BREAKFAST ALTOGETHER.
WARM, CRISP TOAST, HOWEVER, IS SO MUCH NICER. EAT THE TOAST DRY OR TRY ANY OF
THE TOPPING IDEAS BELOW.

TOAST IS ALSO A GOOD WAY OF GIVING A BURST OF LIFE TO BREAD THAT'S STARTING
TO DRY OUT SO YOU DON'T WASTE IT (SEE BELOW).

1 or 2 slices wholemeal or white bread

1. A toaster does all the work for you, but if you don't have one,
preheat the grill to high and position the rack about 10 cm from the
heat. Put the bread on the rack and toast for 2 minutes, or until
golden brown and crisp.

2. Turn the bread over and toast the other side for about 2 minutes
until golden brown. Watch carefully so the toast doesn't become too
brown – the exact time depends on how thick the bread is and how far
the rack is from the heat.

TOPPING IDEAS
▸ Yeast extract
▸ A thin spread of butter with a sprinkling of ground cinnamon and
caster sugar
▸ Honey
▸ Marmalade – keep a selection of flavours in the fridge for variety
▸ Peanut butter – with or without jam or jelly
▸ Fruit Spread (page 153)
▸ Go Continental – top the toast with thinly sliced vegetarian cheese
▸ Scrambled (page 39) or fried (pages 41) free-range eggs

VARIATION
Milk Toast: Spread a slice of toast with Marmite or a thin layer of butter,
and sprinkle with soft light-brown sugar. Tear the toast into a bowl.
Heat 6 tablespoons of milk until almost boiling and pour it over the
bread. Leave the milk to soak in a little, then tuck in. This is a good
way to use bread that is too dry for sandwiches.

Cook's Tip
If you do take your eye off toasting bread and it becomes too brown, hold
the bread over the sink and use a knife to scrape off the brown crumbs.

Eggs & Soldiers

MAKES **1 SERVING** / PREP TIME: **JUST PREHEATING THE GRILL FOR THE TOAST** / COOKING TIME: **3 MINUTES FOR A REALLY RUNNY YOLK WITH AN UNSET WHITE; ABOUT 4 MINUTES FOR A LIGHTLY SET WHITE**

EVEN THOUGH YOUR MUM ISN'T THERE TO PREPARE THIS CHILDHOOD FAVOURITE, THIS REMAINS A COMFORTING START TO THE DAY. SOME AfiCIONADOS INSIST THE SOLDIERS AREN'T PROPERLY DRESSED WITHOUT A SPREAD OF YEAST EXTRACT, WHILE OTHERS CONSIDER IT SACRILEGE. FRUIT JAM IS GOOD, TOO. THE CHOICE IS YOURS. (SEE NOTE ABOUT LIGHTLY COOKED EGGS ON PAGE 42.)

1 large free-range egg
1 slice wholemeal or white bread
Yeast extract, butter or jam

1. If you have a toaster, use it to toast the bread. If not, preheat the grill to high. When the grill is hot, put the bread about 10 cm below the heat and toast for 2 minutes on each side until crisp and golden brown: watch carefully so it doesn't burn.

2. Meanwhile, put the egg in a saucepan and cover it with 2.5 cm water. Set the pan over a high heat and heat until the water comes to a full rolling boil. Immediately reduce the heat to low and leave the egg to simmer for 3 minutes for a runny yolk with an unset white, or about 4 minutes for a lightly set white.

3. Lift the egg out of the water with a large spoon and transfer to an egg cup, rounded side down. Slice off the top of the egg.

4. Spead the toast with yeast extract or butter and cut into thin strips. Dip the 'soldiers' into the egg, then use a small spoon to scoop out the rest of the egg.

Scrambled Eggs on Toast

MAKES **1 SERVING**
PREP TIME: **LESS THAN A MINUTE**
COOKING TIME: **ABOUT 5 MINUTES**

LEARN TO SCRAMBLE EGGS AND YOU'LL NEVER GO HUNGRY. SCRAMBLED EGGS ON TOAST MUST BE ONE OF THE MOST VERSATILE, EASY RECIPES YOU'LL EVER MASTER. AND SCRAMBLED EGGS CAN BE A LIFESAVER WHEN YOU ARE NEW TO COOKING AND ENTERTAINING. IT IS UNUSUAL TO RUIN A WHOLE MEAL WHEN YOU ARE EXPECTING GUESTS, BUT JUST IN CASE THE UNFORTUNATE DOES HAPPEN, KEEP A BOX OF EGGS IN THE FRIDGE. IF ANYTHING GOES WRONG, THIS SIMPLE DISH WILL SAVE YOUR REPUTATION.

SCRAMBLED EGGS ARE ALSO GOOD WHEN YOU ARE FEELING DELICATE AFTER DRINKING TOO MUCH – THEY ARE EASY TO MAKE, EASY TO DIGEST AND GOOD FOR GETTING YOU ON THE ROAD TO RECOVERY. (SEE NOTE ABOUT RAW AND LIGHTLY COOKED EGGS ON PAGE 42.)

1 or 2 slices wholemeal or white bread
A little butter for the toast (optional)
2 free-range eggs
About 2 tablespoons milk
About 15 g butter, or 1 tablespoon sunflower or rapeseed oil
Salt and pepper

1. If you have a toaster, use it toast the bread, otherwise preheat the grill to high and follow the instruction for toasting bread in Eggs & Soldiers (page 38). Spread the toast with a thin layer of butter, if you like, and place on a plate.

2. Meanwhile, heat your frying pan over a medium-high heat. Break your eggs into a small bowl or cup and use a fork to beat together. Add the milk and salt and pepper to taste, and continue beating the eggs – the more you beat the eggs, the more air you will incorporate and the lighter they will be.

3. Melt the butter or heat the oil in the frying pan, tilting the pan so the base is covered. As soon as the butter is foaming or the oil is hot, reduce the heat to medium.

4. Pour the eggs into the pan and use the fork or wooden spoon to stir the eggs constantly until they are thick and fluffy. Just before the eggs begin to look the way you like them cooked, tip them out of the pan on to the toast, as they will continue cooking in the residual heat. And, if you don't have time to wash up the pan, leave it to soak in warm water. That will make the job easier later in the day.

VARIATIONS

▸ Indian Scrambled Eggs: Peel and de-seed a tomato (page 41), then cut it into small dice; trim and finely chop a spring onion; and de-seed and slice $^1/_2$ a fresh green chilli. Prepare the eggs as in Step 2 above, but add a pinch of ground turmeric with salt and pepper to taste. Increase the amount of butter to 40 g or use 1 $^1/_2$ tablespoons oil. Melt the butter or heat the oil as in Step 3 above. Add the spring onion and chilli and stir around until the onion is soft, but not brown. Add the tomato and stir around for about 30 seconds. Stir in the eggs and cook as above. Sprinkle with chopped fresh coriander.

▸ Tex-Mex Eggs: Add $^1/_2$ a de-seeded and chopped green chilli and a finely diced grilled red pepper (page 93) with a pinch of ground coriander and chopped fresh coriander to the eggs in Step 4 of the master recipe.

▸ Herby Eggs: Add 1 tablespoon chopped fresh herbs in Step 2 of the master recipe. Tarragon has a natural affinity with eggs, but only add 1 teaspoon because of its overpowering flavour. Chervil, chives, coriander, dill and parsley are all other suitable herbs to use.

▸ Scrambled Eggs To Go: Fry a thinly sliced $^1/_2$ onion in the pan before you add the eggs, then spoon the scrambled eggs into a toasted pita bread for a breakfast as you run out the door.

▸ To wake up your tastebuds with a blast, add a few drops of hot-pepper sauce with the salt and pepper. Or add a tablespoon or two of Tomato Salsa (page 56) to the eggs in Step 4 after the eggs have cooked for 1 minute.

Successful Scrambled Eggs – Every Time

▸ Add the eggs to hot fat, then *immediately* turn down the heat. If the eggs cook too quickly they will become rubbery.

▸ If you don't have any milk in the fridge, add a small amount of water instead for fluffy eggs.

▸ It's cheap and easy to make scrambled eggs for all your flatmates, but don't start scrambling eggs until everyone is at the table and ready to eat. Cooked eggs kept warm are unappetising.

Lightly Cooked or Raw Eggs

Because of the possible dangers of salmonella food poisoning from lightly cooked or raw eggs, it is recommended that you only eat well-cooked eggs if you are ill or pregnant. You should not serve lightly cooked eggs to young children, the elderly or anyone with a damaged immune system.

Fried-Egg Sandwich

MAKES **1 SANDWICH**
NO PREP TIME
COOKING TIME: **3–4 MINUTES**

OF COURSE, A REGULAR DIET OF FRIED EGGS DOESN'T GET A HEALTH-CONSCIOUS SEAL OF
APPROVAL, BUT THEY ARE QUICK – AND A FRIED EGG CAN BE JUST WHAT YOU CRAVE AFTER
A NIGHT OF TOO MUCH DRINKING. STICK A FRIED EGG BETWEEN TWO SLICES OF BREAD AND
YOU HAVE A BREAKFAST-TO-GO FOR WHEN YOU'RE RUNNING LATE. COOK THE YOLKS LONG
ENOUGH SO THEY DON'T RUN DOWN YOUR CHIN AS YOU GO OUT THE DOOR. (SEE NOTE
ABOUT LIGHTLY COOKED EGGS ON PAGE 40.)

About 1 tablespoon sunflower or olive oil
1 large free-range egg
2 slices wholemeal bread

1. Put the sunflower or olive oil in a frying pan over a medium heat
and swirl the oil around the pan so it coats the base.

2. As soon as the oil is sizzling hot, lower the heat to medium-low and
break the egg into the pan. Use a spoon or the edge of a fish slice to push
the white back towards the yolk so it doesn't spread too much. Fry the
egg for 3–4 minutes, spooning the fat in the pan over the yolks until
the white is set and just lightly coloured at the edge.

3. Use a fish slice to flip the egg over and continue frying for 30 seconds,
or longer if you want a firmly set yolk. Use the fish slice to lift the egg
from the pan and let any oil drip back into the pan.

4. Place the fried egg on one of the slices of bread and top with the
other slice and you're ready to go.

VARIATIONS
▸ Add a slice of tomato
▸ Toast the bread while the egg fries and spread one side of one
slice very lightly with butter or oil before topping with the fried egg
▸ Spread the bread slices with marmalade or jam before adding the egg
▸ Or spread the bread with yeast extract

No Overcrowding
You can fry as many eggs as will fit in a single layer in your pan, adding
an extra tablespoon of oil for each extra egg. If you're cooking for a group
of housemates, however, fry the eggs in batches and serve as soon as
each batch is ready.

Breakfast Drop Scones

MAKES **ABOUT 16**
PREP TIME: **ABOUT 5 MINUTES**
COOKING TIME: **ABOUT 15 MINUTES**

THIS RECIPE IS SO EASY THAT, ONCE YOU MAKE IT, YOU WON'T BE TEMPTED TO BUY DROP SCONES AGAIN.

150 g plain white flour
2 tablespoons sugar
2 teaspoons baking powder
$1/2$ teaspoon salt
250 ml milk
1 large free-range egg
1 tablespoon sunflower or rapeseed oil, plus extra for cooking
Butter and maple syrup to serve

1. Heat the oven on a low setting so you can keep the drop scones warm until all are cooked.

2. Put the flour, sugar, baking powder and salt in a large bowl and stir together. Use the spoon to make an indentation in the centre of the dry ingredients.

3. Measure the milk into a measuring jug, then crack in the egg, add the oil and beat together. Slowly pour these liquid ingredients into the dry ingredients and beat together until a smooth batter forms. If a few lumps remain, don't worry as they will disappear during the cooking.

4. Heat the largest frying pan you have, ideally non-stick, over a medium-high heat. Use a pastry brush or crumpled piece of kitchen paper to lightly grease the base of the pan. Drop the batter by large spoonfuls on to the surface, spacing them well apart. The pancakes should spread to 7.5 cm across. Add as many drop scones as will fit in your pan without them touching.

5. Reduce the heat to medium and leave the drop scones to cook for about 1 minute, or until small bubbles appear all over the surface. Use a fish slice or a metal spatula to flip the drop scones over and leave them to cook for another minute or so until they are set and golden brown on the bottom.

6. Transfer the drop scones to a plate and keep warm in the low oven. Continue as above until all the batter is used. Serve the drop scones with a little butter for smearing over the surface and maple syrup.

VARIATION
Use half white and half wholemeal flours.

Cook's Tips
► Only flip the drop scones once or they will be tough.
► If you don't want to cook all the drop scones at once, store the leftover batter in a clean screw-top jar in the fridge for up to 3 days, and give it a good stir before using.

Eggy Bread

MAKES **6 SLICES**
PREP TIME: **ABOUT 2 MINUTES**
COOKING TIME: **ABOUT 15 MINUTES**

ALTHOUGH THIS IS QUICK AND EASY TO PREPARE, IT'S PROBABLY BEST TO SAVE IT FOR MORE LEISURELY MORNINGS (OR MID-AFTERNOONS, AS THE CASE MIGHT BE) WHEN YOU'VE GOT TIME TO RELAX. THIS IS ALWAYS POPULAR FOR BRUNCH – START WITH A BLOODY MARY (PAGE 216) OR BUCK'S FIZZ. ORDINARY SLICED BREAD THAT IS SEVERAL DAYS OLD IS BEST TO USE.

1 free-range egg
250 ml milk
$^1/_2$ teaspoon ground cinnamon (optional)
About 60 g butter, chopped
6 slices wholemeal or white bread

1. Crack the egg into a pie plate or baking dish large enough to hold a slice of bread flat. Add the milk and use a fork to beat the egg and milk together. Stir in the cinnamon, if using.

2. Melt about $^1/_3$ of the butter in a large frying pan over a medium-high heat. As soon as the butter starts to foam, turn the heat to low.

3. Give the egg-milk mixture another quick stir and add a piece of bread, pressing it down into the liquid. Turn it over and press it down again. Lift up the bread, letting the excess liquid drip off, and put it in the hot butter. Repeat with another slice of bread and ad it to the pan.

4. Cook as many slices as will fit in the pan at one time, adding extra butter as necessary. Leave the bread to cook for 1–2 minutes until it looks golden brown on the edge and the bottom is set and golden brown.

5. Flip the bread over and cook the other side until it is golden brown. Transfer to a plate and add a topping of your choice (page 44).

SERVING IDEAS
- ▸ Maple syrup, golden syrup or honey
- ▸ Spoon sliced strawberries or raspberries over the top, or top with a sliced banana or fresh orange segments
- ▸ Add a slice of tomato
- ▸ Jam or other fruit preserves
- ▸ Fruit Spread (page 153)

Wake-up Smoothies

MAKES **2 GLASSES**
PREP TIME: **ABOUT 2 MINUTES**
NO COOKING

NO MATTER HOW LONG YOU'VE OVERSLEPT, THERE IS ENOUGH TIME TO WHIZ THIS CREAMY BREAKFAST IN A GLASS BEFORE YOU RUN OUT THE DOOR. THE FRUIT SUGARS IN THE BANANA WILL GIVE YOU AN ENERGY BOOST TO KICK-START YOUR BRAIN AND BODY INTO ACTION. THIS WILL ALSO HELP EASE HANGOVERS.

1 banana
1 tablespoon honey or soft light brown sugar
1 tablespoon rolled porridge oats
300 ml milk

1. Peel the banana and cut it directly into chunks into a blender. Add the honey, porridge oats and milk, then blitz until they are well blended.

2. Pour in the milk and blitz again. Now you're all set to drink and run.

VARIATION
Tropical Smoothies: Blend 1 banana, 225 ml of natural yoghurt, 200 ml pint of unsweetened pineapple juice and a pinch of ground ginger together.

Vegan Note
Replace the milk or yoghurt in smoothies with silken tofu.

Almond Smoothies

MAKES **2 GLASSES**
PREP TIME: **ABOUT 5 MINUTES, PLUS OVERNIGHT SOAKING**
NO COOKING

TRY THIS ON A DAY WHEN YOU AREN'T IN A RUSH. IT'S CREAMY AND SATISFYING, AND ONLY TAKES A LITTLE LONGER TO MAKE THAN THE OTHER SMOOTHIES . . . BUT YOU HAVE TO REMEMBER TO SOAK THE NUTS OVERNIGHT.

1 mug blanched almonds
2–3 mugs water
1 banana
Maple syrup or brown sugar to taste (optional)

1. Put the almonds and water in a bowl and leave to soak overnight. The less water you use, the creamier the drink will be.

2. On the next day, drain the almonds and reserve the soaking water. Put the almonds in a blender and blitz until very finely ground. Add the reserved water and blitz again to blend: if it seems too thick, add a little extra water.

3. Peel the banana and cut it directly into chunks into the blender and blitz again. Add maple syrup or brown sugar for sweetness, if you like.

VARIATION
Chocolate-Almond Smoothie: Add 1 tablespoon drinking chocolate with the banana in Step 3.

Vegan Note
Steps 1 and 2 make a thick almond milk that can be used for drinking or in cooking. It is particularly good chilled and poured over ice.

Mixed-Berry Slushies

MAKES **2 GLASSES**
PREP TIME: **ABOUT 2 MINUTES**
NO COOKING

A YEAR-ROUND TREAT – IF YOU KEEP A BAG OF FROZEN SUMMER BERRIES
IN THE ICE-CUBE COMPARTMENT OF YOUR FRIDGE.

250 g frozen mixed berries
200 ml silken tofu or natural yoghurt
About 2 tablespoons orange juice

1. Tip the berries straight from the freezer into a blender. Add the
tofu or yoghurt and orange juice and blitz until slushy crystals form.
You can either sip from a mug or eat with a spoon from a bowl.

Spiced Tea

MAKES **2 MUGFULS**
PREP TIME: **ABOUT 2 MINUTES**
COOKING TIME: **ABOUT 5 MINUTES**

THIS IS THE MILKY MASALA CHAI INDIANS DRINK ALL DAY LONG. MAKE IT AS STRONG
OR AS WEAK AS YOU LIKE, AND DEFINITELY EXPERIMENT WITH THE SPICES.

0.5-cm piece of fresh root ginger
400 ml water
1 teaspoon tea leaves, or 1 tea bag
1 clove
1 green cardamom pod, lightly crushed
Small piece of fresh cinnamon stick
2 tablespoons light-brown sugar
100 ml milk

1. Peel and finely chop the piece of ginger. Put the water and all the
ingredients into a saucepan and bring to the boil, stirring to dissolve.

2. Reduce the heat to low and leave the tea to simmer for about 5
minutes for the flavours to blend. Strain into mugs and add extra milk
or sugar, if desired.

Lime Tea

MAKES **2 MUGFULS**
PREP TIME: **ABOUT 1 MINUTE**
COOKING TIME: **ABOUT 2 MINUTES**

1 piece of lemongrass, about 15 cm long
500 ml water
1 tablespoon sugar
$^1/_2$–1 tablespoon tea leaves, to taste
2 tablespoons freshly squeezed lime juice

1. Peel off the outer layer of the lemongrass, then use a cook's-knife handle or rolling pin to lightly crush the stalk.

2. Put the water, lemongrass and sugar in a saucepan over a high heat and bring to the boil, stirring to dissolve the sugar.

3. Reduce the heat to medium and stir in the tea leaves, at which point the water will turn a pale-brown colour.

4. Switch off the heat and add the lime juice. The liquid will now turn a golden colour. Leave to brew as long as you like, then strain into mugs. This is traditionally drunk without milk.

Cook's Tip
For a refreshing summer drink, leave the tea to cool, then pour it over ice cubes.

Head Clearer

MAKES **1 MUGFUL**
PREP TIME: **ABOUT 5 MINUTES**
NO COOKING

WHETHER YOU'RE fiGHTING A COLD THAT HAS LAID YOU LOW, OR JUST FEELING LOW AFTER DRINKING TOO MUCH, THIS VITAMIN-C BOOSTER SHOULD PICK YOU UP. GINGER IS A GOOD DIGESTIVE, SO IT WILL HELP SETTLE YOUR STOMACH IF YOU ARE HUNG OVER, AND ITS ANTI-BACTERIAL PROPERTIES HELP fiGHT COLDS. IF THERE IS ANY MINT IN THE FRIDGE, IT ALSO HELPS SETTLE YOUR STOMACH.

5cm piece of fresh root ginger
2 fresh oranges
1 lemon
1 sprig fresh mint (optional)

1. Peel and chop the fresh root ginger, then put it in a blender. Cut the oranges and lemon in half and squeeze both lemon halves and 1 orange half into the blender. Add the mint sprig if you have one.

2. Blitz the ingredients until a liquid forms. Squeeze the remaining orange juice into the blender and quickly blitz again.

Cook's Tip
For maximum vitamin C, to boost your immune system, drink the spiced citrus juices as soon as they are blended. To recover from a hangover, however, gently warm the mixture until small bubbles appear around the surface, then take a steaming mug back to bed with you to sip until your stomach settles and your head stops pounding.

GRAZING NOSH

Grazing isn't just for cows. For busy students always on the go, eating little but often is a good way to ensure you get all the nutrients you need for a healthy diet. One of the main benefits of a grazing diet is that you keep your energy levels up so you stay alert, avoiding those all-too-familiar afternoon slumps.

The key to grazing throughout the day is the word 'little'. You can't chow down on big plates of pasta and curries four times a day and call it grazing. If you do, you will soon be as big as a cow!

Many of the recipes in this chapter are snacks that give a healthier option than reaching for a bag of chips or crisps. This chapter also includes lots of salad ideas. If you think a salad is just a few limp lettuce leaves and a soggy tomato, think again. A great salad can be a satisfying meal, with cheese, eggs, olives and fresh fruit.

Sandwiches are a student staple. They are easy to make and quick to eat. But remember, there is more to sandwiches than just bread. It's what's between the slices of bread that counts. And you don't even need to use sliced bread. Take a look at page 50 for ideas.

All these recipes can be adapted to include your favourite ingredients – and there is so little cooking involved, you can't go wrong. Success is guaranteed.

Other good snack recipes to try:
- Artichoke & Pepper Frittata (page 70)
- Bean Patties (page 150)
- Beetroot – Apple Salad (page 76)
- The dip recipes on pages 174–179
- Ginger Fruit Salad (page 194)
- Grilled Pepper Salad (page 93)
- Lentil Burgers (page 145)
- Make a Quiche (page 161)
- Roast Vegetable Crisps (page 152)
- Soda Bread (page 171)
- The soup recipes on pages 163–170
- Spanish Tortilla (page 210)
- Spanish Pimientos (page 180)

Simply Sandwiches

Ever since the 4th Earl of Sandwich demanded something he could hold in his hands so he didn't have to leave the gaming table to eat, the sandwich has been one of the world's favourite snack foods. And when you aren't in the mood and can't be bothered to cook, a sandwich is the solution.

A sandwich is quick and easy to prepare, it can be cheap (a slice of bread with yeast extract folded in half counts) and it can be good for you – or very, very unhealthy. It all depends what you put on the bread. Thin white sandwich loaf smeared with butter and thick slices of vegetarian brie cheese should probably only be an occasional treat. Whereas thick slices of wholemeal bread with spinach leaves, a thin slice of vegetarian brie and sliced grapes is a healthier option. Even the student staple beans on toast has a lot going for it nutritionally. You just don't want to eat it at every meal.

Try these ideas for healthy fill-ups without much effort – or washing-up.
▸ Pita Pockets: Use a serrated knife to slice a wholemeal pita bread along the top and open it up. Stuff with Greek Salad (page 60), shredded lettuce and grilled vegetables (page 156) or shredded lettuce and Chilli sin Carne (page 160). Add a dollop of yoghurt, if you like.
▸ It's a Wrap: Soft flour tortillas make interesting sandwich containers. Spread half a tortilla with roasted garlic (page 177), add shredded lettuce and pepper strips, and wrap up.
▸ Mix grated carrot and radish and very finely chopped celery with a few tablespoons hummus. Spread this on mixed-grain bread and add finely sliced baby spinach or rocket leaves. This is good wrapped in a soft flour tortilla, too.
▸ Chop hard-boiled free-range eggs and stir them with mayonnaise or Greek-style yoghurt and salt and pepper to taste. Stir in chopped watercress leaves and/or cress. Spread on wholemeal bread.
▸ Spread vegetarian Stilton on wholemeal bread and sprinkle with finely chopped walnuts. Thinly sliced pears or halved grapes go well with this.
▸ Cut a ciabatta roll in half and drizzle with olive oil. Add grilled vegetables (page 156) and crumbled vegetarian goat's cheese or feta cheese over. Squeeze the sandwich together so the oil soaks into the bread. Add sliced red onion, if you like.
▸ Top a piece of bread with a tomato. Grate vegetarian cheese over, then add another tomato slice and another slice of bread. Add some lettuce leaves, if you like.

► Crush a garlic clove, chop a spring onion and stone and chop a few black olives. Stir them into vegetarian cream cheese, then spread on a roll. Add a slice of tomato, sliced cucumber and Iceberg lettuce.

► Assemble the Tomato & Mozzarella Salad (page 63) between 2 slices of bread.

► Finely chop a free-range hard-boiled egg and mix it with grated vegetarian cheese, finely chopped celery, a spoonful of Greek-style yoghurt and salt and pepper to taste. Spread on a slice of bread, top with snipped cress or alfalfa sprouts or sesame seeds and add another slice of bread.

For other sandwich recipes see:
► Bruschetta (page 53)
► Tomato Bread (page 52)
► Fried-Egg Sandwich (page 41)
► Toasted Cheese & Chutney (page 65)

Garlic Bread

MAKES **ANY NUMBER OF SERVINGS YOU WANT**
PREP TIME: **ABOUT 2 MINUTES**
COOKING TIME: **10–15 MINUTES**

WASTE NOT, WANT NOT. DON'T LET FRENCH BREAD SIT AROUND AND BECOME SO DRY IT HAS TO BE THROWN AWAY. THIS IS A PARTICULARLY GOOD WAY TO GIVE A BURST OF LIFE TO FRENCH BREAD THAT IS DESTINED FOR THE BIN IN ANOTHER DAY. THIS IS GREAT WITH ITALIAN PASTA, OR TRY IT WITH A BOWL OF MEDITERRANEAN GRILLED VEGETABLES (PAGE 155).

USE AS MUCH GARLIC AS YOU LIKE – YOU KNOW WHO'LL BE CLOSE TO YOU IN THE NEXT COUPLE OF HOURS.

French bread
Olive oil
$^1/_2$–2 garlic cloves, depending on the amount of bread
Any fresh herbs you have in the fridge, such as chives or parsley
    (optional)

1. Preheat the oven to 190°C/375°F/Gas 5. Cut the bread in half lengthwise without cutting it all the way through. Open the bread like a book and brush with olive oil, then set aside to soak in while you chop the garlic and herbs.

2. Peel and chop the garlic. Finely snip the fresh chives or chop any herbs you are using.

3. Lightly brush the crumb-side of the bread again, then sprinkle with the garlic and any herbs. Fold the 2 sides of the bread together. Wrap the bread in a sheet of kitchen foil, shiny side in.

4. Put the bread in the oven for 10–15 minutes until warmed through. Eat within the next couple of hours, because the bread will dry out and there won't be any saving it this time.

VARIATIONS
‣ Spread the bread with roasted garlic (page 177).
‣ Garlic-flavoured olive oil saves having to peel and chop the garlic. Or use any other flavoured oil. The oil from a jar of sun-dried tomatoes is good.

Tomato Bread

MAKES **2 SERVINGS**
PREP TIME: **ABOUT 2 MINUTES**
NO COOKING

A TRADITIONAL CATALAN FAVOURITE FROM BARCELONA.

1 piece French or Italian bread, about 15 cm long
1 ripe, juicy tomato, such as beefsteak
Olive oil (optional)
Salt and pepper

1. Preheat the grill to high and position the rack about 10 cm from the heat. While the grill is heating, cut the bread in half lengthwise and cut the tomato in half.

2. Put the bread under the grill, cut-side up, and toast for about 2 minutes until golden brown and crisp.

3. Hold a tomato half cut-side down and rub it back and froth over the toast, pressing down so the juice, seeds and pulp soak into the bread – when you finish you should just have the skin left in your hand. Repeat with the other tomato half and piece of toast.

4. Drizzle with olive oil, if you like, and sprinkle with salt and pepper.

VARIATIONS
‣ Garlic lovers rub the toast with a cut clove of garlic before the tomato.
‣ Top the tomato-rubbed bread with sliced vegetarian goat's cheese and grill until the cheese is golden and bubbling.

Bruschetta

MAKES **1 SERVING**
PREP TIME: **ABOUT 5 MINUTES**
COOKING TIME: **ABOUT 5 MINUTES**

THIS IS THE ITALIAN VERSION OF OPEN-FACE TOASTED SANDWICHES. IN ITALY THE BREAD
IS TRADITIONALLY CUT FROM A LARGE COUNTRY-STYLE LOAF AND GRILLED OVER AN OPEN
fiRE. YOU CAN USE ANY BREAD, BUT A fiRM LOAF, SUCH AS SOURDOUGH, IS BEST. PICK
UP A BRUSCHETTA TO EAT WITH YOUR fiNGERS, OR USE A KNIFE AND FORK.

1 slice bread
¹/₂ garlic clove
Olive oil

1. Heat the grill to high and position the rack about 10 cm from the heat.
Place the bread on the grill rack and toast for about 2 minutes until
golden brown.

2. Flip the bread over and continue grilling until toasted and golden.

3. Peel the garlic, then rub it back and forth over one side of the toasted
bread. Drizzle with olive oil. Eat the bruschetta plain like this, or add
a topping. The choice is yours.

TOPPING IDEAS
▸ Drained canned broad or cannellini beans tossed with extra-virgin
olive oil, chopped sun-dried tomatoes and lots of any fresh herb you
have in the fridge – parsley, basil and thyme are good.
▸ Smashed Cannellini Bean Spread (page 179) with sliced cherry
tomatoes or stoned olives.
▸ Rocket leaves with Mediterranean Grilled Vegetables (page 156).
▸ Hummus, home-made (page 175) or bought, with sliced tomatoes
and a sprinkling of chopped toasted pine nuts.
▸ Garlic Mushrooms (page 87).

Fried Halloumi

MAKES **1 SERVING**
PREP TIME: **ABOUT 2 MINUTES**
COOKING TIME: **ABOUT 4 MINUTES**

THIS IS LIKE THE LITTLE BLACK DRESS OF SNACK FOODS – IT GOES WITH EVERYTHING. WHEN YOU'RE JUST A LITTLE PECKISH, THE HOT CHEESE WITH PIECES OF FLAT BREAD WILL SATISFY YOU, BUT IF YOU WANT MORE OF A MEAL DRIZZLE THE HALLOUMI WITH OLIVE OIL AND ADD A SALAD. OR EAT IT WITH LOTS OF FRESH VEGETABLE STICKS – HALLOUMI AND RED-PEPPER STRIPS IS A WINNING COMBINATION.

YOU'LL ENJOY THE FRIED HALLOUMI MOST WHEN YOU EAT IT AS SOON AS POSSIBLE AFTER MAKING, ALTHOUGH THE FRIED PIECES WILL KEEP, COVERED, IN THE FRIDGE FOR 2 DAYS TO ADD TO SALADS.

2 tablespoons plain white flour
Salt and pepper
Vegetarian halloumi cheese
Olive, sunflower or rapeseed oil for frying

1. Put the flour on a plate, add salt and pepper to taste and stir to spread the seasoning through the flour.

2. Drain the halloumi and pat it dry with kitchen paper. Use a cook's knife to cut four 0.5cm slices. Most halloumi is sold in a rectangular shape, so cut the slices from the wide side.

3. Dredge the cheese slices in flour on both sides and tap off any extra flour.

4. Heat a thin layer of oil in a frying pan, ideally non-stick, over a medium-high heat. Add the halloumi slices and fry for about 2 minutes until golden brown, then use a knife or palette knife to flip the pieces over and continue frying until golden.

5. Remove the cheese from the pan and drain on crumpled kitchen paper.

SERVING IDEAS
▶ Fried Halloumi Sandwich: Fill a lightly toasted pita bread with sliced lettuce, sliced tomatoes, chopped cucumber and sprouts, and add the hot cheese. Add a spoonful of Tahini-Yoghurt Dip (page 176), if you like.
▶ Serve the hot halloumi with a portion of Catalan Spinach (page 98).
▶ Chop the hot cheese and add it to Mediterranean Grilled Vegetables (page 156) or spoon over hot polenta or couscous.
▶ The hot cheese also tastes great with a squeeze of fresh lemon juice and chopped fresh parsley or mint. Add a sprinkling of cayenne pepper or paprika, if you like.
▶ Sprinkle the hot cheese with finely chopped red onion or spring onions, toasted pine nuts (page 35) and olive oil.

Tandoori Paneer

MAKES **2 SERVINGS**
PREP TIME: **5 MINUTES, PLUS SEVERAL HOURS OPTIONAL
MARINATING** / COOKING TIME: **ABOUT 15 MINUTES**

IF YOU'VE GOT YOUR ACT TOGETHER, LEAVE THE PANEER TO MARINATE BEFORE YOU
RUN OFF TO LECTURES, OTHERWISE SKIP STEP 3.

1 garlic clove
75 g natural yoghurt
$^{1}/_{2}$ teaspoon ground cumin
$^{1}/_{4}$ teaspoon chilli powder, or to taste
$^{1}/_{4}$ teaspoon salt
Pinch of ground turmeric
2 drops of red food colouring (optional; see page 25)
225 g paneer

TO SERVE
Raita (page 178)
Lemon wedges

1. Peel and crush the garlic. Put the garlic in a bowl and stir in the
yoghurt, cumin, chilli powder, salt and food colouring, if you are using.

2. Remove the paneer from its package and drain well. Cut it into bite-
sized cubes, then stir into the yoghurt mixture.

3. Cover the bowl with clingfilm and leave the paneer to marinate for
at least 30 minutes. Give the paneer a stir occasionally.

4. When you are ready to cook, heat the grill to high. Line a baking sheet
with kitchen foil, shiny side down. Put the paneer cubes on the baking
sheet and position the baking sheet about 10 cm under the grill.

5. Grill the paneer cubes for about 15 minutes, turning them several
times, until the marinade looks dry and the edges are charred. These are
particularly good with Raita (page 178) on the side and lemon wedges
for squeezing over.

VARIATION
Tandoori Paneer Kebabs: Marinate the paneer as above. Use long metal
skewers or soak 4 wooden skewers for 30 minutes. Heat the oven to
200°C/400°F/Gas 6. Cut 1 red or green pepper into cubes and 1 onion
into chunks. Thread the marinated paneer, pepper cubes and onion
wedges on to the skewers. Place the skewers on a baking sheet and
roast for 25 minutes, turning them twice, until the peppers and onions
are tender. Serve with Raita and 3–4–1 Rice (page 131).

Tomato Salsa with Corn Chips

 MAKES **2 SERVINGS**
PREP TIME: **ABOUT 10 MINUTES, PLUS OPTIONAL CHILLING**
NO COOKING

2 ripe, juicy tomatoes
1/2 small red onion
1 small green chilli
1/2 lemon
6–8 sprigs fresh coriander or parsley
Salt and pepper
Corn Chips, to serve

1. Cut the tomato in half and use a small spoon to scoop out the cores and seeds. Use a sharp knife to cut the flesh into fine dice. Put the tomato dice in a glass bowl and set aside.

2. Peel and finely chop the red onion, then add it to the tomato. De-seed the chilli if you want a mild salsa or leave the seeds in if you like hot, spicy food. Finely chop the chilli and add it to the other ingredients.

3. Very finely chop the parsley leaves and add them to the other ingredients with salt and pepper to taste. Squeeze over 1 teaspoon of lemon juice and stir all the ingredients together. Taste and adjust the seasoning or lemon juice.

4. Eat at once, or cover and chill until required. Serve with corn chips – or Pita Crisps (page 179), breadsticks or a selection of raw vegetable sticks or slices. Any leftover salsa will keep in the fridge for up to 3 days in a covered container.

VARIATIONS
▶ Salsa Toasts: Spread a slice of wholemeal toast with vegetarian cream cheese, then top with salsa. Or add the salsa to a toasted vegetarian cheese sandwich.
▶ Nachos with Salsa: Line a baking sheet with kitchen foil, and top with a single layer of corn chips. Grate over vegetarian Cheddar cheese, then bake in a preheated 200°C/400°F/Gas 6 oven for about 10 minutes.
▶ Melon Salsa: Peel, seed and dice 1/4 of a cantaloupe melon and toss with a de-seeded and finely chopped green chilli, chopped fresh coriander leaves and lime juice to taste.

Trail Mix

MAKES **AS MANY SERVINGS AS YOU LIKE**
PREP TIME: **ABOUT 5 MINUTES**
COOKING TIME: **UP TO 15 MINUTES IF YOU TOAST THE NUTS**

MAKE UP A BATCH OF THIS AND KEEP IT IN A CUPBOARD FOR A QUICK BURST OF ENERGY.
A LITTLE OF THIS GOES A LONG WAY – IT'S HIGH IN CALORIES AND FAT, BUT CONTAINS LOTS
OF MINERALS – SO DON'T PIG OUT ON THE WHOLE LOT IN ONE GO. IF YOU GO FOR A HIKE
OR CYCLE RIDE, SET OFF WITH A BAG OF THIS IN YOUR BACKPACK.

IF YOU AND YOUR FRIENDS SHOP IN BULK FOR THE INGREDIENTS FOR DIY MUESLI
(PAGE 35) ADD THESE INGREDIENTS TO THE SHOPPING LIST.

Shelled Brazil nuts
Shelled unsalted peanuts
Pecans
Sunflower seeds
Dried apple rings
Dried pineapple rings
Ready-to-eat dried apricots
Ready-to-eat dried cherries or cranberries

1. Toasting the nuts isn't essential but it develops their flavour. If you
have time – it only takes a couple of minutes – toast them as instructed
on page 35. Toast each type of nut separately and immediately tip
them out of the pan.

2. Use a knife or scissors to cut the apricots, apple rings and
pineapple rings into bite-sized pieces. Toss with the nuts and store
in an air-tight jar.

Spiced Nuts & Seeds

MAKES **ABOUT 225 G**
PREP TIME: **LESS THAN 5 MINUTES**
COOKING TIME: **ABOUT 15 MINUTES**

YOUR WEAPON AGAINST SNACK ATTACKS. SAVE THESE FOR AN OCCASIONAL TREAT
THOUGH, AS THEY ARE LOADED WITH FAT. THESE ARE, HOWEVER, A HEALTHY ALTERNATIVE
TO OPENING A BAG OF CRISPS, BECAUSE NUTS AND SEEDS HAVE PLENTY OF ESSENTIAL
MINERALS AND CONTAIN THE 'GOOD' TYPE OF FATS (PAGE 11).

125 g shelled nuts, such as blanched almonds, pistachio nuts
    or walnuts, or a mixture
2 tablespoons olive oil
125 g pine nuts
125 g shelled pumpkin and/or sunflower seeds
1 teaspoon mild or hot paprika, to taste
Salt

1. Preheat the oven to 170°C/325°F/Gas 3. Heat the oil in a roasting tin or large frying pan with an ovenproof handle over a medium-high heat and swirl it round to coat the base.

2. Add the nuts and stir them around until they are all lightly coated with the oil. Stir in the paprika and salt to taste, then spread out the nuts into a single layer.

3. Put the tin in the oven and roast the nuts for about 15 minutes, stirring occasionally, until they are a golden brown. Drain them well on a double thickness of kitchen paper, then leave to cool and store in an air-tight container.

VARIATION
Use ground cumin or coriander if you don't have any paprika.

Toasted Goat's Cheese Salad

MAKES **1 SERVING**
PREP TIME: **ABOUT 2 MINUTES**
COOKING TIME: **LESS THAN 5 MINUTES**

THERE ARE TWO REASONS WHY THIS FEATURES ON JUST ABOUT ALL VEGETARIAN RESTAURANT MENUS. ONE IS BECAUSE IT TASTES GREAT AND THE OTHER IS THAT IT IS SO EASY TO PREPARE. YOU'LL fiND THIS UPMARKET VERSION OF CHEESE ON TOAST IS VERSATILE, TOO. IT'S JUST AS SUITABLE FOR A SOLITARY MEAL WHILE YOU PONDER REQUIRED READING AS IT IS FOR A DINNER PARTY – SERVE 2 CHEESE-TOPPED TOASTS PER PERSON FOR A STARTER OR 4–6 TOASTS FOR A MAIN COURSE WITH PLENTY OF SALAD GREENS.

Mixed salad leaves
Vegetarian goat's cheese with rind
French bread
Olive oil
Vinaigrette Dressing (page 172)

1. Heat the grill to high and position the grill rack about 10 cm from the heat. While the grill is heating, rinse the salad leaves, pat them dry with a clean tea towel and put them in a bowl; set aside.

2. Decide how hungry you are and cut slices of French bread about 0.5 cm thick. Next, cut the same number of cheese slices, also about 0.5 cm thick.

3. Place the bread slices on the grill rack and grill for 2 minutes, or until crisp and golden brown. Turn the slices over and brush the untoasted sides with olive oil, then top each with a slice of cheese.

4. Return the toasts to the grill and continue grilling until the cheese is golden and bubbling.

5. Toss the salad leaves with just enough dressing to lightly coat them. Place the leaves on your plate and top with the cheese toasts.

VARIATIONS
▸ Instead of brushing the untoasted side of the bread with olive oil in Step 3, use Pesto Sauce (page 117) or bottled tapenade.
▸ Slice a drained sun-dried tomato that has been soaked in olive oil and put under the cheese before you grill the cheese.
▸ Replace the goat's cheese with Beer & Cheese Dip (see page 174) spread over the untoasted side of the bread, then toast under the grill until bubbling and golden.

Spinach Salad

MAKES **1 SERVING**
PREP TIME: **UP TO 10 MINUTES, DEPENDING IF YOU HAVE TO MAKE THE DRESSING / NO COOKING TIME**

50 g baby spinach leaves, rinsed
1 orange
2 tablespoons Vinaigrette Dressing (page 172)
50 g vegetarian blue cheese, such as Stilton or Danish blue
Sunflower seeds
A slice of toast

1. Rinse the spinach leaves well and pat them dry with a clean tea towel. Put them in a bowl and set aside.

2. Using a small serrated knife, remove the peel and all white pith from the orange. Cut the segments free and add them to the spinach leaves.

3. Add the dressing to the bowl and toss the leaves so they are all lightly coated.

4. Crumble over the cheese, then sprinkle with a few sunflower seeds. Eat with a slice of toasted wholemeal bread.

See over for variations.

VARIATIONS

‣ Try vegetarian goat's cheese instead of blue cheese, and chopped pecans instead of the sunflower seeds. Or sprinkle the salad with a handful of Spiced Nuts & Seeds (page 57).
‣ Toss in fresh beansprouts or sliced avocado.
‣ Add an extra peppery flavour with rocket and/or watercress leaves.
‣ Omit the vinaigrette and use Tahini-Yoghurt Dip (page 176) instead.

Greek Salad

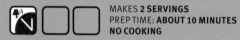 MAKES **2 SERVINGS**
PREP TIME: **ABOUT 10 MINUTES**
NO COOKING

60 g black olives, such as Kalamata
14 cherry tomatoes
10cm piece of cucumber
4 slices Iceberg or Cos lettuce
125 g vegetarian feta cheese, drained
About 1 ¹/₂ tablespoons extra-virgin olive oil
¹/₂ lemon
Salt and pepper

1. Pit the olives – a cherry pitter makes easy work of this, but if you don't have one, use a small knife – and cut them in half. Cut each of the cherry tomatoes in half. Cut the cucumber in half lengthwise and use a small spoon to scoop out the seeds, then slice the cucumber.

2. Rinse the lettuce leaves and pat them dry. Roll them into a tight cylinder, then cut crosswise into slices.

3. Put the cherry tomatoes in a bowl with the olives and cucumber. Crumble in the cheese, then add the shredded lettuce leaves, oil and a squeeze of lemon juice. Toss the ingredients together and add salt and pepper to taste.

VARIATIONS
‣ For a more filling meal, stir in 150 g cooled pasta or rice. Greek orzo is good, but so are Italian twists, corkscrews, snails or macaroni.
‣ Use baby spinach leaves or rocket leaves instead of lettuce.

Thai Mango Salad

MAKES **2–3 SERVINGS**
PREP TIME: **15 MINUTES, PLUS MARINATING**
NO COOKING

¹/₂ red onion
1 ripe mango
¹/₄ cucumber
2 tablespoons salted peanuts, chopped

SPICY CHILLI DRESSING
1 fresh red chilli
1 tablespoon sunflower or rapeseed oil
1 tablespoon lime juice
¹/₂ teaspoon light-brown sugar
1 tablespoon chopped fresh coriander leaves
Salt and pepper

1. To make the dressing, de-seed the chilli and cut it into thin slices. Put the chilli in a bowl with oil, lime juice, sugar and coriander leaves. Add salt and pepper to taste and use a fork to blend the ingredients together, stirring until the sugar dissolves; set aside.

2. Cut the onion into thin half-moon slices. Separate the onion slices and stir them into the bowl with the dressing. Set aside and leave to marinate for 20–30 minutes to soften the onion.

3. Meanwhile, peel, de-seed and cut the mango into thin slices. Cut the cucumber in half, use a teaspoon to remove the seeds, then thinly slice the cucumber flesh.

4. Add the mango and cucumber slices to the bowl with the dressing and onion, and toss together. Chop the peanuts and sprinkle them over the top.

VARIATIONS
► To make more substantial, stir in 75 g cooked rice stick noodles.
► If you don't have any fresh coriander, use fresh parsley or mint.
► When fresh mangoes aren't in season, use orange segments instead. Or buy canned mangos in natural juice.

Lettuce Rolls

MAKES **4 ROLLS**
PREP TIME: **ABOUT 5 MINUTES**
NO COOKING

CRISP AND CRUNCHY, THESE ARE LIKE A SALAD WRAP. AND THEY ARE INfiNITELY
VARIABLE SO USE WHATEVER CRISP VEGETABLES YOU fiND IN THE FRIDGE – TAKE A LOOK
AT THE IDEAS BELOW IF YOU WANT MORE INSPIRATION, BUT IT WON'T BE LONG BEFORE
YOU START MAKING YOUR OWN FLAVOUR COMBINATIONS. THE SKY'S THE LIMIT.

$^1/_2$ red, green or yellow pepper
$^1/_2$ carrot
1 spring onion
3 tablespoons hummus, home-made (page 15) or bought
Finely chopped fresh coriander or parsley
4 large lettuce leaves, such as Iceberg, rinsed and patted dry
Baby spinach leaves (optional)
Salt and pepper

DIPPING SAUCE
2 fresh red chillies, de-seeded and sliced
150 ml water
2 garlic cloves, crushed
$^1/_2$ teaspoon salt
4 tablespoons soft light-brown sugar

1. To make the dipping sauce, put the chilli with half the water in a
saucepan over a medium heat and simmer for 3–5 minutes until the chilli
slices are tender. Add the remaining ingredients and bring to the boil,
stirring to dissolve the sugar. Reduce the heat to very low and leave to
simmer for about 5 minutes. Remove from the heat and leave to cool.

2. Very thinly cut the pepper half into thin strips – a vegetable peeler
is ideal for this, otherwise use the sharpest knife you have. Peel or scrub
the carrot and grate it lengthwise down the medium holes on a grater
to get long strips, or coarsely grate. Very thinly slice the spring onion.

3. Put the hummus or dip in a bowl and stir in the pepper, carrot
and spring onion. Taste and adjust the seasoning if necessary.

4. Put the lettuce leaves, vein-side down, on the work surface. If you
have any spinach leaves scatter them over the lettuce leaves.

5. Divide the vegetable mixture between the lettuce leaves in the centre,
spooning it almost from the top to the bottom of the leaves. Working
with one lettuce leaf at a time, fold down the top part of the leaf and fold
up the bottom part of the leaf. Fold in one side, then roll up. The rolls
are ready to eat as they are, or you can dip them in the sauce.

VARIATIONS

▸ Try a Mexican filling with rinsed canned kidney or cannellini beans, rinsed canned sweetcorn kernels, grated vegetarian hard cheese, a diced tomato and finely chopped red or green fresh chilli. Add a dollop of soured cream or Greek-style yoghurt.

▸ Soak rice vermicelli noodles in hot water for 20 minutes, or boil according to the packet instructions, then drain well. Mix with chopped peanuts, grated carrot, cucumber, radishes and a little sweet soy sauce and Chinese rice wine. Add freshly torn fresh coriander leaves and roll up.

Other Ideas for Fresh Fruit & Veg Salads

▸ Waldorf Salad: Toss grated vegetarian Cheddar cheese, sliced seedless grapes and cored and chopped apples with mayonnaise, then pile on Cos lettuce leaves. Sprinkle with walnut pieces.

▸ Carrot Crudité: Mix the grated rind of 1 orange, 2 tablespoons orange juice and 2 tablespoons extra-virgin olive oil in a bowl. Add salt and pepper to taste, and a crushed garlic clove, if you like. Peel and grate 2 large carrots into the bowl and stir together. Optional ingredients include toasted sesame seeds (page 35), chopped toasted, skinned hazelnuts (page 35) or chopped fresh parsley.

▸ Tomato & Mozzarella Salad: Arrange vegetarian mozzarella and tomato slices on a plate. Add basil leaves and drizzle with olive oil.

▸ Use a small serrated knife to remove the peel and bitter white pith from an orange, then thinly slice the fruit. Thinly slice a fresh fennel bulb. Arrange the orange and fennel slices on a plate, then scatter fresh mint leaves or sliced, stoned olives over. Drizzle with extra-virgin olive oil and freshly squeezed orange juice.

▸ Toss drained kidney beans, chopped tomatoes and sweetcorn kernels together. Stir in Greek-style yoghurt or Vinaigrette Dressing (page 172).

▸ Mix leftover rice with canned black beans, sweetcorn kernels, lots of chopped parsley, then add olive oil and toss together. Throw in a chopped red onion or spring onions, too, if you like.

▸ Add fresh fruit, such as melon cubes, mango slices or pineapple chunks, to cottage cheese. Sprinkle with sesame seeds or toasted pumpkin seeds, or add a handful of golden raisins.

▸ Arrange chicory leaves on a plate and crumble over vegetarian Stilton cheese, or other vegetarian blue cheese, and chopped walnuts. Drizzle with olive oil and balsamic vinegar. Snipped fresh chives are good, too.

Curried Eggs

MAKES **4 SERVINGS**
PREP TIME: **15 MINUTES, INCLUDING HARD-BOILING THE EGGS**
COOKING TIME: **ABOUT 25 MINUTES**

1 onion
1 tablespoon sunflower, rapeseed or groundnut oil
1 teaspoon curry paste – you decide on the heat
1 can (400 g) chopped tomatoes
About 100 ml water
Pinch of soft light-brown sugar
4 large free-range eggs
150 g shelled peas, fresh or frozen
2 tablespoons natural yoghurt
Pinch of garam masala
Salt and pepper
Chopped fresh coriander (optional)

1. Peel and thinly slice the onion. Heat the oil in a large wok or frying pan with a lid, ideally non-stick, over a medium-high heat. Add the onion and stir for 5–8 minutes until golden, but not dark brown.

2. Stir in the curry paste and continue stirring for 2 minutes. Add the tomatoes with their juice, the water, sugar and salt and pepper to taste, and bring to the boil. Reduce the heat to low, half cover the pan and leave to simmer for 15 minutes. Check occasionally to make sure the tomato mixture isn't drying out and stir in a little extra water if necessary.

3. Meanwhile, to hard-boil the eggs, put the eggs in a saucepan and cover with 5 cm water. Set the pan over a high heat and bring the water to a full boil. Immediately turn the heat to low and leave the eggs to simmer for 10 minutes longer: start counting from the time the water boils.

4. Drain the eggs and run cold water over them for 1–2 minutes to stop the cooking. Tap the eggs on the side of the sink to crack the shells, then peel off the shells and cut each egg in half, from top to bottom.

5. Stir the frozen or fresh peas into the tomato mixture after 10 minutes to cook in the sauce.

6. Add the eggs to the pan and spoon the sauce over. Leave them just long enough to warm through. Put the yoghurt in a small cup and stir several spoonfuls of the tomato mixture into it, then stir this mixture into the pan: do not boil. Sprinkle with garam masala and chopped coriander.

Toasted Cheese & Chutney

  MAKES **1 SANDWICH**
PREP TIME: **ABOUT 2 MINUTES**
COOKING TIME: **ABOUT 5 MINUTES**

IF YOU CAN'T EVEN BE BOTHERED TO TOAST THIS SANDWICH – OR ANY VARIATIONS BELOW
– IT IS JUST AS TASTY. EXPERIMENT WITH DIFFERENT BREADS FROM THE SUPERMARKET,
OR MAKE YOUR OWN (PAGE 171).

2 slices wholemeal bread
About 30 g vegetarian hard or semi-hard cheese, such as Cheddar or Edam
Mango chutney – or your favourite chutney

1. Heat the grill to high and position the rack about 10 cm from the heat.

2. Grate the cheese over one slice of bread. Spread some chutney over
the other slice of bread and put it, chutney-side down, on top of the
cheese. Squeeze the 2 slices of bread together.

3. Put the sandwich under the grill and grill for 2 minutes, or until the
top slice of bread is golden brown. Flip the sandwich over and toast the
other side, by which time the cheese will have melted. Cut the sandwich
in half and let it cool for a few minutes before you bite – the melted
cheese will be hot.

VARIATIONS
▸ Toasted Cheese & Onion: Replace the chutney with thin red onion
or white onion slices, or finely chopped spring onions. Add chopped
fresh parsley, coriander, dill or chives, and toast as above.
▸ Try mango chutney and vegetarian goat's cheese.
▸ Or try vegetarian goat's cheese with Tomato Salsa (page 56).
▸ When you're feeling hung over, add a sliced banana. The potassium
it contains will help you feel better.
▸ Beer & Cheese Dip (page 174) makes a good toasted or cold sandwich
filling, too.
▸ Add a leftover fried Aubergine Slice (page 72) with a thin slice of
vegetarian halloumi cheese or crumbled feta cheese. Add a tomato
slice too, if you like.
▸ For even quicker toasted sandwiches, use a soft flour tortilla. Put
the tortilla in a frying pan over a high heat. Spread half the tortilla with
chutney and top with the grated cheese. Fold the tortilla in half to
enclose the cheese. Flip the tortilla over (if you don't have asbestos
fingers use a knife or palette knife) and continue toasting until it is
golden brown on both sides. Middle Eastern flatbread works just as well.

Japanese Mushroom Broth

MAKES **2 SERVINGS**
PREP TIME: **ABOUT 12 MINUTES**
COOKING TIME: **ABOUT 7 MINUTES**

AN ORIENTAL VEGETARIAN VERSION OF CHICKEN SOUP – THIS WILL WARM YOU UP
WHEN YOU'RE FEELING UNDER THE WEATHER.

75 g shiitake mushrooms
75 g broccoli florets
4 spring onions
2-cm piece of fresh root ginger
2 shallots
1 large garlic clove
1 green chilli
1 tablespoon sunflower or rapeseed oil
500 ml water
2 sachets instant miso soup mix
1 tablespoon dark soy sauce or tamari
1 tablespoon rice vinegar
Large handful of fresh watercress leaves

1. Wipe the shiitake mushrooms with a damp cloth and cut off the ends of the stalks, then thinly slice the caps and stalks. Cut the broccoli florets into small pieces. Trim and chop the spring onions.

2. Peel and thinly slice the ginger. Peel and thinly slice the shallots. Peel and crush the garlic. De-seed and thinly slice the chilli, or leave the seeds in if you like very hot, spicy food.

3. Heat the oil in a saucepan over a medium-high heat. Add the ginger, shallots and garlic and stir around for a couple of minutes until they are soft, but not brown.

4. Stir in the water and miso soup mix, then add the mushrooms, broccoli, chilli, soy sauce and rice vinegar and bring to the boil, stirring. Reduce the heat to low and simmer for 3–5 minutes until the mushrooms and broccoli are tender.

5. Stir in the watercress. Taste and add extra soy sauce or rice vinegar, if necessary.

VARIATION

For a more substantial meal, include 150 g of cooked medium rice sticks.

GET YOUR 5-A-DAY ... & POTATOES, TOO

Remember when your mum used to tell you to eat your greens? Well, she was right. Nutritional experts around the world agree that eating lots of fruit and vegetables every day is good for your health. Current recommendations are that you have at least five portions of different fruit and vegetables a day. For healthy vegetarians, that's easy peasy – even a glass of juice counts (but only one glass counts).

The recipes in this chapter will help you towards hitting your 5-a-day goal. Often if you stop at the supermarket late in the day fresh produce is on sale. Pick up a bargain and hopefully the recipes in this book will help transform it into a meal or two. (If you don't find what you're looking for in this chapter, try the index.)

If 5-a-day sounds like a lot, it's not. A portion can be as small as 4 tablespoons of chopped French beans or half a red pepper. Take a look at the chart on the following page and you'll see how easy it is to have several portions of fruit or vegetables in a single meal.

Alas, the nation's favourite vegetable, the potato, doesn't count towards your 5-a-day no matter how you cook it. But it still plays an important part in a healthy, balanced diet by contributing complex carbs, a variety of nutrients and fibre. There are many options besides chips.

Mixed fruit and veg dishes, such as Couscous with Moroccan Vegetables (page 138), are a real bonus for chasing the 5-a-day goal.

More-than-one-portion-of-fruit-or-veg dishes to try:
- Big Bowls of Spinach Salad (page 59)
- Cider-Barley Stew (page 142)
- Curried Veg & Semolina (page 144)
- Mediterranean Grilled Vegetables (page 155)
- Minestrone (page 165)
- Overnight Dried Fruit Salad (page 36)
- Vegetable Bake (page 184)

HOW MUCH IS A PORTION?

Fruit:

Apple	1 medium
Apple, dried rings	4 rings
Apricot, dried	3 whole
Avocado	$1/2$ an avocado
Banana chips	1 handful
Banana, fresh	1 medium
Blackberries	1 handful (9 or 10)
Cherries, dried	1 heaped tablespoon
Dried fruit, mixed	1 heaped tablespoon
Fig, dried	2 figs
Fruit juice	150 ml (only 1 glass a day counts)
Fruit salad, canned	3 heaped tablespoons
Fruit salad, fresh	3 heaped tablespoons
Fruit smoothie	150 ml
Orange	1 orange
Peach, dried	2 halves
Peach, fresh	1 medium
Pear, dried	2 halves
Pear, fresh	1 medium
Pineapple, canned	1 heaped tablespoon
Pineapple, dried	1 heaped tablespoon
Pineapple, fresh	1 large slice
Plum	2 medium
Prune, dried	3 prunes
Raisins	1 tablespoon
Raspberries, fresh	2 handfuls
Strawberries, fresh	7 strawberries
Sultanas	1 heaped tablespoon

Vegetables:

Aubergine	$1/3$ aubergine
Beans, baked	3 heaped tablespoons (only 1 serving a day counts)
Beans, barlotti	3 heaped tablespoons
Beans, black-eyed	3 heaped tablespoons
Beans, broad	3 heaped tablespoons
Beans, butter	3 heaped tablespoons
Beans, cannelloni	3 heaped tablespoons
Beans, French	4 heaped tablespoons
Beans, kidney	3 heaped tablespoons
Beansprouts, fresh	2 handfuls
Broccoli	2 spears
Cabbage, shredded	3 heaped tablespoons
Carrots, fresh slices	3 heaped tablespoons
Cauliflower	8 florets
Celery	3 sticks
Chickpeas	3 heaped tablespoons
Courgettes	$1/2$ large
Cucumber	5cm piece
Leeks	1 leek (white portion)
Lentils	3 tablespoons
Lettuce (mixed leaves)	1 cereal bowl
Mangetout	1 handful
Mushrooms, button sliced	14 mushrooms, or 3–4 tablespoons,
Onion	1 medium
Parsnip	1 large
Peppers, fresh	$1/2$ pepper
Spring onions	8 onions
Sweetcorn, canned	3 heaped tablespoons
Tomato, fresh	1 medium or 7 cherry
Tomato, sun-dried	4 pieces

Artichoke & Pepper Frittata

MAKES **4–6 SERVINGS**
PREP TIME: **ABOUT 5 MINUTES**
COOKING TIME: **ABOUT 15 MINUTES**

FRITTATAS ARE FLAT, SET OMELETTES THAT ARE WORTH LEARNING TO MAKE. LIKE ALL FRITTATAS, THIS RECIPE TASTES EQUALLY GOOD HOT OR AT ROOM TEMPERATURE. IT CAN SEEM LIKE A LIFESAVER IF YOU HAVE HALF A FRITTATA WAITING IN THE FRIDGE WHEN YOU STAGGER IN AFTER A LONG SESSION AT THE PUB. AND THIS WILL DO FOR BREAKFAST AS WELL.

A NON-STICK PAN IS BEST FOR THIS, BUT AN ORDINARY PAN WORKS fiNE AS LONG AS YOU CHECK THE BOTTOM OF THE FRITTATA DURING COOKING TO MAKE SURE IT DOESN'T STICK AND BURN.

1 onion
1–2 garlic cloves, to taste
2 or 3 tablespoons olive oil
1 red pepper
1 green pepper
400 g bottled artichoke hearts in oil
5 large free-range eggs
$^1/_2$ teaspoon dried mixed herbs (optional)
About 50 g vegetarian Parmesan-style cheese
Salt and pepper

1. Heat the grill to high. Peel and thinly slice the onion. Peel and crush the garlic cloves.

2. Heat the oil in a 20 or 22cm (ideally non-stick) frying pan with a flameproof handle, over a medium-high heat. Swirl the oil around so it coats the base and side of the pan. Add the onion and fry for 3–5 minutes, stirring occasionally, until it is soft but not brown.

3. Meanwhile, cut the peppers in half, remove the cores and seeds and thinly slice the flesh. Remove the artichoke hearts from the oil and cut them into quarters lengthwise.

4. Add the pepper to the pan and fry for 2–3 minutes, stirring frequently. Add the artichokes and gently stir.

5. Crack the eggs into a small bowl and beat them with a fork. Add the mixed herbs and salt and pepper to taste, and beat again.

6. Scrape off any crusty bits from the base of the pan. If you're not using a non-stick pan, add another tablespoon of oil to the pan and swirl it around. Pour the egg mixture into the pan, letting it run to the edge. Shake the pan back and forth over the heat until the eggs just begin to set.

7. Use a fork or metal spatula to push the cooked egg and vegetables to the centre of the pan, so the uncooked egg mixture can run underneath.

8. Reduce the heat to medium and continue cooking for 4–5 minutes until the under-side of the omelette is set. Use a metal spatula or knife to lift an edge – it should be golden brown and set.

9. Grate the cheese over the top of the frittata, then put it under the grill until the top is golden brown and set. The frittata should slide on to a plate, but if it has stuck on the bottom cut it into wedges and serve straight from the pan.

VARIATIONS
▶ Onion Frittata: Omit the artichokes and peppers, and instead use 3 sliced large onions and 6 chopped spring onions.
▶ Spinach Frittata: Fry the onion as above, then add 250 g of rinsed baby spinach leaves and fry the spinach for about 3 minutes until it wilts. Pour the spinach and onions into the egg mixture in Step 5. Continue with the recipe as above from Step 6.

Roasted Asparagus

MAKES **2–3 SERVINGS**
PREP TIME: **ABOUT 5 MINUTES**
COOKING TIME: **UP TO 15 MINUTES**

ONCE YOU'VE EATEN ROASTED ASPARAGUS, YOU'LL BE HOOKED. THIS TECHNIQUE ELIMINATES THE DANGER OF OVERCOOKING ASSOCIATED WITH STEAMING ASPARAGUS. ENJOY THE SPEARS WITH A DASH OF BALSAMIC VINEGAR AND A FINE SHAVING OF VEGETARIAN PECORINO CHEESE ON TOP. OR CUT COLD SPEARS INTO BITE-SIZED PIECES AND TOSS WITH LEFTOVER RICE TO MAKE A SALAD.

450 g fresh asparagus
Olive oil
Salt

1. Heat the oven to 230°C/450°F/Gas 8. Rinse the asparagus well and pat dry. Hold one end of each asparagus spear in your hand and bend it back on itself – it will snap where the stalk becomes too woody to eat; discard the woody ends.

2. Rub olive oil all over the asparagus spears, then sprinkle with salt. Place them in a single layer in a roasting pan and roast for 10–15 minutes until they are just beginning to turn brown. The exact length of time depends on the thickness – when you pick up a spear it should be tender, but not falling over.

Aubergine Slices
with Yoghurt Sauce

MAKES **2–3 SERVINGS**
PREP TIME: **ABOUT 10 MINUTES, PLUS 45 MINUTES STANDING**
COOKING TIME: **ABOUT 15 MINUTES**

EAT THE AUBERGINE SLICES AND YOGHURT SAUCE WITH SOME PLAIN BOILED RICE ON THE SIDE. OR SERVE THE AUBERGINE MEZE-STYLE WITH FRIED HALLOUMI (PAGE 54), CHILLED MEDITERRANEAN BROAD BEANS (PAGE 75), A BOWL OF HUMMUS, HOME-MADE (PAGE 175) OR BOUGHT, AND TOASTED PITA BREAD.

1 aubergine, about 500 g
Olive, sunflower or rapeseed oil
Salt and pepper
Chopped fresh coriander to garnish (optional)

FOR THE YOGHURT SAUCE
2 garlic cloves, or to taste
150 ml Greek-style yoghurt

1. Rinse and dry the aubergine. Cut the aubergine into round discs about 1 cm thick. Place the slices in a colander set in the sink, sprinkle with salt and set aside for at least 45 minutes. (This is called 'degorging' and stops the aubergine from becoming soggy when it cooks.)

2. Meanwhile, peel and finely chop the garlic cloves for the sauce – use as many or as few as you like. Put the yoghurt in a bowl and stir in the garlic and $^1/_2$ teaspoon of salt. Cover the bowl with clingfilm and chill until you are ready to serve. Line a large plate with a double thickness of crumpled kitchen paper and set aside.

3. Rinse the aubergine slices to remove the salt and bitter juices, then pat dry. It is important that they are completely dry.

4. Heat a thin layer of oil in a large frying pan until a cube of bread sizzles and browns in 30 seconds.

5. Add as many aubergine slices as will fit in a single layer without overcrowding the pan. Fry the slices for about 2 minutes until golden brown, then flip them over and fry on the other side. Immediately transfer the aubergine slices to the kitchen paper to drain, and pat the excess oil off the top with more crumpled paper. If you have more aubergine slices to fry, cover the plate with aluminium foil to keep them warm.

6. Serve the hot aubergine slices with a dollop of cool yoghurt sauce on top. If you have any fresh coriander, sprinkle it over the top.

VARIATION
▸ Greek Yoghurt-Mint Sauce: Add thinly sliced fresh mint leaves to the yoghurt sauce just before serving. (If you add the mint leaves too far in advance they will turn an unappetising colour). If you don't have fresh mint, dried mint is perfectly acceptable. Or, for a slightly less authentic version, use fresh or dried dill, fresh coriander or even fresh basil – all complement the aubergines and yoghurt.
▸ Use courgette slices, rather than aubergine slices.
▸ Don't throw away any leftover aubergine slices because they can be turned into a salad. Chop the leftover aubergine into cubes and fold them into the yoghurt sauce. Although you can fry the aubergine slices up to a day in advance, don't mix with the yoghurt sauce in advance, because the salt in the sauce will make the aubergines soggy.

VEGAN NOTES
▸ Top the fried aubergine slices with toasted pine nuts (see page 35), chopped fresh parsley or coriander and a few red onion rings. Squeeze over fresh lemon juice.
▸ Put the fried aubergine slices in a saucepan and add one quantity of Essential Tomato Sauce (see page 154) and slowly bring to the boil. Reduce the heat to low, cover the pan and simmer for about 10 minutes. Serve this with steamed rice for a filling meal.

CUT THE FAT
Make sure you have a roll of kitchen paper handy before you start frying the aubergine slices. Aubergines are notorious for soaking up fat – they will absorb as much as you give them. To remove the excess fat, as the aubergine slices come out of the pan, drain them on a double thickness of kitchen paper and use more paper to pat the tops.

Steamed Green Beans with Almonds

MAKES **2 SERVINGS**
PREP TIME: **ABOUT 10 MINUTES**
COOKING TIME: **ABOUT 5 MINUTES**

20 g almond slivers
Several sprigs fresh parsley, or a mixture of fresh parsley and mint
150 g thin green beans
2 teaspoons extra-virgin olive oil
Salt and pepper

1. Put a thin layer of water in the bottom of a saucepan that will hold your steamer. It is important that the water does not to touch the perforations of the steamer. Cover the steamer and bring the water to the boil.

2. Meanwhile, toast the almond slivers (page 35). Remove the leaves from the herb sprigs, and chop so you have about 2 tablespoons. You can cut off the ends of the beans or leave them, as you like, but leave the beans whole.

3. Add the beans to the steamer, re-cover and steam them for about 5 minutes, shaking the pan once or twice, until they are tender but still slightly crisp.

4. Transfer the beans to a bowl, add the oil, chopped herbs and salt and pepper to taste, and toss together. Sprinkle with the almonds and toss again.

VARIATION

Replace the toasted almonds with very finely chopped raw red onion or toasted hazelnuts.

ALL STEAMED UP

▸ It's no sweat when all you want to eat is a simple bowl of veggies and rice. Steaming is a very easy technique that leaves vegetables with a tender-crisp texture and fresh flavour. Inexpensive collapsible metal steamers or Chinese bamboo steamers work fine.
▸ Many people steam, rather than boil, vegetables because fewer water-soluble vitamins are thrown down the drain.
▸ Make sure the water in the pan is shallow enough that it doesn't touch the food being steamed or the food can become soggy.
▸ Use a pan large enough to let the steam circulate around the vegetables, so they cook evenly.
▸ If your pan's lid doesn't fit tightly, cover the pan with a piece of kitchen foil before adding the lid.

Mediterranean Broad Beans

MAKES **2 SERVINGS**
PREP TIME: **ABOUT 5 MINUTES, UNLESS YOU ARE PEELING
THE BEANS** / COOKING TIME: **ABOUT 5 MINUTES**

SOME LIKE IT HOT AND SOME LIKE IT COLD . . . AND THIS IS A VEGETABLE DISH THAT
CATERS FOR ALL TASTES.

200 g fresh or frozen shelled broad beans
Small bunch of fresh dill sprigs
1 $^1/_2$ tablespoons extra-virgin olive oil
$^1/_2$ lemon
30 g vegetarian feta cheese
Salt and pepper

1. Bring a kettle of water to the boil. If you're in a hurry you can skip this
step, but the beans taste and look so much more exciting when you take
the time to remove the tough outer green-grey skins. To do this, put the
beans in a heatproof bowl, straight from the freezer if frozen, and pour
over enough boiling water to cover. Leave the beans to stand for about
5 minutes, then drain.

2. Meanwhile, remove the feathery dill leaves from the stems and
finely chop, then set aside. As soon as the beans are cool enough to
handle, use you fingers to 'pop' the bright-green peas out of the skins.

3. Bring another kettle of water to the boil. Put the beans in a saucepan
over a high heat. Pour over enough boiling water to cover and boil for
2–3 minutes until tender. Drain the beans and shake off the excess
water.

4. Tip the beans into a bowl, add the oil and salt and pepper while
they are still hot, and toss together. Squeeze over about $^1/_2$ a tablespoon
of lemon juice, crumble the cheese over and toss all the ingredients
together. Taste and add extra oil, lemon juice or salt and pepper
as required.

Cook's Tip
If you do peel the beans, save the skins for adding to a batch of
vegetable stock (page 164).

Roasted Beetroots

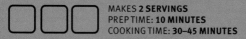

MAKES **2 SERVINGS**
PREP TIME: **10 MINUTES**
COOKING TIME: **30–45 MINUTES**

FORGET ABOUT SHARP-TASTING BEETROOT IN VINEGAR YOU MIGHT HAVE HAD IN THE PAST. THIS WILL MAKE YOU A FAN. IN FACT, IT MAKES SENSE TO ROAST EXTRA BEETROOTS, AS THE LEFTOVERS MAKE EXCELLENT SALADS.

SERVE THESE SLICED WITH STEAMED GREEN VEGGIES, SUCH AS SPROUTING BROCCOLI OR MANGETOUT.

2 medium beetroots
Olive oil

TO SERVE
Greek Yoghurt-Mint Sauce (page 73)
2 tablespoons sesame seeds

1. Heat the oven to 200°C/400°F/Gas 6. Use a small brush to scrub the beetroots under cold running water, taking care not to break the skins. Trim the stems until they are about 4 cm long.

2. Use kitchen paper to dry the beetroots, then rub oil all over them. Put them in a roasting tin and roast for 30–45 minutes, occasionally turning them over, until they are tender and you can insert a knife without any resistance.

3. Meanwhile, make the Greek Yoghurt-Mint Sauce and set aside. Put the sesame seeds in a small dry frying pan over a high heat, stirring, for about 30 seconds or until they are light-golden brown: immediately tip the seeds out of the pan.

4. When the beetroots are cool enough to handle, use a small knife or vegetable peeler to peel them, then cut them into 0.5-cm slices. Arrange the slices on plates, spoon the yoghurt sauce along side and sprinkle with the sesame seeds.

VARIATIONS:
▶ Russian Salad: Dice leftover cool beetroot and place in a large bowl. Add diced cooked new potatoes, cooked peas and diced cooked carrots. Add enough mayonnaise to bind together and gently stir in drained and rinsed capers, chopped fresh parsley and chopped fresh dill. Pile the salad on baby spinach leaves and add quartered hard-boiled eggs.
▶ Beetroot-Apple Salad: Dice peeled cold roasted beetroot and toss with diced crisp apple and chopped walnuts. Drizzle with walnut oil and balsamic dressing, then serve on a bed of baby beetroot leaves or mixed salad greens.

▸ Toss diced leftover cold beetroot in Raita (page 178). The yoghurt will turn bright pink.

▸ Sprinkle the beetroot slices with Garlic-flavoured Vinaigrette Dressing (page 172), then crumble vegetarian feta cheese over. Add mâche or rocket leaves, too.

▸ Serve the roasted beetroot slices alongside Fried Halloumi (page 54) and Roasted Asparagus (page 71). Sprinkle with chopped toasted pecans or hazelnuts (page 35).

Cook's Tip
Large beetroots will take up to 1 hour to roast.

Stir-fried Broccoli & Peppers

MAKES **2 SERVINGS**
PREP TIME: **ABOUT 10 MINUTES**
COOKING TIME: **ABOUT 8 MINUTES**

SERVE THIS WITH A BOWL OF RICE (PAGE 131) FOR A CHINESE MEAL THAT WILL BE ON YOUR PLATE QUICKER THAN YOU CAN STOP FOR A TAKE-AWAY.

$^1/_2$ red onion
250 g broccoli
1 large red, green, orange or yellow pepper
1 large garlic clove
3 tablespoons vegetable stock, home-made (page 164) or from a cube, or water
2 tablespoons bottled black-bean sauce
1 tablespoon sunflower or rapeseed oil
50 g fresh beansprouts
Salt and pepper
Sesame seeds to garnish (optional)

1. Peel and finely chop the onion. Cut the broccoli florets and stalks into small pieces. De-seed and thinly slice the pepper. Peel and finely chop the garlic. Mix the stock or water and black-bean sauce together in a small bowl and set aside.

2. Heat a wok with a lid or a large frying pan with a lid over a high heat until a splash of water 'dances' on the surface. Add the oil and swirl it around.

3. Add the broccoli stalks and stir around for about 2 minutes, constantly tossing. Add the onion, garlic and pepper and continue stir-frying for 2 minutes longer.

4. Stir in the broccoli florets, beansprouts, stock mixture and salt and pepper to taste, and stir around. Cover the pan and leave over a high heat for 2–3 minutes until the broccoli florets and stalks are tender when you pierce them and the florets are bright green.

5. Stir in the coriander leaves, then adjust the seasoning, if necessary. A sprinkling of sesame seeds adds extra crunch and flavour, if you like.

SUCCESSFUL STIR-FRYING

▸ Have all your ingredients prepared before you start cooking. Once the cooking starts, everything happens fast.

▸ Chop ingredients into similar-size pieces so they are all tender at the same time.

▸ Add the thickest ingredients to the wok or pan first because they take longer than thinner ingredients to cook.

▸ Always heat the wok or pan before you add the oil. This prevents food from sticking.

▸ Use chopsticks or a wooden spoon to constantly toss and stir the ingredients while they are cooking.

Baked Red Cabbage

MAKES **2–3 SERVINGS**
PREP TIME: **ABOUT 10 MINUTES**
COOKING TIME: **ABOUT 1 HOUR**

A REAL WINTER WARMER. TRY THIS ALONGSIDE A BAKED JACKET SWEET POTATO AND YOU'LL FEEL WARM AND CONTENT. ADD A FEW SLICES OF GARLIC BREAD (PAGE 51) FOR A MORE fiLLING MEAL.

500 g red cabbage
2 cooking apples, such as Granny Smith
1 onion
1 teaspoon caraway weeds
50 g raisins or sultanas
2 teaspoons soft light-brown sugar
250 ml dry cider or vegetarian dry red wine
Salt and pepper

1. Heat the oven to 180°C/350°F/Gas 4. Cut the thick core out of the cabbage, then slice the leaves. Cut the apples in half, remove the cores and cut each half into 4 or 5 slices. Peel and chop the onion.

2. Heat a dry frying pan over a high heat. Add the caraway seeds and stir them around for about 30 seconds or until they start to brown and you can smell the aroma: watch carefully because they burn quickly. Immediately tip the seeds out of the pan.

3. Put the red cabbage, apples, onion, caraway seeds, raisins or sultanas, brown sugar, cider or wine and salt and pepper to taste in a large flameproof casserole and stir together.

4. Bring to the boil on the hob, stir again and cover the casserole. Transfer it to the oven and bake for 45 minutes, without lifting the lid. Uncover the casserole and use a fork to check if the cabbage is tender. If not, re-cover the casserole and return it to the oven. Taste and adjust the seasoning, if necessary.

Cook's Tip
If you've bought a whole head of cabbage, use the leftovers raw in salads. Toss finely chopped or grated red cabbage with walnuts and a handful of raisins. Add a little Vinaigrette Dressing (page 172) and toss again. Add finely sliced celery and chopped fresh parsley, too, if you like. Grapes and vegetarian feta cheese are other options.

Bubble & Squeak

MAKES **2–3 SERVINGS** / PREP TIME: **ABOUT 10 MINUTES, PLUS
MAKING THE POTATOES** / COOKING TIME: **10–15 MINUTES,
DEPENDING ON THE SIZE OF YOUR PAN**

GET IN THE HABIT OF MAKING EXTRA MASHED POTATOES (PAGE 96) AND THIS TRADITIONAL
BRITISH DISH WILL BE A FLASH IN THE PAN. MAKE A MEAL OUT OF THIS WITH STEAMED
LEEKS, SPINACH OR BROCCOLI, OR ADD A FREE-RANGE FRIED EGG (PAGE 41) ON TOP.

250 g green cabbage
4 spring onions
1 quantity Creamy Mashed Potatoes (page 96)
Pinch of grated nutmeg
About 1 ¹/₂ tablespoons sunflower or rapeseed oil
Salt and pepper

1. Put a thin layer of water in a saucepan that will hold your steamer
without the water touching the perforations. Cover the pan and bring
the water to the boil.

2. Remove the core from the green cabbage and finely shred the leaves.
Trim and finely chop the spring onions.

3. Put the cabbage and spring onions in the steamer, re-cover and steam
for 5 minutes, or until tender.

4. Meanwhile, put the mashed potatoes in a bowl and stir in the grated
nutmeg. Add the cabbage and spring onions and stir together. Taste
and adjust the seasoning, if necessary.

5. Heat 1 tablespoon of the oil in a large frying pan, ideally non-stick,
over a medium heat. Add the potato-and-cabbage mixture and spread
it out with the back of a spoon or metal spatula.

6. Cook the potatoes and cabbage for about 5 minutes, or until the
bottom surface is brown and crisp.

7. Cut the potatoes-and-cabbage layer in half and slide the portions
out of the pan. If the pan looks too dry, add a little more oil and heat.

8. Slide the vegetable portions back into the pan, raw-side down, and
press down. Continue cooking for about 5 minutes longer, or until the
second side is crisp and golden.

Glazed Carrots

MAKES **2–3 SERVINGS**
PREP TIME: **LESS THAN 5 MINUTES**
COOKING TIME: **10–15 MINUTES**

500 g carrots
200 ml water
30 g butter
1 teaspoon soft light-brown sugar
Salt and pepper

1. Scrub or peel the carrots, then cut them into thin slices.

2. Put the carrots in a saucepan or frying pan with the water, butter, sugar and salt and pepper to taste. Bring the water to the boil, stirring to dissolve the sugar.

3. Reduce the heat to low, cover the pan and leave the carrots to cook for 10–15 minutes until they are tender and the liquid is absorbed. If the carrots are soft before all the liquid is absorbed, uncover the pan and increase the heat and leave to cook until the liquid evaporates.

4. Taste and adjust the seasoning, if necessary.

Cauliflower à la Grecque

MAKES **2–3 SERVINGS**
PREP TIME: **ABOUT 5 MINUTES, PLUS SEVERAL HOURS CHILLING**
COOKING TIME: **10–15 MINUTES**

KEEP A BOWL OF THESE VEGGIES IN THE FRIDGE TO FIGHT OFF SNACK ATTACKS OR
MIDNIGHT FEASTS. TRY THESE WITH TOMATO BREAD (PAGE 52) OR A SALAD OF MIXED
LEAVES ON THE SIDE.

1 cauliflower head
2 garlic cloves
1 tablespoon coriander seeds
6 sprigs fresh parsley
400 ml vegetarian dry white wine
4 tablespoons olive oil
2 sprigs fresh thyme
1 bay leaf
1 tablespoon soft light-brown sugar
Salt and pepper

1. Cut the cauliflower florets from the thick stalk, then cut the florets into
bite-sized pieces – it is important to make the florets about the same size
so they cook in the same time; set aside. Use the back of a wooden
spoon to lightly smash the parsley stalks.

2. Peel and finely chop the garlic. Put the coriander seeds in a mortar
and use a pestle to lightly crush, or use the back of a wooden spoon.

3. Put the cauliflower florets and other ingredients in a saucepan over
a high heat and bring to the boil, stirring to dissolve the sugar.

4. Reduce the heat to very low and leave the cauliflower to simmer,
uncovered, for 10–15 minutes until they are tender when you pierce
them with the tip of a knife. Start testing after 10 minutes so they
don't overcook and become mushy.

5. Use a slotted spoon to transfer the cauliflower to a bowl. Return
the cooking liquid to the boil, and boil until reduced by half.

6. Strain the liquid over the cauliflower, then set aside to cool
completely. When the liquid is cool, cover the dish with clingfilm and
chill for 2–3 hours. Serve at room temperature.

VARIATION

Many other vegetables lend themselves to this treatment, which is
popular throughout the Mediterranean and Middle East. Try French
beans, courgettes, mushrooms and button onions.

Celeriac Rémoulade

MAKES **2–3 SERVINGS**
PREP TIME: **ABOUT 15 MINUTES, PLUS OPTIONAL CHILLING**
NO COOKING

FOR A FRENCH-STYLE SALAD SUPPER, SERVE THIS WITH CARROT CRUDITÉ (PAGE 63) AND
GRATED ROASTED BEETROOT (PAGE 76) TOSSED WITH VINAIGRETTE DRESSING (PAGE 172).
AND FRENCH BREAD, OF COURSE.

$^1/_2$ head celeriac
2 tablespoons mayonnaise
$^1/_2$ tablespoon Dijon mustard, or to taste
$^1/_2$ tablespoon white-wine vinegar
1 teaspoon capers, rinsed (optional)
Salt and pepper

1. Bring a saucepan of water to the boil over a high heat. Put a sieve in
the sink. Meanwhile, use a vegetable peeler or small knife to peel the
celeriac. Be very careful as the knobbly surface makes it easy to cut
yourself if you are using a knife.

2. Cut the peeled celeriac into large chunks, then coarsely grate the
chunks. Drop the celeriac in the pan of boiling water and leave just long
enough for the water to return to the boil. Drain the celeriac in the sieve,
then immediately put it under cold water to stop the cooking and retain
the crunch.

3. Pat the celeriac completely dry with a clean tea towel. Beat the
mayonnaise, mustard, vinegar and salt and pepper to taste in a bowl.
Stir in the celeriac and capers, if using.

4. Taste and adjust the seasoning, if necessary, or add a little more
mustard or vinegar. This is ready to eat but it tastes better if you chill
it for at least 30 minutes.

Cook's Tips
▸ The remaining celeriac can be peeled, chopped and boiled with
potatoes to make Mashed Celeriac – follow the technique for Creamy
Mashed Potatoes (page 96).
▸ Once the celeriac is cut, the exposed flesh will quickly brown, so
wrap the unused half in clingfilm. If you aren't going to cook the grated
celeriac straight away in Step 2, leave it in a bowl of cold water with
a slice of lemon to prevent it from becoming brown.

Courgette Gratin

MAKES **4–6 SERVINGS** / PREP TIME: **ABOUT 15 MINUTES**
COOKING TIME: **ABOUT 1 HOUR, DEPENDING ON HOW LARGE
YOUR FRYING PAN IS**

1 garlic clove
6 courgettes
1 onion
Several sprigs mixed fresh herbs, or all one herb
About 4 tablespoons olive or sunflower oil, plus extra for the dish
200 g vegetarian Parmesan-style cheese, or mature vegetarian
   Cheddar cheese
2 free-range eggs
125 ml milk
125 ml double cream
Grated fresh nutmeg
Salt and pepper

1. Heat the oven to 190°C/375°F/Gas 5. Rub a little oil over the base
and side of an ovenproof serving dish. Cut the garlic clove in half and
rub it over the base and side, pressing down firmly; discard the clove.
Place the dish on a baking sheet and set aside.

2. Thinly slice the courgettes into 0.5cm slices. Peel and thinly slice
the onion. Finely chop the herb leaves to make about 2 tablespoons.

3. Use the largest frying pan (ideally non-stick) you have, or 2 frying
pans. Heat a thin layer of oil in the frying pan over a medium-high heat.
Add as many courgettes as will fit in a single layer and fry for 2–3 minutes
until golden, then flip over and fry on the other side. Continue until
all the courgettes are fried.

4. Use a fish slice to transfer the courgettes to a plate lined with kitchen
paper. Heat a little extra oil in the pan, if necessary, then add the onion
and stir around until very soft and pale brown. Watch carefully so it
doesn't burn.

5. Spread half the courgettes over the base of the dish. Top with the
onions and half the herbs. Grate over slightly less than half the cheese.

6. Mix together the milk and cream with nutmeg and salt and pepper
to taste. Pour this mixture over the courgettes and onion. Grate the
remaining cheese over the top.

7. Transfer the dish and baking sheet to the oven and bake for 35–45
minutes until it is golden brown and set if you stick a knife in the centre.
Leave to stand for about 5 minutes before serving.

Hot Kale

MAKES **2 SERVINGS** / PREP TIME: **ABOUT 10 MINUTES**
COOKING TIME: **ABOUT 20 MINUTES**

KALE AND OTHER LEAFY GREENS CAN BE A REAL BARGAIN IN MARKETS, SO GRAB
A BUNCH WHEN YOU SEE THEM. LARGE SPINACH LEAVES AND SPRING GREENS CAN
ALSO BE PREPARED THIS WAY, ALTHOUGH SPRING GREENS MIGHT NEED LONGER
COOKING IN STEP 1, WHEREAS SPINACH WILL BE TENDER QUICKER.

TRY THIS SPOONED OVER GRILLED SEMOLINA GNOCCHI (PAGE 143), MOUNDS
OF POLENTA WITH CHEESE (PAGE 140) OR A BOWL OF PLAIN RICE (PAGE 131).

450 g kale or other greens
2 large tomatoes, such as beefsteak
1 onion
2 tablespoons unsalted peanuts
1 $^1/_2$ tablespoons sunflower or rapeseed oil
Hot-pepper sauce
$^1/_2$ lemon
Salt and pepper

1. Rinse the kale in lots of cold water to remove any dirt. Cut out any
tough stems, then chop the leaves. Put the leaves in a pan with water
to cover and a pinch of salt, and bring to the boil. Reduce the heat, cover
the pan and simmer for 10–12 minutes until they are tender. Drain the
kale well and set aside.

2. Meanwhile, cut the tomatoes in half and use a small spoon to scoop
out the cores and seeds, then chop the flesh. Peel and chop the onion.
Finely chop the peanuts and set aside.

3. Heat the oil in a large frying pan or saucepan with a tight-fitting lid
over a medium-high heat. Add the onion and stir for 3–5 minutes until
soft. Stir in the tomatoes and hot-pepper sauce to taste, then tip into
a bowl.

4. Put the kale in the bottom of the pan and spoon the tomato mixture
over the top with salt and pepper to taste. Cover the pan and leave to
simmer for 8 minutes.

5. Squeeze the lemon over the kale, then taste and adjust the seasoning
if necessary. Sprinkle with the peanuts and serve.

Stir-fried Mangetout

MAKES **2 SERVINGS**
PREP TIME: **ABOUT 10 MINUTES**
COOKING TIME: **ABOUT 5 MINUTES**

EAT THIS WITH A BOWL OF RICE OR EGG NOODLES.

150 g mangetout
1 large garlic clove
$^1/_2$-cm piece of fresh root ginger
1 tablespoon sesame seeds
1 tablespoon sunflower, rapeseed or groundnut oil
$^1/_2$ teaspoon cornflour
3 tablespoons vegetable stock
$^1/_2$ tablespoon dark soy sauce or tamari
Salt and pepper

1. Top and tail the mangetout. Peel and crush the garlic clove. Peel and very finely chop the ginger. Put the cornflower in a small bowl and very slowly stir in the stock, stirring until a thin paste forms and there aren't any lumps.

2. Heat a wok or large frying pan over a high heat until a drop of water 'dances' on the surface. Add the sesame seeds and stir-fry them, constantly tossing and turning them, for 30 seconds, or until they turn a light-golden brown. Immediately tip them out of the pan and set aside.

3. Add the oil to the wok or pan and swirl it around. Add the garlic and ginger and stir-fry for about 1 minute. Add the mangetout and continue stir-frying for about 30 seconds.

4. Stir in the cornflour paste, soy sauce and salt and pepper to taste, and continue stir-frying for 1–2 minutes until the mangetout turn vibrant green and are tender-crisp. Sprinkle with the sesame seeds.

VARIATIONS
► Add a handful of fresh beansprouts in Step 4.
► Replace the mangetout with sliced courgettes, sliced chestnut mushrooms, thinly sliced red, green, yellow or orange peppers, or small cauliflower florets.

Garlic Mushrooms

MAKES **2 SERVINGS**
PREP TIME: **ABOUT 10 MINUTES**
COOKING TIME: **ABOUT 10 MINUTES**

QUICK AND EASY, THIS SIMPLE DISH IS PARTICULARLY TASTY MADE WITH SEVERAL VARIETIES OF MUSHROOMS, BUT CAN ALSO TRANSFORM ORDINARY BUTTON MUSHROOMS.
   ITALIANS SERVE THESE SPOONED OVER GRILLED POLENTA (PAGE 140), BUT THE MUSHROOMS ALSO MAKE A GOOD TOPPING FOR BRUSCHETTA (PAGE 53) OR BAKED JACKET POTATOES (PAGE 94).

100 g fresh shiitake or other wild mushrooms
100 g chestnut or brown mushrooms
2 large garlic cloves – or more if you like
Fresh parsley sprigs or chives (optional)
1 ¹/₂ tablespoons sunflower or rapeseed oil
Salt and pepper

1. Use a damp cloth to wipe the mushrooms, then trim the end of the stalks. Thickly slice the caps and stalks. Peel and very finely chop the garlic. Chop 1 ¹/₂–2 tablespoons parsley leaves or snip the chives, if you are using.

2. Heat the oil in a large frying pan or wok, ideally non-stick, over a high heat. Add the mushrooms and garlic to the pan and stir around for 2–3 minutes until the mushrooms absorb the oil.

3. Reduce the heat to low and add salt and pepper to taste. When the juices have come out of the mushrooms, increase the heat to high again and continue stirring for 4–5 minutes until all the moisture is absorbed and the mushrooms are golden brown and tender.

4. Stir in the herbs, if you are using. Taste and adjust the seasoning, if necessary.

VARIATIONS

▸ Peppers & Mushrooms: Finely slice a cored and de-seeded red, green, yellow or orange pepper and thinly slice an onion. Heat 1 tablespoon oil in the pan, then fry the pepper and onion, stirring frequently, for about 5 minutes. Add another tablespoon of oil to the pan, if necessary, and continue with the recipe above. This will serve 2–3.
▸ If you don't have any fresh herbs, use 4 finely chopped spring onions.

Mushroom Magic
Revive shrivelled mushrooms at the bottom of the fridge by loosely wrapping the mushrooms in kitchen paper and covering with more damp kitchen paper.

Stuffed Mushroom Caps

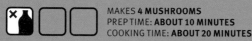

MAKES **4 MUSHROOMS**
PREP TIME: **ABOUT 10 MINUTES**
COOKING TIME: **ABOUT 20 MINUTES**

TRY THESE WITH HOT GARLIC BREAD (PAGE 51), OR SPOONED OVER MOUNDS OF POLENTA WITH CHEESE (PAGE 140).

2 large Portobello mushroom caps
1–2 garlic cloves, to taste
About 6 sprigs fresh parsley
Olive oil
Salt and pepper

1. Heat the oven to 190°C/350°F/Gas 4. Lightly grease an ovenproof dish that will hold the mushrooms.

2. Wipe the mushroom caps with a damp cloth and remove the stalks. Peel and finely chop the garlic cloves. Very finely chop the parsley stalks and leaves. Mix together the parsley and garlic with salt and pepper to taste.

3. Place the mushrooms in the dish, gill-side up, then spoon in the parsley stuffing. Drizzle with olive oil.

4. Place the mushrooms in the oven and bake for about 20 minutes until they are hot and tender.

VARIATION
Sprinkle the mushroom caps with pine nuts after 10 minutes' cooking, then return to the oven.

Cook's Tips
The mushroom stalks will add an earthiness to a pot of Vegetable Stock (page 164).

Mushroom Stroganoff

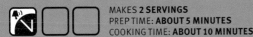

MAKES **2 SERVINGS**
PREP TIME: **ABOUT 5 MINUTES**
COOKING TIME: **ABOUT 10 MINUTES**

DINE LIKE AN IMPERIAL RUSSIAN FOR PENNIES. THIS IS A VEGETARIAN VERSION OF A
RUSSIAN CLASSIC, NAMED AFTER COUNT PAUL STROGANOV, A 19TH-CENTURY RUSSIAN
DIPLOMAT. IF YOU'RE PUSHING OUT THE BOAT, SERVE IT WITH VEG & RICE PILAF (PAGE 133),
BUT FOR SUPPER IN FRONT OF THE TV SERVE IT WITH BOILED WHOLEMEAL TAGLIATELLE
OR SPOONED OVER TOASTED BREAD.

400 g chestnut or button mushrooms, or a mixture of mushrooms
1 onion
1 large garlic clove
2 tablespoons sunflower or rapeseed oil
4 tablespoons dry white wine
2 teaspoons Dijon or wholegrain mustard
150 ml soured cream
Pinch of paprika (optional)
Salt and pepper
Chopped fresh parsley to serve

1. Wipe the mushrooms with a damp cloth and trim the stalks, then
thinly slice the caps and stalks. Peel and finely chop the onion. Peel
and finely chop the garlic.

2. Heat the oil in a large frying pan or wok, ideally non-stick, over
a medium heat. Add the onion and garlic and stir around for 2 minutes:
do not let the garlic brown. Add the mushrooms with a pinch of salt
and stir for 3–5 minutes until they give off their liquid.

3. Increase the heat, add the wine and continue stirring until it bubbles
and evaporates.

4. Stir in the mustard, then add the soured cream and stir until the sauce
thickens and the mushrooms are tender. Add a pinch of paprika, if you
have any, and salt and pepper to taste. Sprinkle with parsley if there is
any in the fridge.

Curried Peas & Mushrooms

MAKES **4 SERVINGS**
PREP TIME: **ABOUT 10 MINUTES**
COOK TIME: **ABOUT 10 MINUTES**

ANOTHER INDIAN TAKE-AWAY FAVOURITE THAT IS EASY PEASY. AS PART OF A MEAL,
EAT THIS WITH BOILED BASMATI RICE (PAGE 132) AND RAITA (PAGE 178), OR A NAAN
FROM THE SUPERMARKET.

1 large tomato
1 large onion
300 g chestnut or button mushrooms
2 tablespoons sunflower or rapeseed oil
1 teaspoon cumin seeds
$^1/_2$ teaspoon black mustard seeds
$^1/_2$ teaspoon onion seeds
$^1/_2$ teaspoon turmeric
Pinch of cayenne pepper, to taste
300 g shelled peas, fresh or frozen
Salt and pepper

1. Hold the tomato in your hand and rub it up and down over the large
holes on a grater into a bowl, pressing down firmly.

2. Peel and chop the onion. Wipe the mushrooms with a damp cloth
and trim the ends of the stalks, then thickly slice the caps and stalks.

3. Heat the oil in a wok or large frying pan over a medium-high heat.
Add the cumin, black mustard and onion seeds and stir for 20–30
seconds until they pop and crackle: watch carefully because the
cumin seeds can burn quickly.

4. Stir in the turmeric and cayenne, then add the peas and stir. Add
the tomato and mushrooms with a pinch of salt and continue stirring
for 8–10 minutes until the mushrooms are soft and the peas are tender.
Taste and adjust the seasoning, if necessary.

Peas & Paneer

MAKES **2 SERVINGS**
PREP TIME: **ABOUT 15 MINUTES**
COOKING TIME: **ABOUT 10 MINUTES**

1 large juicy tomato, such as beefsteak
1 onion
1 garlic clove
1-cm piece of fresh root ginger
175 g paneer
3 tablespoons sunflower, rapeseed or groundnut oil
$1/2$ teaspoon turmeric
300 g shelled peas, fresh or frozen
$1/4$ teaspoon garam masala
Pinch cayenne pepper, or to taste
Salt

1. Hold the tomato in your hand and rub it up and down over the large holes on a grater into a bowl, pressing down firmly.

2. Peel and chop the onion. Peel and crush the garlic clove. Peel and finely chop the ginger. Drain the paneer well and pat dry with kitchen paper, then cut into 1-cm cubes.

3. Heat 2 tablespoons of the oil in a wok or large frying pan over a medium heat. Add as many paneer cubes as will fit in a single layer and fry to brown on all sides, carefully turning the cubes over so they don't break up – you might have to do this in batches. Remove the paneer from the pan and drain it well on kitchen paper.

4. Add the remaining 1 tablespoon oil to the pan and heat. Add the onion and stir for 3–5 minutes until soft, then add the garlic and turmeric and stir for a minute or so.

5. Add the peas and continue stirring until the peas are tender and hot – fresh peas will take 2–3 minutes and frozen peas about 5 minutes.

6. Return the paneer to the pan and continue cooking for about 2 minutes until it is hot. Add the garam masala and cayenne, and salt to taste.

Halloumi-stuffed Peppers

MAKES **4 SERVINGS**
PREP TIME: **ABOUT 10 MINUTES**
COOKING TIME: **ABOUT 30 MINUTES**

EAT THESE WITH A SALAD FOR A MAIN MEAL, OR SERVE HALF A PEPPER AS A fiRST COURSE IF YOU ARE HAVING A DINNER PARTY.

4 red peppers
1 garlic clove
250 g vegetarian halloumi cheese, drained
About 2 tablespoons olive oil
Grated rind of 1 lemon
8 fresh mint leaves, or $1/_2$ tablespoon dried mint
$1/_2$ tablespoon dried thyme
2 tablespoons pine nuts
Pepper

1. Heat the oven to 200°C/400°F/Gas 6 and lightly grease the base and side of a roasting tray or ovenproof dish large enough to hold 8 pepper halves. Cut each pepper in half from top to bottom and use the tip of the knife to scrape out the cores and seeds; set aside. Peel and very finely chop the garlic. Finely dice the halloumi cheese.

2. Rub the outside of each pepper half with a little oil. Place them in the roasting tray or dish, skin-side down. Sprinkle a little garlic in each pepper half. Divide the cheese between the pepper halves, then add torn mint leaves, lemon rind, any remaining garlic, the thyme, pine nuts and pepper to taste: you won't need to add salt as the cheese is salty.

3. Place the peppers in the oven and roast for 30 minutes, or until the pepper flesh is tender and lightly charred. These are best served straightaway or the cheese will become rubbery as it cools.

Plan Ahead
If you want to serve these for a dinner party, the pepper halves can be prepared through Step 2 several hours in advance and kept in the fridge. Remove them from the fridge about 10 minutes before they go in the oven to bring them back to room temperature.

Grilled Pepper Salad

MAKES **4–6 SERVINGS**
PREP TIME: **ABOUT 5 MINUTES**
COOKING TIME: **ABOUT 10 MINUTES**

GRILLED PEPPERS AND VEGETARIAN DIETS GO HAND-IN-HAND. GRILL AND PEEL EXTRA PEPPERS TO KEEP, SUBMERGED IN OLIVE OIL, IN AN AIR-TIGHT CONTAINER IN THE FRIDGE FOR UP TO 3 DAYS. THEY ARE IDEAL TO ADD TO SANDWICHES, EAT AS A SNACK WITH CHEESE OR TO TOSS WITH PASTA. FRENCH BREAD IS PARTICULARLY GOOD WITH THIS TO MOP UP THE DELICIOUS DRESSING.

4 red, green, yellow and/or orange peppers, any combination you like
60 g vegetarian feta cheese, drained
3 tablespoons chopped fresh herbs, such as parsley, coriander, mint, chives or dill

GARLIC-LEMON DRESSING
1 garlic clove
1 tablespoon lemon juice
1 teaspoon clear honey
Pinch of paprika or cayenne pepper
5 tablespoons extra-virgin olive oil

1. Heat the grill to high and position the rack about 15 cm from the heat. When the grill is hot, place the peppers on the rack and grill, turning them occasionally, until they are charred all over.

2. Remove the peppers from the grill rack, cover them with a tea towel and leave to stand until cool – the steam that forms under the skins makes them easier to peel.

3. While the peppers are cooling, make the dressing. Peel and crush the garlic clove. Put the garlic in a jar with a screw top, add the lemon juice, honey, paprika or cayenne, and 5 tablespoons of olive oil, then shake until blended; set aside.

4. Use your fingers and a small knife to peel the skins off all the peppers. Cut the peppers in half and scrape out the cores and seeds, then cut the flesh into thin strips.

5. Arrange the pepper strips on a large plate. Give the dressing a good shake again and pour it over the peppers. Crumble the cheese over and then scatter with the herbs.

See over for variations.

VARIATIONS
‣ Scatter pitted black olives over the salad
‣ If you don't have any paprika or cayenne, use a pinch of ground cumin or marjoram. Some versions also add toasted cumin seeds.

Vegan Note
Omit the cheese and use brown sugar instead of honey in the dressing.

Plan Ahead
If you want to serve this for a party, grill, peel and cut the peppers into strips a day ahead. Put them in a bowl with the dressing and put in the fridge until about 15 minutes before you will be serving to let them come back to room temperature.

Baked Jacket Potatoes

MAKES **1 SERVING**
PREP TIME: **A MINUTE OR SO**
COOKING TIME: **45 MINUTES–1 HOUR**

THE ULTIMATE COMFORT FOOD – ESPECIALLY TOWARDS THE END OF TERM IF YOUR BANK ACCOUNT IS LOOKING SAD. A DAILY DIET OF JACKET POTATOES MIGHT GET JUST A BIT TOO BORING FOR WORDS, BUT WHEN YOU VARY THE TOPPINGS – AND THE LIST IS LITERALLY ENDLESS – YOU'LL FIND THESE FIT THE BILL FOR HEALTHY, CHEAP FOOD.

AND WHEN YOU'RE BAKING ONE POTATO, IT MAKES SENSE TO BAKE A COUPLE, AS THEY CAN BE REHEATED FOR A SECOND, QUICKER MEAL (SEE HOT POTATOES, RIGHT). BE SURE TO ADD EXTRA NUTRITIONAL VALUE TO YOUR TATTIE WITH A GOOD VEGGIE TOPPING. TRY CHILLI SIN CARNE (PAGE 160), FOR EXAMPLE.

1 large flour potato
Olive, sunflower or rapeseed oil
Salt, ideally coarse sea salt

1. Heat the oven to 230°C/450°F/Gas 8. Scrub the potatoes, then thoroughly dry them with a clean tea towel. Use a fork to poke the potato all over.

2. Using your hands, rub the potato all over with a small amount of oil so it is coated. Sprinkle it all over with a thin coating of salt.

3. Place the potato directly on the rack and bake for 45 minutes–1 hour, depending on the size, until the skin is crisp and brown and the flesh feels very soft when you squeeze the sides. If you poke it with a knife or the tines of a fork there shouldn't be any resistance.

4. Slice the potato lengthwise along the top, then push on both ends to open it out before adding a topping of your choice.

TOPPING IDEAS
► Drained canned corn kernels, tossed with grated vegetarian Cheddar cheese and spring onions
► Try blue cheese smashed with snipped chives and/or chopped spring onions
► Chopped Mediterranean Grilled Vegetables (page 156) with crumbled feta cheese
► Tahini-Yoghurt Dip (page 156) and drained canned chickpeas
► Babaganoush (page 177) and toasted sesame seeds

VARIATIONS
► Baked Sweet Potato: Use an orange-fleshed sweet potato and bake as above. All the topping ideas above are ideal, but it is also exceptionally good with Chimichurri Sauce, an all-purpose sauce from Argentina. (It's worth keeping a jar of this in the fridge to brush on grilled vegetables or tofu as they cook.) To make, combine 2 finely chopped spring onions with 3 tablespoons finely chopped fresh flat-leaf parsley, 2 tablespoons red-wine vinegar, 1 1/2 tablespoons olive oil, 1/2 a teaspoon dried oregano, a pinch of paprika and salt and pepper, and bottled hot-pepper sauce to taste.
► Baked New Potatoes: Heat the oven to 220°C/425°F/Gas 7. Scrub the new potatoes and rub them with oil and salt as above, then bake for 30–45 minutes until the skins are crisp and wrinkled. These don't need a topping and can be served hot straight from the oven, or at room temperature with a bowl of Tahini-Yoghurt Dip (page 176). Or serve them with Mediterranean Grilled Vegetables (page 156).

Hot Potatoes
Reheat leftover jacket potatoes at 180°C/350°F/Gas 4 for 15–20 minutes.

Creamy Mashed Potatoes

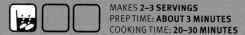

MAKES **2–3 SERVINGS**
PREP TIME: **ABOUT 3 MINUTES**
COOKING TIME: **20–30 MINUTES**

OF COURSE A PACKET OF INSTANT MASH IS QUICKER BUT IT DOESN'T COME CLOSE TO
MAKING THE REAL THING. WHEN YOU'RE FEELING DOWN IN THE DUMPS, TRY A BOWL OF
MASH. IT'S COMFORTING AND HOMELY. AND IF YOU'VE HAD TOO MUCH TO DRINK THE
NIGHT BEFORE THESE ARE EASY TO DIGEST WHEN YOU ARE STILL FEELING ILL.

2 floury potatoes, such as King Edwards
4–6 tablespoons milk
45 g butter
Salt and pepper

1. Bring a saucepan of salted water to the boil. Meanwhile, peel the
potatoes and cut them into small chunks.

2. Add the potatoes to the saucepan and return the water to the boil.

3. Continue boiling the potatoes for 20–30 minutes until they are
very tender and a knife slides through them without any resistance.
Start checking after 15 minutes, so the potatoes do not overcook
and become soggy.

4. Set a colander or sieve in the sink and drain the potatoes, shaking
off the excess water. Return the potatoes to the pan and set them over
a low heat for 1–2 minutes to remove excess moisture, stirring.

5. Meanwhile, put the milk in a small saucepan over a low heat and
warm just until bubbles appear around the edge: do not boil.

6. Tip the potatoes into a large bowl and add the butter. Use a hand-held
electric mixer on low speed to mash the potatoes. Or, if you don't have
an electric mixer, mash firmly and quickly with a masher. As the butter
melts, gradually beat in the milk, tablespoon by tablespoon, until the
potatoes are smooth, but still with enough body that they don't run off
the spoon. Season the potatoes generously with salt and pepper.

Aloo Gobi

MAKES **4–6 SERVINGS**
PREP TIME: **ABOUT 10 MINUTES**
COOKING TIME: **ABOUT 25 MINUTES**

1 small head of cauliflower
400 g new potatoes
2 garlic cloves
1 fresh green chilli
3 tablespoons sunflower, rapeseed or groundnut oil
1 tablespoon cumin seeds
1 teaspoon turmeric
1 teaspoon salt
Chopped fresh coriander to garnish (optional)

1. Cut the cauliflower in half, remove the thick core and cut the head into florets. Scrub the potatoes and cut them into quarters.

2. Peel and crush the garlic cloves. De-seed the chilli if you like mild food or leave the seeds in if you prefer hot, spicy food, then slice the chilli.

3. Heat a large wok or frying pan, ideally non-stick with a tight-fitting lid, over a medium-high heat until a splash of water 'dances' on the surface. Add 2 tablespoons of the oil and swirl it around.

4. Add the cumin seeds and stir them around until they crackle. Stir in the garlic, turmeric and salt.

5. Add the cauliflower and potatoes and stir. Reduce the heat to medium-low, cover the pan and leave to cook for about 20 minutes or until the potatoes are tender and there isn't any resistance when you pierce them with a knife.

6. Sprinkle with coriander, if you have any.

VARIATION
Add 150 g frozen peas with the cauliflower and potatoes in Step 5.

Catalan Spinach

MAKES **4 SERVINGS**
PREP TIME: **ABOUT 10 MINUTES**
COOKING TIME: **ABOUT 10 MINUTES**

600 g fresh spinach leaves
1 large garlic clove
1 1/2 tablespoons olive oil
75 g raisins
4 tablespoons pine nuts
Salt and pepper

1. Pick over the spinach leaves and remove any wilted leaves or any thick stems. Rinse them well in cold water to remove any dirt, then shake to remove most of the water. Peel and coarsely chop the garlic clove.

2. Heat the oil in a large frying pan, ideally non-stick, over a medium heat. Add the garlic and stir it around just until it begins to colour, then scoop it out with a spoon and discard: this is to flavour the oil.

3. Add the raisins and pine nuts to the pan and stir for 1–2 minutes until the pine nuts just begin to brown: watch carefully because they can burn quickly.

4. Stir the spinach into the pan with just the water clinging to the leaves, adding a small amount to begin with and pushing it down with a wooden spoon. When the first batch wilts, stir in the remaining spinach. Season with salt and pepper to taste.

5. Cover the pan and leave the spinach to cook for about 5 minutes until it is all wilted. Taste and adjust the seasoning, if necessary.

Baked Spinach & Eggs

MAKES **2 SERVINGS**
PREP TIME: **ABOUT 5 MINUTES**
COOKING TIME: **ABOUT 20 MINUTES**

TRY THIS FOR A TV DINNER ON A TRAY. ALL IT NEEDS IN THE WAY OF ACCOMPANIMENT IS A CHUNK OF WHOLEMEAL BREAD. (SEE NOTE ABOUT LIGHTLY COOKED EGGS ON PAGE 42.)

250 g baby spinach leaves
1 red onion
1 tablespoon olive oil
2 tablespoons double cream
Freshly grated nutmeg
1 tablespoon pine nuts
2 large free-range eggs
Vegetarian Cheddar, red Leicester or Wenslydale cheese
Salt and pepper

1. Heat the oven to 200°C/400°F/Gas 6. Lightly grease an ovenproof dish. Rinse the spinach leaves under cold water, then shake dry. Peel and finely chop the onion.

2. Heat the oil in a saucepan over a medium heat. Add the onion and stir for 3–5 minutes until soft. Add the spinach with only the water clinging to their leaves. Use a wooden spoon to push the leaves into the pan.

3. Reduce the heat to low, cover the pan and leave the spinach to wilt for 2–3 minutes. Tip the spinach into a sieve over the sink and use a wooden spoon to press out as much liquid as possible.

4. Return the spinach to the pan. Stir in the cream, add a few gratings of nutmeg and salt and pepper to taste. Stir in the pine nuts.

5. Spoon the spinach into the dish and level out. Use the back of a wooden spoon to make 2 indentations in the spinach.

6. Crack an egg into each indentation and grate a little cheese over each. Put the dish in the oven and bake for 15 minutes, or until the eggs are just set.

Spiced Winter Squash Stew

MAKES **4–6 SERVINGS**
PREP TIME: **ABOUT 15 MINUTES**
COOKING TIME: **ABOUT 45 MINUTES**

THIS IS SO BRIGHT AND COLOURFUL IT JUST HAS TO BE GOOD FOR YOU! YOU CAN EAT
IT LIKE A CHUNKY SOUP WITH PITA BREAD OR IRISH SODA BREAD (PAGE 171), OR SPOON
IT OVER POLENTA, COUSCOUS OR RICE. AND AFTER YOU'VE HAD A FEW MEALS FROM THIS
BATCH, YOU CAN BLITZ ANY LEFTOVERS IN THE BLENDER WITH VEGETABLE STOCK OR
MORE TOMATO JUICE TO MAKE A THICK SOUP.

   MAKE UP A BATCH OF THIS BEFORE YOU GO OUT PARTYING. EVEN IF YOU CAN BARELY
CRAWL OUT OF BED THE NEXT DAY, THIS DOESN'T TAKE MUCH EFFORT TO REHEAT AND IS
EASY TO DIGEST – JUST AVOID BITING INTO ONE OF THE CLOVES. THIS IS GOOD FOR YOU.

900 g butternut or acorn squash
1 turnip
1 large carrot
1 large parsnip
1 large onion
2 large garlic cloves
1 fresh red chilli
1 $^1/_2$ tablespoons sunflower or rapeseed oil
350 ml passata (Italian bottled sieved tomatoes)
1 cinnamon stick
6 whole cloves
Salt and pepper
Chopped fresh parsley, coriander or mint to garnish (optional)

1. Cut the squash in half and scoop out the seeds and fibres. Peel the
squash, then cut it into bite-sized pieces. Peel and chop the turnip.
Peel, core and chop the parsnip. Scrub or peel the carrot.

2. Peel and chop the onion. Peel and crush the garlic cloves. De-seed
the chilli if you want a moderately spiced dish, or leave the seeds in
if you like a lot of heat, and thinly slice the chilli.

3. Heat the oil in a flameproof casserole or large saucepan with a tight-
fitting lid. Add the onion and fry for 3–5 minutes until soft. Add the
garlic and stir around for another 1–2 minutes.

4. Stir in the squash, turnip, carrot, parsnip, passata, cinnamon, cloves
and salt and pepper to taste. Bring to the boil, then reduce the heat to
low, partially cover the pan and leave to simmer for 25–30 minutes until
the passata has evaporated and the squash and root vegetables are
tender. Check occasionally to make sure the pot isn't boiling dry –
add water or vegetable stock if it is.

5. Taste and adjust the seasoning if necessary. Sprinkle with fresh herbs.

Baked Spaghetti Squash

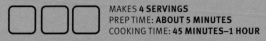

MAKES **4 SERVINGS**
PREP TIME: **ABOUT 5 MINUTES**
COOKING TIME: **45 MINUTES–1 HOUR**

1 spaghetti squash

TO SERVE
1 quantity Essential Tomato Sauce (page 154)
Vegetarian Parmesan-style or pecorino cheese
Salt and pepper

1. Heat the oven to 200°C/400°F/Gas 6. Bring a kettle of water to the boil. Cut the spaghetti squash in half lengthwise and use a spoon to scoop out the seeds.

2. Place both halves in a roasting tin, cut-side down. Pour about 2 ½ cm of boiling water into the tin, then tightly cover the top with kitchen foil. Take care to seal the foil around the edge of the tin, so steam doesn't escape.

3. Place the tin in the oven and leave for 45 minutes. Test to see if the squash is tender by poking it with a fork. If not, return the tin to the oven for a further 10–15 minutes.

4. Meanwhile, reheat the tomato sauce. Remove the squash from the tin and place cut-side up on a plate. Use 2 forks to scrape the flesh, which will separate into spaghetti-like strands.

5. Transfer the squash strands to plates and season with salt and pepper. Spoon the tomato sauce over, then grate the cheese over.

Sweet & Sour Mixed Veg

MAKES **2–3 SERVINGS**
PREP TIME: **10–15 MINUTES, DEPENDING ON THE VEGETABLES USED** / COOKING TIME: **ABOUT 5 MINUTES**

TRY THIS SWEET-AND-SOUR SAUCE ONCE AND YOU WILL STOP REACHING FOR THE EXPENSIVE BOTTLED SAUCES AT THE SUPERMARKET – WITHOUT ANY PRESERVATIVES THIS HAS A CLEANER, FRESHER FLAVOUR. AND YOU CAN ALTER THE FLAVOUR TO BE AS SWEET, HOT OR SOUR AS YOU LIKE. SERVE WITH BOILED RICE (PAGE 131) OR EGG NOODLES, OR A NAAN BREAD.

400 g mixed vegetables, such as broccoli, carrots, celery, garlic cloves, leeks, mushrooms, onions, peppers, or spring onions
2 tablespoons sunflower or rapeseed oil
3 tablespoons vegetable stock, home-made (page 164) or from a cube
2 tablespoons bottled hoi sin sauce
50 g fresh beansprouts
Dark or mushroom soy sauce or tamari, to taste

FOR THE SWEET-AND-SOUR SAUCE
1 1/2 tablespoons cornflour
200 ml water
3 tablespoons red-wine or white-wine vinegar
2 teaspoons Chinese rice wine
1–1 1/2 tablespoons soft light brown sugar, to taste
About 1 teaspoon hot-pepper sauce, to taste

1. Begin by making the sauce. Put the cornflour in a saucepan and very slowly stir in the water to avoid lumps forming (See Cook's Tips below). Stir in the remaining ingredients and bring to the boil, stirring to dissolve the sugar. Reduce the heat and leave the sauce to simmer for just a few minutes until it thickens. Remove the pan from the heat and set aside.

2. Prepare the vegetables: cut broccoli florets and stalks into small pieces; peel and thinly slice carrots; cut celery into thin slices; peel and chop garlic; slice and rinse leeks; wipe mushrooms with a damp cloth, trim the ends of the stalks and thinly slice the caps and stalks; peel and chop onions; de-seed and slice peppers; chop spring onions. The idea is to get similar-sized pieces so they cook in the same amount of time.

3. Mix the vegetable stock and hoi sin sauce together in a small bowl and set aside. Heat a large wok over a high heat until a splash of water 'dances' on the surface. Add the oil and swirl it around.

4. Add the thickest vegetables, such as broccoli stalks, and stir-fry for 2 minutes. Add the remaining vegetables and continue stir-frying for 2 minutes.

5. Stir in the beansprouts with the vegetable stock and hoi sin mixture and stir-fry for about 15 seconds, constantly turning all the ingredients, until the liquid evaporates. Add the sweet-and-sour sauce and stir together until it is bubbling.

VARIATION
If you don't have vegetable stock or Chinese rice wine, use water.

Cook's Tips
▸ If lumps form when you combine the cornflour and water in Step 1, add the remaining ingredients, then use a wooden spoon to press them all through a fine sieve into a bowl. Return the mixture to the pan, bring to the boil and continue with Step 1.
▸ Save time and make double the quantity of the sauce. It will keep, covered, in the fridge for up to 3 days, ready to use in another meal.
▸ If you think the sauce is too spicy hot, stir in extra sugar.

Tray of Roast Veg

MAKES **4 SERVINGS**
PREP TIME: **ABOUT 10 MINUTES**
COOKING TIME: **ABOUT 50 MINUTES**

450 g new potatoes
2 carrots
2 red peppers
1 red onion
Olive oil
8 garlic cloves
Salt and pepper – sea salt is ideal

1. Heat the oven to 210°C/425°F/Gas 7. Scrub and dry the potatoes, then cut them into 1-cm dice. Scrub or peel the carrots and cut them into 1-cm slices. Core and de-seed the peppers, then cut them into thick strips. Cut the onion into wedges.

2. Pour a thin layer of olive oil into a large roasting tin. Add the vegetables and the unpeeled garlic cloves and stir them around in the oil. Drizzle with a little extra oil and sprinkle with salt; you don't want the veggies 'swimming' in oil.

3. Put the tray in the oven and roast for 45–50 minutes until the potatoes and carrots are tender. Dish up the veg. Everyone can pop the garlic cloves out of their skins, then smear the soft flesh on the potatoes.

PLENTY OF PASTA

Things have moved on from the days when students seemed to live on nothing but Spag Bol, but no doubt pasta will be a staple ingredient in your kitchen. There are endless pasta shapes to choose from, and you can eat pasta hot or cold. It is so easy to cook you can knock up a meal in minutes while you watch TV. Cooking pasta is one of the easiest meals you can prepare. When you stock up on bags of dried pasta and cans of chopped tomatoes you'll always have something to eat.

And it's not just Italians who eat pasta. Have you ever been to a noodle bar? Chinese and Japanese noodles are just pasta by another name (see The World of Pasta, page 128). This chapter includes many quick Asian recipes, including ones with egg-free noodles that suit vegans. A few years ago you might have had to go to an Asian food store for ingredients, but now you'll find them at the supermarket.

Most traditional pasta sauces are meat free, so making pasta meals is ideal for vegetarians. A tomato-based sauce with a chopped onion and garlic and a little olive oil is a great TV dinner. If you want to be more adventurous, add broccoli with chilli flakes.

Other pasta dishes to try:
- Japanese Mushroom Broth with rice sticks (page 66)
- Minestrone (page 165)
- Spiced Noodle & Fruit Pudding (page 202)

Boiling Italian Pasta

You don't have to be reading nuclear physics to master cooking pasta. There are only two things to remember: use the largest pot or pan you have so the pasta has plenty of water to boil in, and don't walk away and forget about the pasta or it will overcook and become a soggy, inedible mess.

Cooking perfect pasta is as easy as 1-2-3:

1. Bring the water to a full rolling boil in a covered pan over a high heat. Uncover the pan and add 1 teaspoon salt for each litre of water.

2. Add the pasta and stir with a wooden spoon. Make sure the water comes back to the boil, then continue to boil, uncovered, until the pasta is tender, or what the Italians describe as 'al dente' (see How Done is Done? on page 106).

3. Have a colander or sieve waiting in the sink. Pour the pasta and water into the colander or strainer, let the water drain off and then give it a few shakes to remove any excess water. Voilà! There you have it – perfect pasta.

Cook's Tips

▸ The size of your largest pan determines how many people you can cook pasta for at any one time. Ideally you want a pan large enough to hold 4 litres water for each 450 g pasta. As you are unlikely to have a pot that large, only cook one or two portions at a time.

▸ Covering the pan while you heat the water helps it boil faster.

▸ The water should be boiling the whole time the pasta is cooking.

▸ Don't forget to salt the cooking water. If you don't add salt then your pasta will taste bland, no matter how flavoursome the sauce.

▸ Save a few tablespoons of the pasta cooking water before draining. If the sauce is too thick, thin it with this water, without diluting the flavour.

▸ Do not rinse pasta after it is drained: the starch helps the sauce adhere to the pasta.

▸ Pasta is best piping hot. Take a tip from Italian cooks and return the drained pasta to the still-hot pan it was boiled it in, then add the hot sauce and toss together.

Vegan Note

Vegans take care – although many of the sauces in this section of the chapter are fit for your diet, they are served with Italian pasta, and most pasta from Italy contains eggs. Read the labels carefully. Most of the

Asian noodle recipes that follow will be more suitable for you, but experiment and mix and match these sauces with rice sticks, mung-bean or buckwheat noodles until you find a combination you like.

HOW DONE IS DONE?

It's one thing to read a recipe that tells you to cook pasta until it is 'al dente', but it is another thing to know what it means when you are new to cooking. 'Al dente' literally translates as 'tender to the bite'. The only accurate way to check if pasta is cooked is to fish out a piece and bite: there shouldn't be any chalky whiteness in the centre and it should feel tender, but still slightly firm. The residual heat will finish the cooking and the pasta won't become mushy.

For dried pasta, follow the timings on the packet. Fresh pasta, however, cooks in 3–5 minutes.

HOW MUCH IS ENOUGH?

Everyone has different appetites, but plan on 80–100 g for a main-course portion, depending on how filling the sauce is. After you cook pasta a couple of times you will know how much fills you up.

MIXING & MATCHING

Many cookbooks make a big deal about matching specific sauces to specific shapes of pasta, but there are no firm rules. One reason pasta is such an appealing ingredient for new cooks is that it is so versatile.

Pasta with Squash

MAKES **2 SERVINGS**
PREP TIME: **10–15 MINUTES**
COOKING TIME: **ABOUT 20 MINUTES**

225 g butternut or acorn squash
1 garlic clove
Several sprigs fresh parsley or sage, or a pinch of dried sage
1 1/2 tablespoons olive, sunflower or rapeseed oil
200 g dried pasta shapes, such as twists or macaroni
200 ml water
40 g mature vegetarian Parmesan-style or Cheddar cheese
Freshly grated nutmeg (optional)
Salt and pepper

1. Use a vegetable peeler or knife to peel the piece of squash. Cut out and discard any seeds and fibres in the centre. Cut the flesh into 1-cm pieces.

2. Peel and crush the garlic. Finely chop the parsley or sage leaves – add as much parsley as you like, but go lightly with the sage as it has such a pronounced flavour.

3. Heat 1 $1/2$ tablespoons oil in a large wok, frying pan or saucepan, ideally non-stick, with a lid over a medium heat. Add the squash pieces and stir around until they brown on the sides.

4. Stir in the garlic and water with salt and pepper to taste. Bring to the boil, then reduce the heat, cover the pan tightly and leave the pumpkin to simmer for 20 minutes, or until the pieces can easily be mashed.

5. Meanwhile, bring a large saucepan of water to the boil. When the water has reached a rolling boil, add salt and the pasta. Stir and continue boiling for 10 minutes, or the time specified on the packet, until the pasta is al dente.

6. When the squash is tender, uncover the pan. If any liquid remains, turn up the heat and let it bubble away. Stir in the herb and a few gratings of nutmeg, if you are using.

7. Drain the pasta well and shake off any excess water. Add the pasta to the squash and toss together, breaking up the squash as you combine the two ingredients. Grate the cheese over and toss again.

VARIATIONS
- Vegetarian Stilton or goat's cheese also work well in this dish.
- For a spicy flavour, add a pinch of dried chilli flakes to the squash in Step 3.
- Sprinkle the top with toasted pine nuts (page 35).

Cook's Tip
Use leftover uncooked squash in Spiced Winter Squash Stew (page 100).

Pasta with Spinach & Cheese

MAKES **2 SERVINGS**
PREP TIME: **ABOUT 5 MINUTES**
COOKING TIME: **ABOUT 10 MINUTES**

HUNG OVER? TOO TIRED TO THINK STRAIGHT? IT DOESN'T MATTER – YOU STILL HAVE TO EAT. THIS RECIPE REQUIRES LESS EFFORT THAN GETTING OUT OF BED AND GETTING DRESSED.

200 g small pasta shapes, such as macaroni or spirals
2 spring onions (optional)
225 g baby spinach leaves
75 g vegetarian Stilton or Cheddar cheese
1 tablespoon olive, sunflower or rapeseed oil
Grated nutmeg (optional)
Salt and pepper

1. Bring a large saucepan of water to the boil over a high heat. Add salt and the pasta and stir. Continue boiling the pasta for 10 minutes, or according to the timings on the packet.

2. Meanwhile, trim and finely chop the spring onions, if using. Rinse the spinach leaves and remove any thick stalks

3. Crumble the cheese into a bowl large enough to hold all the pasta. Add the spring onions and oil, and beat together until a thick paste forms. Add pepper to taste: do not add any salt at this point. If you have any nutmeg in the cupboard add several gratings.

4. Just before the pasta is cooked, stir the spinach into the boiling water and leave for 10–15 seconds to wilt. Set aside 4 tablespoons of the pasta cooking water before you drain the pasta.

5. Drain the pasta and spinach and shake off excess water. Immediately add it to the bowl with the sauce, and toss together: the heat of the pasta will melt the cheese. If the sauce is too thick, very slowly stir in the reserved cooking water until you have a consistency you like. Taste and adjust the seasoning, if necessary.

Hot Tomatoes & Noodles

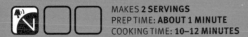

MAKES **2 SERVINGS**
PREP TIME: **ABOUT 1 MINUTE**
COOKING TIME: **10–12 MINUTES**

TOSSING CHERRY TOMATOES INTO A SALAD MIGHT BE SECOND NATURE, BUT TRY THEM HOT WITH PASTA. THIS IS BLINDINGLY SIMPLE AND WITH SUN-RIPE TOMATOES THE TASTE IS UNBEATABLE.

200 g dried spaghetti or noodles, such as tagliatelle
14 cherry tomatoes
Small bunch fresh flat-leaf parsley
15 g butter
1 tablespoon olive oil
Salt and pepper

1. Bring a large saucepan of water to the boil over a high heat. Add salt and the pasta and stir. Continue boiling the pasta for 10 minutes, or according to the instructions on the packet.

2. Meanwhile, use a small knife to remove the green leaf and stem from each tomato. Finely chop the parsley leaves.

3. Melt the butter with the oil in a large frying pan or wok over a medium-high heat. Add the tomatoes, sprinkle with a little salt and pepper and stir for 6–8 minutes, or until the skins begin to wrinkle.

4. Toss in the parsley and continue stirring for another minute.

5. Drain the pasta and add it to the tomatoes, using 2 forks to mix all the ingredients together.

VARIATIONS
▸ Try the cooked tomatoes on their own without pasta – they are good hot, lukewarm or at room temperature. Any leftovers can be smashed together and used in a toasted cheese sandwich.
▸ Add diced, drained vegetarian mozzarella cheese to the pan with the pasta in Step 5.

Vegan Note
For a vegan meal, omit the butter and egg noodles. Use 1 $^1/_2$ tablespoons olive oil and spoon the tomatoes and pan juices over couscous or boiled rice at the end of Step 4.

Mediterranean Pasta

MAKES **2 SERVINGS**
PREP TIME: **ABOUT 10 MINUTES**
COOKING TIME: **ABOUT 20 MINUTES**

$^1/_2$ onion
1 garlic clove
60 g black olives
1 $^1/_2$ tablespoons olive oil
$^1/_2$ tablespoon dried oregano or dried mixed herbs
$^1/_2$ teaspoon fennel seeds
Pinch of dried red chillies, or to taste
1 tin (400 g) chopped tomatoes
Pinch of sugar
200 g dried pasta – use any shape
Salt and pepper
Vegetarian feta cheese to serve (optional)

1. Peel and chop the onion. Peel and crush the garlic. Remove the stones from the olives – a cherry pitter makes the job easy, but you can use a small knife.

2. Heat the oil in a large frying pan with a lid or saucepan over a medium-high heat. Add the onion and stir for 2–3 minutes. Add the garlic and stir for a minute longer.

3. Stir in the oregano or mixed herbs and fennel seeds. Add the tomatoes with their juice, sugar and salt and pepper to taste, and bring to the boil. Reduce the heat to low, half cover the pan and leave to simmer for about 20 minutes.

4. Meanwhile, bring a large pan of water to the boil over a high heat. Add the pasta and salt and continue to boil for 10–12 minutes, or according to the packet instructions.

5. Drain the pasta and add it to the sauce, using 2 forks to mix all the ingredients together. Taste and adjust the seasoning, if necessary. Top with crumbled feta cheese if a vegan isn't eating with you.

VARIATIONS
▸ If you have any Mediterranean Grilled Vegetables (page 53) in the fridge, cut them into bite-size pieces and add them to the sauce just before the pasta finishes cooking so they have time to warm through.
▸ Add $^1/_2$ tablespoon of rinsed capers.

Lemon Pasta

MAKES **2 SERVINGS**
PREP TIME: **ABOUT 10 MINUTES**
COOKING TIME: **ABOUT 10 MINUTES**

1 large lemon
200 g small pasta shapes, such as orzo, macaroni or spirals
1 large garlic clove
Small bunch fresh parsley
2 tablespoons olive oil
60 g vegetarian Parmesan-style cheese
Salt and pepper

1. Bring a large pan of water to the boil over a high heat. Use the small holes on a grater to remove the rind from the lemon: take care not to include any of the bitter white pith. Then roll the lemon back and forth on the work surface, pressing down firmly. Cut the lemon in half and squeeze out all the juice. Set aside the rind and juice in a bowl large enough to hold the cooked pasta.

2. When the water boils, add salt and the pasta, and continue boiling for 10 minutes, or until the pasta is tender.

3. While the pasta boils, peel and finely chop the garlic. Very finely chop the parsley leaves and stems – it is the stems that have the most flavour. Grate the cheese.

4. Add the garlic, parsley and oil to the lemon rind and juice, and stir together until blended.

5. Drain the pasta and add it to the bowl with the other ingredients and toss together. Season with salt and pepper and serve.

VARIATIONS
▸ Thinly slice 6 stoned black olives and add them to the sauce with the pasta in Step 4.
▸ Add drained and rinsed tinned cannellini or flagolet beans.

Pasta with Broccoli & Chilli

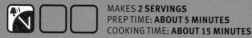

MAKES **2 SERVINGS**
PREP TIME: **ABOUT 5 MINUTES**
COOKING TIME: **ABOUT 15 MINUTES**

400 g fresh broccoli
2 large garlic cloves
200 g dried orecchiette or other small pasta shapes
3 tablespoons olive oil
¼ teaspoon dried red chilli flakes
Salt and pepper
Grated vegetarian Parmesan-style cheese, to serve (optional)

1. Bring a large saucepan of water to the boil over a high heat.
Meanwhile, chop the broccoli florets and stalks into small pieces.
Peel and finely chop the garlic and set aside.

2. Add salt and the broccoli florets and stalks to the boiling water,
cover the pan and return the water to the boil. When the water boils,
uncover it and continue boiling the broccoli for 10 minutes.

3. Use a slotted spoon to remove the broccoli from the water and
set aside. Stir in the pasta and continue boiling for 10–12 minutes,
or according to the packet instructions.

4. After 8 minutes return the broccoli to the pan and continue boiling
until the pasta is al dente and the broccoli is very tender. Drain well,
shaking the pan to remove the water that will be trapped in the pasta.

5. While the pasta is cooking, put the oil, chilli flakes and garlic in a
large frying pan over a medium heat and stir just until the garlic starts
to brown: do not burn.

6. Tip the pasta and broccoli into the oil and toss together. Add salt and
pepper to taste, although remember, if you are sprinkling with Parmesan
cheese be very light handed with the salt as the cheese will be salty.

VARIATION
Cauliflower is a good alternative to the broccoli.

Vegan Note
Try the broccoli without the egg noodles. Just cook the broccoli for
less time, so it still retains some crunch. If you want something more
substantial, add a de-seeded, chopped tomato to the frying pan just
before you add the broccoli.

Baked Macaroni & 4 Cheeses

MAKES **3–4 SERVINGS**
PREP TIME: **ABOUT 15 MINUTES**
COOKING TIME: **25 MINUTES**

THIS IS GROWN-UP MACARONI CHEESE. IT'S COMFORT FOOD WITH STYLE.

THINK OF THIS AS A TWOFER – A TWO-IN-ONE RECIPE. FOLLOW THE WHOLE RECIPE AND YOU HAVE A BAKED fiLLING DISH WITH A CRUNCHY BREADCRUMB-AND-CHEESE TOPPING FOR SHARING WITH FLATMATES OR FRIENDS. BUT IF YOU CAN'T BE BOTHERED TO WAIT FOR THE DISH TO BAKE, BOIL THE PASTA FOR THE FULL COOKING TIME SPECIfiED ON THE PACKET AND WARM IT IN CHEESE SAUCE AT THE END OF STEP 5.

RICH AND fiLLING, THIS GOES WELL WITH A TOSSED GREEN SALAD ON THE SIDE OR STEAMED CARROTS OR BROCCOLI.

75 g vegetarian Cheddar cheese
75 g vegetarian mozzarella cheese, drained
50 g vegetarian dolcelette or other vegetarian blue cheese
400 ml milk
Olive, sunflower or rapeseed oil for the dish
350 g dried macaroni or other pasta shapes, such as shells or snails
60 g butter
55 g fine breadcrumbs (page 114)
2 tablespoons plain wholemeal or white flour
Pinch of cayenne pepper
Pinch of grated nutmeg (optional)
4 tablespoons grated vegetarian Parmesan-style cheese
Salt and pepper

1. Preheat the oven to 200°C/400°F/Gas 6. Bring a large pan of water to the boil. Add salt and the pasta to the boiling water and boil for 2 minutes less than specified on the packet. Drain the pasta and immediately rinse with cold water to stop the cooking; set aside.

2. While the pasta is cooking, grate the Cheddar cheese and cut the mozzarella and the dolcelette cheeses into small pieces; set aside. Put the milk in a saucepan over a medium heat and heat until small bubbles appear around the edge: do not boil. Rub a small amount of oil over the base and sides of a 1-litre flameproof dish; set the dish aside.

3. Melt half the butter in a saucepan over a medium heat. Put the breadcrumbs in a bowl, pour the butter over and stir together; set aside.

4. Melt the remaining butter in the same pan over low heat. Sprinkle in the flour and stir constantly for one minute to remove the raw taste of the flour. Remove the pan from the heat and slowly stir in the milk, stirring constantly so lumps do not form.

5. Return the pan to the heat and simmer, stirring constantly, until the sauce becomes thick. Turn off the heat and stir in the Cheddar, mozzarella and dolcelette cheeses. Add the pasta with the cayenne, salt and pepper to taste and a little grated nutmeg, if you are using. Stir all the ingredients together so each piece of pasta is coated with the sauce.

6. Spoon the pasta and sauce into the dish and sprinkle the Parmesan cheese and breadcrumbs over the top. Bake for 25 minutes until golden and crisp on top. Use oven gloves to remove from the oven and place on a heatproof surface for 2 minutes before serving.

Plan Ahead
You can assemble the dish through Step 5 up to a day in advance, ready for sprinkling with the breadcrumbs and Parmesan cheese just before baking. Just remember to let the sauce cool before you put it in the fridge, then take the dish out of the fridge to return to room temperature while the oven heats.

Making Breadcrumbs
Day-old bread is best to make crumbs from. If you have a food processor, just tear pieces of bread into the bowl and whiz until crumbs form. Otherwise, rub the bread up and down over the coarse holes on a grater. Store leftover crumbs in an air-tight container in the fridge for up to 3 days.

PASTA SAUCES

A bowl of pasta without sauce is like a pub without beer. It just isn't worth thinking about. Here are some ultra-easy ideas that will keep you fed and happy without much effort. Each is intended for 200 g of freshly cooked pasta, except the pesto sauce, which makes double that amount – spread it on bruschetta (page 53).

No-cook Tomato Sauce

MAKES **2 SERVINGS**
PREP TIME: **ABOUT 10 MINUTES, PLUS OPTIONAL MARINATING
NO COOKING**

WHAT MORE CAN YOU ASK FOR? THIS IS AS QUICK AND EASY AS 'COOKING' GETS. THE MOST DIFFICULT THING IS TO REMEMBER TO BUY THE TOMATOES. (FOR A SLOW-COOKED TOMATO SAUCE, SEE ESSENTAIL TOMATO SAUCE, PAGE 154.)

1 large garlic clove
2 large juicy beefsteak tomatoes
1 tablespoon olive oil
$^1/_2$ tablespoon tomato purée
Pinch of sugar
20–24 fresh basil leaves
Salt and pepper

1. Peel and crush the garlic. Place the garlic in a serving bowl that will be large enough to hold all the cooked pasta.

2. Use the coarse holes on a grater to grate the tomatoes directly into the bowl, rubbing them back and forth and pressing down firmly. Stir in the tomato purée, sugar and salt and pepper to taste.

3. Tear the basil leaves into thin strips and stir it into the other ingredients. At this point you can set the sauce aside for up to 2 hours for the flavours to blend and develop.

4. When you are ready to use the sauce, give it a good stir, taste and adjust the seasoning, if necessary. Add hot freshly boiled pasta to the sauce and toss together.

Sweet Ways
Get in the habit of adding a pinch of sugar when cooking with tomatoes. It helps counter the acidity in the tomatoes.

Fresh Herb & Garlic Sauce

MAKES **2 SERVINGS**
PREP TIME: **ABOUT 5 MINUTES, PLUS AT LEAST 20 MINUTES**
MARINATING / COOKING TIME: **ABOUT 2 MINUTES**

IF YOU STOP AT THE SUPERMARKET AT THE END OF THE DAY, YOU'LL OFTEN fiND PACKETS OF
FRESH HERBS MARKED DOWN. GRAB A PACKET OR TWO. THEY WILL HAVE TO BE USED
WITHIN A DAY OR WILL START TO COLOUR AND BECOME LIMP. THIS SIMPLE SAUCE LETS
YOU TAKE ADVANTAGE OF THE BARGAIN.

GARLIC SAUCE IS ONE TO SHARE WITH ONLY CLOSE FRIENDS. SPAGHETTI, LINGUINI
AND THIN NOODLES ARE MOST SUITABLE TO USE WITH THIS BUT, OF COURSE, ANY PASTA
SHAPE WILL DO.

1 large lemon
1 large garlic clove
Small bunch fresh chives
Small bunch fresh parsley
A few sprigs fresh tarragon
2 $^1/_2$ tablespoons olive oil
Salt and pepper

1. Finely grate the rind from the lemon. Peel and crush the garlic clove.

2. Put the garlic and olive oil in a large frying pan over a medium-low heat
and heat for about 2 minutes, just until the garlic begins to sizzle: do not
let it brown. Immediately remove the pan from the heat.

3. Stir in the lemon rind and set the oil aside for at least 20 minutes to let
the flavours blend.

4. Meanwhile, finely chop the chives, parsley and tarragon: you need
about 3 tablespoons of chopped fresh herbs in total.

5. Just before you drain the pasta, stir the herbs into the oil. Add the
hot pasta and toss together. Season with salt and pepper to taste.

VARIATIONS

► For a Mediterranean twist, add 1 tablespoon drained and rinsed
capers.
► Or add a finely sliced sun-dried tomato that has been preserved in
oil to the pasta just before it finishes boiling. Use the oil for the jar of
tomatoes in place of some or all of the olive oil in the recipe.
► For a touch of heat, add a pinch of dried red chilli flakes to the sauce
with the salt and pepper.
► If you don't have a selection of herbs, just use about 3 tablespoons
all parsley or chives. Fresh thyme is also good, as are torn basil leaves.
Tarragon has too strong a flavour to use on its own.

Cook's Tips
► If you make double the quantity of the flavoured oil, the leftovers can be strained and used in salad dressings.
► Don't throw away the lemon after you have grated it. It will have to be used quickly before it dries out, but the juice can be added to salad dressings or squeezed over Fried Halloumi (page 54).

Pesto Sauce

MAKES **4 SERVINGS**
PREP TIME: **ABOUT 10 MINUTES**
NO COOKING

2 bunches fresh basil
1–2 garlic cloves, to taste
2 tablespoons toasted pine nuts (page 35)
125 ml extra-virgin or ordinary olive oil
Salt
Vegetarian Parmesan cheese

1. Tear the leaves from the basil stems and discard all but the thinnest, most delicate stems. Crush the garlic cloves.

2. Put the basil leaves, garlic, pine nuts, 4 tablespoons of the oil and a pinch of salt in a blender and blitz until chopped and blended. Scrape down the side of the blender, then replace the lid and gradually add the remaining oil while the motor is running. Taste and adjust the salt, if necessary. Or use a stick blender and add all the oil at once.

3. If you don't have a blender, pound and grind the ingredients together in a mortar with a pestle.

4. The sauce is now ready to toss with hot pasta, or you can store it in the fridge for up to a week, or the freezer for up to a month. Use the leftovers in Minestrone (page 165) or Pesto-Yoghurt Dip (page 176).

VARIATIONS
► Parsley Pesto: Follow the above recipe, but substitute fresh flat-leaf parsley leaves for the basil and add the grated rind of 1 lemon and lemon juice to taste.
► Pasta al Genovese: In Genoa it's traditional to add cooked sliced new potatoes and French beans to linguini or spaghetti and pesto sauce – a filling dish in a bowl!

Parmesan Sauce

MAKES **2 SERVINGS**
PREP TIME: **ABOUT 5 MINUTES**
NO COOKING

75 g vegetarian Parmesan-style cheese
About 2 tablespoons olive oil
Salt and pepper

1. Grate the cheese into a bowl large enough to hold all the pasta. Add the oil and beat together until a thick paste forms.

2. Set aside 4 tablespoons of the pasta cooking water before you drain the pasta. Add the hot freshly drained pasta to the bowl with the sauce and toss together: the heat of the pasta will melt the cheese and make a creamy coating sauce. If the sauce is too thick, very slowly stir in the reserved cooking water until you have a consistency you like. Taste and adjust the seasoning, if necessary.

VARIATIONS
▶ Parmesan is the traditional Italian choice for this sauce, but other vegetarian cheeses, such as Cheddar, red Leicester, Edam or feta, also make a quick sauce.
▶ Add thinly sliced sun-dried tomatoes with the hot pasta to the cheese sauce.
▶ For a more substantial meal, add frozen peas or small broccoli florets to the pasta as it boils.

Other Ideas for Easy Pasta Meals

▶ Heat Tomato Salsa (page 56) until warm. Toss with boiled pasta and stir in diced vegetarian mozzarella.
▶ Mix small pasta shapes with Mediterranean Broad Beans (page 75). Greek orzo is ideal for this, but macaroni and shells are good, too.
▶ Make a pasta salad with cooked and cooled pasta, chopped sun-dried tomatoes, chopped cherry tomatoes, torn fresh basil leaves and a little Vinaigrette Dressing (page 172). Sprinkle with toasted pine nuts.
▶ Toss wholemeal pasta shapes with Catalan Spinach (page 98).
▶ Put chopped artichoke hearts in oil, sun-dried tomatoes in oil, and a little of the oil from either in a bowl with chopped fresh parsley. Add hot pasta and toss together. Grate over a little vegetarian cheese.

OODLES AND OODLES OF NOODLES

When you're hungry and don't want to spend much time in the kitchen, get your wok out and start cooking Asian noodles. You'll soon find Asian noodles are difficult to beat when it comes to fast food.

Some Asian noodles are made with eggs, but vegans will still find lots of options here with rice noodles, cellophane noodles and several varieties of wheat noodles made without eggs.

WATCH POINT – SOFTENING RICE NOODLES

Rice noodles are firm and brittle when you buy them and have to be softened before you can cook with them. When you buy rice noodles (also called rice sticks) at the supermarket the labels will often instruct you to pour boiling water over them and leave them to soak for up to 10 minutes until they are pliable. This does work, but when you stir-fry the noodles they will often break up and be overcooked.

Instead, if you aren't in a hurry, put the noodles in a large bowl, pour over enough cold water to cover and leave to stand for 30–60 minutes before draining.

SHAKE IT UP

When you drain noodles that have been soaking, give the colander or strainer a good shake. You don't want the noodles dripping with water when they hit the hot wok.

Tofu Chow Mein

MAKES **2 SERVINGS**
PREP TIME: **ABOUT 15 MINUTES, INCLUDING MARINATING**
COOKING TIME: **ABOUT 4 MINUTES**

HEAT UP YOUR WOK AND GET COOKING. THIS IS A STRAIGHTFORWARD STIR-FRY RECIPE, BUT IT HAS A WHOLE LOT GOING FOR IT. AFTER YOU'VE MADE IT A FEW TIMES IT WILL BE WHAT POPS INTO YOUR HEAD WHEN YOU WANT FAST FOOD. AND, OF COURSE, ONCE YOU'VE GOT THE HANG OF THIS, VARIATIONS WILL BE LIMITLESS – GO FOR IT!

125 g firm tofu
1 garlic clove
1-cm slice fresh root ginger
1 tablespoon Chinese rice wine
1 tablespoon mushroom or dark soy sauce
150 g dried thin Chinese egg noodles

1 carrot
75 g mangetout
2 spring onions
30 g unsalted cashew nuts
1 tablespoon sunflower or rapeseed oil
50 g fresh beansprouts
1 teaspoon toasted sesame oil (optional)
Vegetable stock, home-made (page 164) or from a cube, or water
Chopped fresh coriander or parsley (optional)

1. Bring a kettle of water to the boil. Cut the tofu into small cubes. Peel and finely chop the garlic. Peel and finely chop the ginger.

2. Put the garlic and ginger in a bowl with the rice wine and soy sauce and stir together. Add the tofu and gently stir again so it is coated. Set aside and leave to marinate while you prepare and cook the other ingredients.

3. Put the egg noodles in a heatproof bowl and pour over enough boiling water to cover and leave for 5 minutes, or boil according to the packet instructions.

4. While the noodles are soaking, peel the carrot, then cut it in half lengthwise and then into very thin long slices. Cut the mangetout into thin, long strips. Trim the ends off the spring onions and finely chop. Coarsely chop the cashews.

5. Drain the noodles, shaking off any excess water. Heat a wok over a high heat until a few drops of water 'dance' on the surface. Add the oil and swirl it around.

6. Add the carrot, mangetout and spring onions, and stir-fry for about 2 minutes, constantly stirring and turning the ingredients.

7. Tip in the tofu with the marinade, the noodles, the beansprouts, cashews, and sesame oil, if you are using, and continue stir-frying and mixing the ingredients together for about 2 minutes until everything is hot. If the mixture seems too dry, stir in 1–2 tablespoons of vegetable stock or water. Sprinkle with coriander or parsley, if you have any.

VARIATION
Other vegetables that can be used in place of any of the ones listed above include thinly sliced red, green or yellow peppers; small broccoli florets; sliced mushrooms; well-drained canned sweetcorn kernels.

Vegan Note
Replace the egg noodles with soaked rice sticks.

Buckwheat Noodles with Miso Dip

MAKES **2 SERVINGS**
PREP TIME: **ABOUT 10 MINUTES, PLUS CHILLING**
COOKING TIME: **ABOUT 3 MINUTES**

JAPANESE STUDENTS EAT THIS COLD NOODLE DISH DURING THE SUMMER MONTHS. THIS
IS VERY EASY TO PREPARE, BUT IT ISN'T A SPUR-OF-THE-MOMENT DISH. THE NOODLES HAVE
TO BE BOILED AND THE DIPPING SAUCE MADE WELL IN ADVANCE SO THEY WILL BE CHILLED
WHEN YOU WANT TO EAT. HAVE IT WAITING WHEN YOU COME HOME FROM LECTURES OR
A NIGHT ON THE TOWN.

BUCKWHEAT NOODLES ARE ALSO LABELLED AS 'SOBA NOODLES'.

125 g dried thin buckwheat noodles
2 red radishes
1 large spring onion
Pickled red ginger
Wasabi paste
1 sheet nori seaweed (optional – see Cook's Tip, page 122)

MISO DIPPING SAUCE
150 ml water
1 sachet instant miso soup
2 tablespoons dark soy sauce
2 tablespoons rice-wine vinegar
2–3 tablespoons Chinese rice wine

1. A couple of hours in advance, bring a saucepan of water to the boil
over a high heat. Add the noodles and boil for 3 minutes, or according
to the packet instructions, until they are soft. Drain the noodles, then
put them in a bowl of cold water and swish them around to remove the
starch. Drain them again and rinse the bowl. Fill it with fresh cold water,
add the noodles, cover and chill until you are ready to serve.

2. Meanwhile, bring the water for the dipping sauce to the boil in a
small pan over a high heat. Stir in the miso soup and leave to stand for
5 minutes. Place a fine sieve over a small bowl and strain the soup.

3. Wash and rinse the pan. Return the strained miso soup to the pan.
Stir in the soy sauce, wine vinegar and rice wine and bring to the boil.
Boil for 1 minute, then remove from the heat and leave to cool
completely. Pour into a bowl, cover and chill.

4. When you are ready to eat, grate the radish and finely chop the spring
onion. Divide the noodles between 2 plates and arrange the pickled
ginger, spring onion, radish and wasabi paste round the rim, keeping
each separate. Divide the dipping sauce between small bowls.

5. You eat this by using chopsticks or a fork to pick up some noodles and then quickly dip them in the dipping sauce and then flavour them with one of the garnishes.

Cook's Tip
Toasted nori is the traditional garnish for these noodles. It is sold in very thin sheets at Japanese and whole-food shops. Hold one sheet about 7 1/2 cm above a gas flame with a pair of tongs and toast on both side. Use a pair of scissors to cut the nori into very thin strips, then sprinkle them over the noodles.

Noodle-Egg Pancake

   MAKES **1 PANCAKE**
PREP TIME: **15 MINUTES**
COOKING TIME: **5 MINUTES**

40 g dried thin cellophane noodles
1 spring onion
1 large free-range egg
Sunflower or rapeseed oil
Salt and pepper

1. Bring a pan of water to the boil over a high heat. Add the noodles and cook for 15 minutes, or according to the packet instructions.

2. Meanwhile, trim and finely chop the spring onion. Crack the eggs into a large bowl and beat together, then add salt and pepper to taste.

3. Drain the noodles and cut them into 12.5-cm pieces.

4. Heat a 20-cm frying pan, ideally non-stick, over a high heat. Add 1 tablespoon of oil and swirl it around.

5. Pour the egg-and-noodle mixture into the pan and tilt the pan so the base is covered. Reduce the heat to medium and leave to cook for about 1 minute until the base is set.

6. If you're feeling confident, give the pan a good shake to flip the pancake over, otherwise slide it on to a plate. Turn the pancake over and slide it back into the pan. Continue cooking until the bottom is set.

Sweet Chilli-Coriander Noodles

MAKES **2 SERVINGS**
PREP TIME: **ABOUT 10 MINUTES**
COOKING TIME: **ABOUT 5 MINUTES**

125 g dried Chinese egg noodles
30 g shelled peanuts, without any papery skins
Bunch fresh coriander
2 sprigs fresh mint (optional)
1 tablespoon lime juice
1 tablespoon sweet soy sauce
1 tablespoon bottled sweet chilli sauce
$^1/_2$ tablespoon Chinese rice wine
1 teaspoon sesame oil
125 g drained canned sweetcorn kernels
1 tablespoon sunflower or groundnut oil

1. Bring a kettle of water to the boil. Put the noodles in a heatproof bowl, pour over enough boiling water to cover and leave for 5 minutes, or boil according to packet instructions. Drain well and shake off any excess water.

2. Meanwhile, coarsely chop the peanuts. Finely chop the coriander stalks and leaves, and mint leaves, if you are using.

3. Mix the lime juice, sweet soy sauce, sweet chilli sauce, rice wine and sesame oil together in a bowl. Add the noodles and sweetcorn, and toss together.

4. Heat a wok, ideally non-stick, over a high heat until a splash of water 'dances' when it hits the surface. Add the noodles and liquid, and stir around for about 3 minutes. Transfer the noodles to bowls and sprinkle with peanuts.

Singapore-style Noodles

MAKES **2 SERVINGS**
PREP TIME: **ABOUT 20 MINUTES, INCLUDING SOAKING THE NOODLES** / COOKING TIME: **8–10 MINUTES**

125 g vermicelli rice noodles
60 g Chinese cabbage
1 onion
1 garlic clove
$^1/_2$-cm piece of fresh root ginger
60 g sugar-snap peas or mangetout
$^1/_2$ red, green, yellow or orange pepper
1 tablespoon sunflower or rapeseed oil
1 tablespoon curry paste – you determine the heat
1 teaspoon turmeric
$^1/_2$ teaspoon sugar
60 g shelled peas, fresh or frozen
4 tablespoons vegetable stock (page 164), or water
$^1/_2$ teaspoon salt
Chopped fresh coriander (optional)
Mushroom or dark soy sauce to serve (optional)

1. Put the noodles in a large bowl and pour over enough luke warm water to cover, then set aside to soak for 20 minutes, or boil according to packet instructions. Drain well, shaking off any excess water.

2. Meanwhile, remove the core from the Chinese cabbage and finely shred the leaves. Peel and finely chop the onion. Peel and finely chop the garlic. Peel and finely chop the ginger. Top and tail the sugar-snap peas or mangetout. De-seed and finely chop the pepper.

3. Heat a wok over a high heat until a splash of water 'dances' when it hits the surface. Add the oil and swirl it around.

4. Add the onion and stir-fry for 2–3 minutes. Add the garlic and ginger and continue stir-frying for a minute longer.

5. Stir in the curry paste, turmeric and sugar. Add the sugar-snap peas or mangetout, pepper, shelled peas and cabbage, and stir-fry for about 2 minutes, constantly tossing and stirring.

6. Stir in the vegetable stock and salt. Add the noodles and use 2 forks to mix all the ingredients together, and continue stir-frying until the noodles are hot and the liquid evaporates.

7. Put the noodles in bowls and sprinkle with coriander, if you have any. Taste and add soy sauce, if you like.

Stir-fried Udon Noodles

MAKES **2 SERVINGS**
PREP TIME: **ABOUT 15 MINUTES, PLUS MARINATING**
COOKING TIME: **ABOUT 5 MINUTES**

TRY THIS FOR AN ULTRA-QUICK MEAL. IN THE SUPERMARKET UDON NOODLES WILL BE
SOLD AS 'STRAIGHT TO WOK', OR YOU CAN BUY THEM IN A CHINESE-FOOD SHOP.

40 g mangetout
$^1/_2$ red onion
1 red, green, yellow or orange pepper
$^1/_2$ fresh red chilli
Several sprigs fresh coriander or parsley
2 teaspoons Chinese rice wine
1 $^1/_2$ tablespoons sunflower oil
1 teaspoon mushroom or dark soy sauce
1 teaspoon sesame oil
300 g fresh udon noodles
30 g fresh beansprouts
Toasted sesame seeds (page 35)
Pink pickled ginger (optional)

1. Cut the mangetout into long, thin strips. Peel and finely chop the
onion. De-seed and thinly slice the pepper. Finely chop the coriander
or parsley.

2. Combine the rice wine, soy sauce and sesame oil in a bowl. Add
the vegetables and beansprouts and use your hands to stir together.

3. Heat the wok over a high heat until a splash of water 'dances' on
the surface. Add the sunflower oil and swirl it around.

4. Tip the noodles, vegetables and any liquid into the wok and stir-fry,
constantly tossing and stirring the ingredients, for about 3 minutes,
or until the vegetables are just tender.

5. Add the chopped coriander or parsley and a few sesame seeds,
and mix in. Transfer to plates and add pickled ginger, if you have any.

Thai Vegetable Laksa

MAKES **4 SERVINGS**
PREP TIME: **ABOUT 40 MINUTES, INCLUDING SOAKING
THE NOODLES** / COOKING TIME: **25–30 MINUTES**

THIS IS THE VEGETARIAN VERSION OF THAILAND'S FAVOURITE STREET FOOD.

DON'T LET THE APPEARANCE OF THE LONG LIST OF INGREDIENTS AND PREPARATION
AND COOKING TIMES PUT YOU OFF THIS RECIPE. THE LAKSA PASTE AND STOCK SIMMER
AND NOODLES SOAK UNATTENDED SO YOU CAN GET ON WITH OTHER THINGS.

MAKE EXTRA OF THE CHILLI-FAVOURED COCONUT BASE TO KEEP IN THE FRIDGE
AND YOU'LL HAVE ANOTHER MEAL READY IN LESS TIME THAN IT WILL TAKE TO WALK TO
THE LOCAL THAI RESTAURANT. AND IF YOU HAVE SOME OF THE COCONUT BROTH ON
HAND, REHEAT A MUGFUL AND SIP SLOWLY TO HELP YOU RECOVER FROM A HANGOVER.

1 teaspoon sunflower or canola oil
500 ml vegetable stock, home-made (page 164) or from a cube
60 g coconut cream, dissolved in 500 ml boiling water
100 g dried medium rice sticks
6 fresh coriander sprigs
1 lime
1 fresh red chilli
2 red peppers
100 g fresh shiitake mushrooms
100 g broccoli florets
50 g fresh beansprouts
Salt and pepper
Chopped fresh coriander leaves to garnish (optional)

FOR THE LAKSA PASTE
3 large garlic cloves, or to taste
1 fresh red chilli
1 lemongrass stalk
4-cm piece of fresh root ginger
$1/2$ teaspoon turmeric
$1/4$ teaspoon salt

1. Begin by making the laksa paste. Peel and chop the garlic cloves.
De-seed and thinly slice the chilli. Remove and discard the outer leaves
from the lemongrass stalk, then finely chop the central part. Peel and
chop the ginger.

2. Put the garlic cloves in a mortar and use a pestle to pound and grind
them to a paste. Add the chilli and continue grinding to incorporate,
then add the lemongrass, ginger and turmeric the same way.

3. Put the oil in a large saucepan or deep frying pan over a medium heat. Add the paste and stir-fry for 1–2 minutes until you can just smell the aromas. Stir in the stock and dissolved coconut and bring to the boil.

4. Reduce the heat to low, cover the pan and leave the broth to simmer for 30 minutes.

5. Meanwhile, put the noodles in a large bowl, pour over enough lukewarm water to cover and leave to soak for 20 minutes, or until tender, or cook the noodles according to the packet instructions.

6. Finely grate the lime rind and squeeze the juice, then set both aside separately. De-seed and finely slice the chilli. Halve, core and thinly slice the red peppers. Wipe the mushrooms with a damp cloth, trim the base of the stalks and thinly slice the caps and stalks. Cut the broccoli into small florets.

7. Add the chilli, red peppers, mushrooms and broccoli to the broth, increase the heat slightly and simmer, uncovered, for 4–6 minutes until all the vegetables are tender.

8. Add the lime rind and $^1/_2$ a tablespoon of lime juice to the soup with salt and pepper to taste. Taste and add extra lime juice or pepper, if necessary.

9. Drain the noodles and shake off the excess water. Divide the noodles between 4 bowls and spoon the broth and vegetables over. Sprinkle with chopped coriander, if you have any.

Plan Ahead
If you want to serve this at a dinner party, the recipe can be prepared through Step 4 up to 3 days in advance. After the broth has simmered for 30 minutes, transfer it to a bowl and leave to cool completely, cover with clingfilm and chill. Just remember to reheat the broth before adding the vegetables in Step 7.

THE WORLD OF PASTA

The choice of pasta sold in supermarkets, ethnic grocery shops and whole-food shops appears endless. It is said Italy alone is home to more than 200 shapes. Here's a guide to some of the selection you might find:

ASIAN PASTA

Cellophane noodles: Thin, flat noodles made from ground mung beans which develop a slippery texture and glossy appearance when cooked; also called bean thread noodles or transparent noodles.

Egg noodles: Round noodles made with eggs and wheat; available in a variety of thicknesses. The coiled dried noodles in supermarkets are most likely egg noodles. Very quick and easy to cook.

Green tea noodles: Expensive Japanese noodles made with both buckwheat and wheat flours; look like Italian spinach pasta when boiled.

Hokkien noodles: Thick round Chinese noodles with a bright golden colour, made without eggs; sold fresh or dried.

Rice noodles: As the name implies, made from ground rice with wheat and water. Medium and wide flat noodles that should be soaked before boiling; often labelled as 'rice sticks'.

Soba noodles: Thin Japanese noodles made from buckwheat with a rectangular shape, like Italian tagliarini.

Udon noodles: Japanese rice noodles; usually sold fresh in vacuum packs labelled 'straight to wok'.

Vermicelli noodles: Thin, round rice noodles that look like Italian spaghetti.

GREEK PASTA

Orzo: Small shapes of pasta that look like grains of rice.

INDIAN PASTA

Vermicelli: Very thin spaghetti-like noodles; used in sweet desserts.

ITALIAN PASTA

Bucatini: Hollow spaghetti; comes in several thicknesses.
Canelloni: Large hollow tubes for stuffing.
Capelli d'angelo: Translates as 'angel hair'. Extra-thin noodles.
Cappelletti: Stuffed small hat shapes.
Conchiglie: Shell shape; comes in many sizes.
Farfalle: Look like bows or butterflies.
Fettuccine: Long, flat noodles that come in several thicknesses; often sold in bundles or 'nests'.
Fusilli: Long or short coils or spirals.
Lasagne: Wide flat noodles that are layered and baked with vegetable and/or cheese sauces; look for the variety labelled 'par-boiled' or 'ready-to-cook' to save time.
Linguine: Very thin, flat noodles; about the thickness of spaghetti.
Lumache: Snail-like shape; comes in many sizes.
Maccheroni: Short hollow tubes called 'elbow macaroni' are most common, but can be longer.
Manicotte: Large hollow tubes like cannelloni.
Paglia e Fieno: Spinach (green) and egg (plain coloured) noodles sold in 'nests'.
Pastine: Tiny shapes for using in soups and casseroles.
Penne: Quill-like shapes; short tubes with angled ends; ridged penne are called penne rigate.
Ravioli: Square or round stuffed pasta.
Rigatoni: Short ridged tubes.
Ruote: Cartwheel shape.
Spaghetti: Long thin 'strings' of pasta; spaghettini is very thin.
Tagliatelle: Long, flat noodles like fetuccine; very thin ones are called taglierini.
Vermicelli: Very thin spaghetti-like noodles

GR8 GRAINS, RICE & PULSES

You'll hear people joking about vegetarians just eating brown rice and lentils. But the joke is actually on them. Grains, rice and pulses are delicious. They feature in dishes around the world. Can you imagine an Indian or Chinese meal without rice? And think of the creamy risottos from the Italians, or the spicy dahls without which an Indian meal wouldn't be complete.

Cans of beans and bags of grains and rice should join pasta in your cupboard. These are all cheap and easy to cook – and good for you, too. Like pasta, these are complex carbohydrates that give you energy and fill you up for very little money.

'Pulses' is a term used to describe dried beans, peas and lentils. They are an excellent source of protein for vegetarians.

One reason you might not be familiar with some of the pulses and grains in this chapter is because they used to take for ever to prepare and were almost abandoned in the age of fast cooking. For generations, you had to soak dried beans overnight before hours of simmering to make them edible. But today you can buy inexpensive cans of beans that are ready to use. Dried lentils, however, are handy, because unlike the other dried pulses they don't require soaking. You can use them straight from the bag. Instant versions of Italian polenta and North African couscous also speed up cooking times.

For meals that pack a nutritional punch, use brown rice instead of white. If you aren't familiar with its slightly nutty flavour and chewy texture you are in for a great surprise. Give it a try.

Other grain, rice and pulse recipes:
- Chilli sin Carne (page 160)
- Italian Beans & Tomatoes (page 159)
- Lentil Loaf (page 189)
- Rice 'Soup' (page 33)
- Smashed Cannellini Bean & Garlic Spread (page 179)

RICE IS NICE

Rice should be one of the staple grains of your diet. It's a cheap, low-fat source of carbohydrate that's a real all-rounder: you can use it in sweet and savoury recipes, and it fits in with most meals, from breakfast through to midnight feasts.

And, of course, rice is the perfect accompaniment to spicy food. There is a big mark-up on rice at your local Indian and Chinese take-aways, so if you want to save money get cooking. You know it makes sense.

There are literally thousands of varieties of rice, but they are all classified as long, medium or short grain. The long-grain varieties contain less starch so the grains remain separate. These are used most often in savoury recipes. Medium-grain rice becomes 'gluey' with grains that stick together when cooked, and it is used for Italian risottos and Spanish paellas. Short-grain rice becomes very sticky, which is why the Chinese favour it to eat with chopsticks.

Brown rice is the entire grain with only the inedible outer husk removed, so it has a more chewy texture and nutty flavour. It also contains more nutrients and tends to be used mostly in savoury recipes. Although white rice has less fibre than brown rice, it still contains many nutrients and is low in fat.

3–4–1 Rice

MAKES **2–3 SERVINGS**
PREP TIME: **2–3 MINUTES**
COOKING TIME: **ABOUT 40 MINUTES**

'3-4-1' IS ALL YOU HAVE TO REMEMBER TO COOK TENDER LONG-GRAIN BROWN RICE FOR THE REST OF YOUR LIFE, EVEN IF YOU DON'T HAVE A KITCHEN SCALE OR MEASURING JUG HANDY: USE 3 CUPS OF WATER FOR EACH 1 CUP OF RICE. IT DOESN'T MATTER IF YOU USE A TEACUP, A MUG OR A MEASURING JUG, USE TRIPLE THE AMOUNT OF WATER. IF YOU BUY RICE AT THE SUPERMARKET, FOLLOW THE COOKING INSTRUCTIONS ON THE PACKET, OTHERWISE USE THIS SIMPLE TECHNIQUE.

ALWAYS COOK MORE RICE THAN YOU THINK YOU WILL NEED TO USE IN EGG-FRIED RICE & VEG (PAGE 135).

1 mugful long-grain brown rice
1 teaspoon salt

1. Bring a kettle of water to the boil. Tip the rice into a sieve and rinse it under cold water to reduce the starch.

2. Put the rice and salt in a saucepan with a tight-fitting lid and pour over 3 mugfuls of boiling water. Return the water to the boil, stir, cover the pan and reduce the heat to its lowest setting.

3. Leave the rice to simmer, without lifting the lid, for 35–40 minutes until the grains are tender and all the liquid has been absorbed. The surface of the rice will be covered with small holes.

4. Remove the pan from the heat and leave covered for 5 minutes. Use a fork to fluff rice and serve.

Cook's Tips
▸ If the water is not absorbed and the rice isn't tender at the end of the cooking time, re-cover the pan and continue cooking for about 2 minutes longer.
▸ If all the water is not absorbed, but the rice grains are tender, uncover the pan, increase the heat slightly and simmer to evaporate the water. However, if the water is absorbed before the grains are tender, add a few tablespoons boiling water and continue cooking.

Cooking White Long-grain Rice
White rice absorbs less water than brown, so cook it as above, but use the formula 2-4-1 and decrease the cooking time to 15–18 minutes.

Beautiful Basmati
Basmati rice, grown in the Himalayas and valued for its fragrance and flavour, is available in both brown and white. Some supermarket basmati rice comes ready to cook, but basmati bought in bulk will need rinsing and soaking before cooking. Rinse the rice, as above, until the water runs clear. Tip the rice into a bowl, add enough cold water to cover and leave to stand for 30 minutes. Drain and continue with the recipe as above, cooking for 15 minutes for white, or 35 minutes for brown.

'Head' Veg & Rice Pilaf

MAKES **2 SERVINGS**
PREP TIME: **ABOUT 10 MINUTES**
COOKING TIME: **ABOUT 20 MINUTES, PLUS 5 MINUTES STANDING**

THIS IS A BASIC RECIPE THAT CAN BE ADAPTED FOR WHATEVER YOU FIND IN THE KITCHEN. IT GETS ITS TITLE BECAUSE YOU USE YOUR HEAD TO DECIDE WHAT INGREDIENTS TO INCLUDE.

ALMOST ANYTHING GOES, BUT DO USE COMMON SENSE – DON'T SELECT COURGETTES TURNING TO MUSH, GREEN SPROUTING POTATOES, ULTRA-SOFT PARSNIPS OR ANYTHING SMELLING LIKE THE INSIDE OF YOUR TRAINERS. THOSE BELONG IN THE BIN!

About 200 g mixed veg – use whatever you have in the fridge, but crisp, firm ones are best: carrots, celery, mangetout, onions, peppers, spring onions, peas and/or drained canned and rinsed sweetcorn kernels and chickpeas
1 garlic clove
1 1/2 tablespoons sunflower or canola oil
200 g American long-grain rice
400 ml vegetable stock, home-made (page 164) or from a cube, or water
1 1/2 teaspoons salt
Pepper

1. Peel and chop the vegetables as required into small pieces. Peel and crush the garlic clove.

2. Heat the oil in a flameproof casserole or large saucepan with a tight-fitting lid over a medium-high heat. Add the garlic and stir it around for 1 minute. Add the firmest vegetables, such as carrots, celery and onions, and continue stirring for 2 minutes.

3. Add the remaining vegetables and stir for about 1 minute.

4. Add the rice and stir it for 1–2 minutes until the grains are coated with oil and become translucent. Stir in the stock or water, salt and pepper to taste, and bring to the boil.

5. Stir once, reduce the heat to low, cover the pan and leave to cook, without uncovering, for 18 minutes until the liquid is absorbed and the surface of the rice is covered with small indentations.

6. Remove the pot from the heat, re-cover and leave to stand for 5 minutes. Fluff the rice with a fork and adjust the seasoning, if necessary.

Golden Lentils & Rice

MAKES **2 SERVINGS**
PREP TIME: **ABOUT 10 MINUTES, PLUS SOAKING THE RICE**
COOKING TIME: **ABOUT 20 MINUTES**

FOR A PROTEIN-RICH MEAL, SERVE WITH RAITA (PAGE 178) AND A NAAN OR CHAPATTI FROM THE SUPERMARKET.

125 g basmati rice
1 onion
2 tablespoons sunflower, canola or groundnut oil
$^1/_2$ teaspoon curry powder – mild, medium or hot, as you like
$^1/_4$ teaspoon turmeric
$^1/_2$ teaspoon salt
Pinch of ground asafoetida (optional)
125 g split red lentils
450 ml vegetable stock, home-made (page 164) or from a cube, or water
Chopped fresh coriander leaves (optional)

1. Put the rice in a sieve and rinse under cold water until the water runs clear. Tip the rice into a bowl, cover with fresh cold water and leave to soak for 30 minutes. Drain the rice well, shaking off any excess water.

2. Meanwhile, thinly slice the onion.

3. Heat the oil in a flameproof casserole or saucepan with a tight-fitting lid over a medium-high heat. Add onion and stir for 3–5 minutes until soft.

4. Stir in the curry powder, turmeric, salt and asafoetida. Add the rice and lentils and continue stirring until the rice looks translucent.

5. Add the vegetable stock and bring to the boil. Stir once, reduce the heat to low, cover the pan and leave to cook, without lifting the lid, for 15 minutes until the rice and lentils are tender and the surface is covered with small indentations.

6. Re-cover the pan and leave to stand for 5 minutes. Use a fork to fluff the rice and lentils, and stir in the coriander, if using.

VARIATION
Add finely chopped smoked tofu to the top of the rice when you check it for doneness in Step 5. It will heat through while the rice stands in Step 6.

Egg-fried Rice & Veg

MAKES **2 SERVINGS**
PREP TIME: **ABOUT 10 MINUTES**
COOKING TIME: **ABOUT 8 MINUTES**

THIS IS A GREAT WAY TO USE UP LEFTOVER COOKED RICE AND VEG.

1 onion
1 garlic clove
About 100 g cooked vegetables
1 large free-range egg
1 teaspoon dark or mushroom soy sauce
$^1/_4$ teaspoon sesame oil
200 g cold, leftover cooked rice
1 $^1/_2$ tablespoons sunflower or rapeseed oil
50 g fresh beansprouts (optional)
Salt and pepper

OPTIONAL EXTRAS
Chopped fresh coriander or parsley
Sesame seeds

1. Peel and finely chop the onion. Peel and crush the garlic. Cut the vegetables into small, equal-sized pieces.

2. Break the egg into a small bowl. Add the soy sauce and sesame oil, and beat with a fork. Use the fork to separate the grains of rice.

3. Heat a wok or large frying pan, ideally non-stick, over a high heat until a splash of water 'dances' on the surface. Add the oil and swirl it around. Add the onion and stir-fry for 2–3 minutes. Add the garlic and continue stir-frying for about a minute.

4. Add the vegetables and stir-fry, stirring constantly, for 2–3 minutes until they are heated through.

5. Push the vegetables to the side of the pan. Pour the egg into the other side of the pan and stir-fry for about 30 seconds until it is scrambled and set.

6. Add the rice and beansprouts, if you are using, and salt and pepper to taste, and stir-fry, tossing all the ingredients together, until the rice is hot. Sprinkle with chopped fresh herbs or sesame seeds if you have any.

VARIATION
Add any nuts in the cupboard with the beansprouts in Step 6.
Try peanuts or cashews.

Pea & Mint Risotto

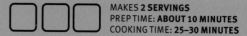

MAKES **2 SERVINGS**
PREP TIME: **ABOUT 10 MINUTES**
COOKING TIME: **25–30 MINUTES**

A FASHION FOR ALL THINGS ITALIAN HAS GIVEN THE HUMBLE RISOTTO A SOPHISTICATED IMAGE, BUT THAT IS FAR FROM REALITY. RISOTTOS, WHICH ARE CREAMY RICE DISHES, SHOWCASE BASIC VEGETARIAN COOKING. PEAS . . . MUSHROOMS . . . ASPARAGUS . . . COURGETTES . . . ARTICHOKES . . . PEPPERS . . . JUST ABOUT ANY VEGETABLE YOU THINK OF CAN BE USED TO MAKE RISOTTO. (WHEN THE CUPBOARD IS REALLY BARE, A RISOTTO BIANCO, SIMPLY FLAVOURED WITH VEGETARIAN PARMESAN-STYLE CHEESE IS ONE OF LIFE'S COMFORT FOODS.)

THE ONLY THINGS YOU HAVE TO REMEMBER WHEN MAKING RISOTTOS ARE TO USE THE CORRECT RICE – MEDIUM GRAIN – AND DON'T TAKE SHORTCUTS WITH THE SLOW COOKING AND STIRRING. DON'T START A RISOTTO IF YOU ARE PLANNING TO FLOP IN FRONT OF THE TV.

TREAT THIS AS A MASTER RECIPE FOR THE PROPORTION OF RICE TO LIQUID, BUT EXPERIMENT WITH THE OTHER VEGETABLES.

$^1/_2$ onion
1 garlic clove
Several sprigs fresh mint
750 ml vegetable stock, either home-made (page 164) or from a cube
2 tablespoons olive oil
200 g medium-grain Italian rice, such as Arborio or carnoli, or Spanish paella rice
4 tablespoons dry white wine (optional)
150 g frozen shelled peas
30 g butter
30 g vegetarian Parmesan-style cheese
Salt and pepper

1. Peel and finely chop the onion. Peel and crush the garlic. Remove the mint leaves from the stalks and slice them. Put the stock in a small pan and bring to the boil, then add the mint stalks and reduce the heat so it just simmers with small bubbles around the edge.

2. Heat the oil in a large saucepan over a medium-high heat. Add the onion and garlic and stir around for 3 minutes.

3. Add the rice to the pan and stir around so the grains are coated in oil. Add the wine, if you want, and stir until it evaporates, which will only take a minute or so.

4. Reduce the heat to low and add a ladleful of simmering stock. Use a long wooden spoon to stir the rice until all the liquid is absorbed. Continue adding ladlefuls of stock after the previous one has been absorbed, stirring constantly, for about 20 minutes or until about 150 ml of stock is left.

5. Stir in the peas straight from the freezer and add another ladleful of stock. Continue slowly adding the stock as before.

6. Add the mint leaves with the last addition of stock and continue stirring until all the liquid is absorbed. You want a creamy, still-liquid texture, which Italians describe as *all'onda*, or 'in the waves'.

7. Stir in the butter and grate the cheese into the pan, stirring until the cheese melts. Add salt and pepper to taste, but go lightly on the salt as the cheese is salty.

VARIATION
Mushroom Risotto: For a strong flavour, use dried mushrooms, such a porcini. Soak 40 g of dried mushrooms in 800 ml of boiling water for about 20 minutes, or until tender. Strain the mushrooms through a sieve lined with a piece of muslin, a clean tea towel or a piece of kitchen paper and reserve. Use the strained mushroom liquid in place of the vegetable stock. Slice and dry the mushrooms, then fry them in 1 tablespoon oil and a pinch of salt until they give off and reabsorb their liquid. Remove them from the pan and set aside. Heat another 1 1/2 tablespoons oil in the pan and continue with the recipe, as above, returning the mushrooms to the pan in Step 5. Replace the mint with finely chopped parsley and/or fresh thyme leaves.

Couscous with Moroccan Vegetables

MAKES **4 SERVINGS**
PREP TIME: **ABOUT 15 MINUTES**
COOKING TIME: **ABOUT 30 MINUTES**

COUSCOUS IS PASTA IN DISGUISE. THE WORD 'COUSCOUS' DESCRIBES BOTH NORTH AFRICA'S NATIONAL DISH AND THE TINY PIECES OF PASTA USED TO MAKE THE DISH. TRADITIONAL RECIPES SLOWLY STEAM COUSCOUS, LIKE A GRAIN, OVER THE POT OF SIMMERING STEW IT IS SERVED WITH. NOW YOU CAN BUY INSTANT COUSCOUS, SO ALL YOU HAVE TO DO IS POUR BOILING WATER OVER, LEAVE IT TO STAND AND IT WILL BE TENDER AND READY TO EAT IN MINUTES. YOU CAN EAT IT HOT WITH VEGETABLES, OR LEAVE IT TO COOL AND MAKE IT INTO A SALAD.

1 large red onion
2 large garlic cloves
1 red pepper
1 green pepper
1 carrot
1 can (400 g) butter beans or chickpeas
1 1/2 tablespoons olive oil
1 1/2 teaspoons ground coriander
1 1/2 teaspoons ground cumin
1 teaspoon turmeric
1/4 teaspoon cayenne pepper, or to taste
1 can (400 g) chopped tomatoes
200 ml water
60 g dried apricots
60 g dried figs
40 g golden raisins or raisins
4 spring onions
Several sprigs fresh coriander or parsley
150 g instant couscous
30 g butter
Salt and pepper

1. Peel and chop the onion. Peel and crush the garlic cloves. Core, de-seed and chop the peppers. Peel or scrub the carrot and cut into thick slices.

2. Place a sieve in the sink and tip the butter beans or chickpeas into it, then rinse them under cold water and set aside.

3. Heat the oil in a flameproof casserole or large saucepan with a tight-fitting lid over a medium-high heat. Add the onion and stir for 3 minutes. Add the garlic, coriander, cumin, turmeric and cayenne, and continue stirring for 1–2 minutes until the onions are soft.

4. Stir in the tomatoes with the juices, the water, the butter beans or chickpeas and the dried fruit. Bring to the boil, stirring, then reduce the heat to low, cover the pan and leave to simmer for about 20 minutes, or until the carrots are tender.

5. Meanwhile, bring a kettle of water to the boil. Put the couscous in a heatproof bowl with the butter and a large pinch of salt. Pour over enough water to cover by about 1 cm, cover the bowl with a clean tea towel and set aside until all the liquid is absorbed.

6. Trim and thinly slice the spring onions. Finely chop the coriander or parsley leaves.

7. When the carrots are tender, taste and add salt and pepper. Stir the spring onions and chop the herbs into the couscous. Serve the couscous in bowls with the fruit and vegetables spooned over.

VARIATIONS

► Add other root vegetables instead of the carrot. Try peeled, cored and chopped parsnip, peel and chopped turnip or peeled and chopped swede. Unpeeled, chopped new potatoes are good, too.
► Vary the dried fruit – try dates, prunes, dried cherries, currants and mangoes.
► If you don't have any couscous, serve this over 3-4-1 Rice (page 131).

Mounds of Polenta with Cheese

MAKES **2–3 SERVINGS**
NO PREP TIME
COOKING TIME: **5–6 MINUTES**

POLENTA IS AN ITALIAN CORNMEAL MUSH THAT CAN BE SERVED AS SOON AS IT COOKS, OR IT CAN BE CHILLED TO SLICE AND GRILL LATER. EITHER VERSION MAKES A GOOD ACCOMPANIMENT TO SERVE WITH VEGETABLES – THIS IS PARTICULARLY GOOD WITH CATALAN SPINACH (PAGE 98). TRY POLENTA FOR A CHANGE FROM PASTA OR RICE.

400 ml milk, or milk and water combined
100 g instant polenta
60 g vegetarian dolcelatte or other vegetarian blue cheese
Pinch paprika
Salt and pepper

1. Bring the milk, or milk and water, to the boil in a saucepan over a high heat.

2. Hold the polenta in one hand and a whisk or wooden spoon in your other hand. Let the polenta slowly fall through your fingers into the pan while whisking constantly until the liquid is absorbed. Italian culinary tradition insists you stir in only one direction.

3. Reduce the heat to low and continue whisking for 2–3 minutes until the polenta has the consistency of mashed potatoes and doesn't taste 'raw'. The only way you can test is to taste some, but be careful as it will be hot and can burn your tongue.

4. Cut or crumble the cheese into small pieces, then stir them into the hot polenta, until they melt. Stir in the paprika and salt and pepper to taste.

VARIATION
Grilled Polenta: At the end of Step 3 season the polenta to taste with salt and pepper; omit the cheese. Line the bottom of a loaf pan with a piece of greaseproof paper cut to fit, then grease the paper and sides of the pan. Spoon in the polenta and smooth the top. Set aside until the polenta is completely cool, then cover and chill for at least 1 hour until set. When you are ready to grill the polenta, heat the grill to high and lightly grease a baking sheet. Run a metal spatula or table knife around the side of the polenta, then tip the polenta on to a plate, giving the pan a firm shake. Cut the polenta into 1-cm slices and place the slices on the baking sheet. Brush with olive oil and sprinkle with paprika. Grate vegetarian Parmesan-style cheese over the top. Grill the polenta for 4–5 minutes until golden brown and the cheese is bubbling.

Tabbouleh

MAKES **4 SERVINGS**
PREP TIME: **20 MINUTES SOAKING**
NO COOKING

WHEN IT COMES TO QUICK-AND-EASY 'COOKING', BULGAR WHEAT IS A TREAT. BULGAR IS A CRACKED WHEAT GRAIN WITH A NUTTY FLAVOUR. ALL YOU HAVE TO DO IS ADD BOILING WATER AND LEAVE THE GRAINS TO SOAK UNTIL THEY BECOME TENDER.

USE BULGAR WHEAT IN PLACE OF RICE IN SALADS, OR AS A SIDE DISH. IT IS A GOOD LOW-FAT SOURCE OF fiBRE, AS WELL AS IRON.

175 g bulgar wheat
2 large beefsteak tomatoes
6 spring onions
$^1/_2$ bunch fresh flat-leaf parsley
$^1/_2$ bunch fresh coriander
About 2 tablespoons extra-virgin olive oil
1 lemon
Salt and pepper
Toasted pita bread to serve (optional)

1. Bring a kettle of water to the boil. Put the bulgar wheat in a large heatproof bowl, pour over enough boiling water to cover and stir. Cover the bowl with a clean tea towel and leave to soak for 20–30 minutes until the grains are tender. Test for doneness by scooping out a few grains with a spoon and biting.

2. Meanwhile, bring another kettle of water to the boil. Cut a small 'X' in the top of each tomato and put the tomatoes in a heatproof bowl. Pour over enough water to cover and leave for 2 minutes, or until the skins split. Use a large slotted spoon to remove the tomatoes from the water. Use your fingers and a small knife to peel off the skins.

3. Cut the tomatoes in half, scoop out the seeds and cores and cut the flesh into dice. Finely chop the parsley leaves and stalks together, and finely chop the coriander leaves.

4. Drain the bulgar wheat and use your hands to squeeze it dry.

5. Put the bulgar wheat in a bowl. Add the tomatoes, spring onions, coriander and parsley, and toss together. Add 2 tablespoons olive oil and salt and pepper to taste, and toss again.

6. Cut the lemon in half and squeeze half over the salad. Toss again, then taste and add extra oil, lemon juice or salt and pepper as desired. This is good eaten with pita bread.

Cider-Barley Stew

MAKES **4 SERVINGS**
PREP TIME: **ABOUT 15 MINUTES**
COOKING TIME: **ABOUT 1 HOUR**

1 carrot
1 large onion
1 sweet potato
1 parsnip
1 leek
1 large garlic clove
300 ml vegetable stock, home-made (page 164) or from a cube
300 ml dry cider
175 g pot barley
1 bay leaf
Salt and pepper
Chopped fresh parsley to garnish (optional)

1. Scrub or peel the carrot and cut it into large chunks. Peel the onion and coarsely chop. Peel the sweet potato and cut it into large chunks. Peel the parsnip, cut in half lengthwise and remove the core, then cut into large chunks. Trim the leek and cut it into thick slices and rinse under cold water to remove the dirt between layers.

2. Put the vegetables in a large flameproof casserole or large saucepan with a tight-fitting lid. Peel and slice the garlic clove and add it to the pan with the vegetable stock, pearl barley, bay leaf and salt and pepper to taste.

3. Bring to the boil over a high heat, then reduce the heat to low, cover the pan tightly and leave to simmer for about 45 minutes, or until the barley and vegetables are tender. Taste and adjust the seasoning, if necessary. Sprinkle with lots of parsley if you have any.

VARIATION
If you don't have pot barley, substitute brown rice.

Grilled Semolina Gnocchi

MAKES **2 SERVINGS**
PREP TIME: **2 MINUTES, PLUS SETTING TIME**
COOKING TIME: **UP TO 5 MINUTES**

SAVOUR SIMPLE SEMOLINA. SEMOLINA MIGHT HAVE A BAD REPUTATION FROM HORRIBLE SEMOLINA PUDDING SERVED FOR SCHOOL DINNERS, BUT IT DESERVES BETTER. MADE FROM fiNELY GROUND DURUM WHEAT, IT IS VERY QUICK AND EASY TO COOK.

250 ml milk
Freshly grated nutmeg
100 g semolina
40 g vegetarian Parmesan-style cheese, plus a little extra to finish
1 large free-range egg yolk
Olive oil
Salt and pepper
Essential Tomato Sauce (page 154) or Mediterranean Grilled Vegetables
   (page 156)

1. Lightly grease a flameproof dish, such as a quiche dish, with olive oil. Rinse a saucepan with water.

2. Add the milk and nutmeg and salt and pepper to taste to the pan over a high heat and bring to the boil. When the milk is boiling, pour in the semolina, stirring constantly.

3. Remove the pan from the heat. Grate the cheese into the pan, then beat in the egg yolk. Pour the mixture onto a greased work surface and use a wet knife to smooth in a layer about 0.5-cm thick. Set aside and leave to set, which should only take a couple of minutes.

4. Meanwhile, preheat the grill to high. Use a round biscuit cutter to cut the set semolina into circles. If you don't have a cutter, use a knife to cut squares or rectangles.

5. Put the semolina trimmings in the base of the dish. Arrange the semolina circles or squares over the surface, overlapping the pieces. Drizzle with olive oil.

6. Grill the semolina for 3 minutes. Grate a little cheese over the top, and continue grilling until the cheese bubbles. Leave the semolina gnocchi to stand for a couple of minutes before serving with tomato sauce spooned over, or with grilled vegetables.

Curried Veg & Semolina

MAKES **2 SERVINGS**
PREP TIME: **ABOUT 10 MINUTES**
COOKING TIME: **ABOUT 10 MINUTES**

THIS SOUTHERN INDIAN DISH IS A GOOD WAY TO TRANSFORM SMALL AMOUNTS OF
VEGETABLES IN THE FRIDGE INTO A MEAL. TRY THIS WITH TANDOORI PANEER (PAGE 55).

100 g vegetables – mixed or one type – such as aubergine, broccoli,
    courgettes, peppers, peas, mangetout
1 onion
1–2 fresh green chillies
1 large, juicy tomato
1 tablespoon groundnut, sunflower or canola oil
$^1/_4$ teaspoon black mustard seeds
$^1/_4$ teaspoon cumin seeds
3 or 4 dried curry leaves (optional)
$^1/_2$ tablespoon garam masala
Pinch of turmeric
120 g semolina
250 ml hot water
$^1/_2$ lime or lemon
Salt
Chopped fresh coriander leaves (optional)

1. Prepare the vegetables as necessary, cutting them into small pieces
that will cook quickly. Peel and thinly slice the onion.

2. De-seed and slice the chillies, or leave the seeds in if you like a really
spicy, hot dish. Cut the tomato in half and scrape it up and down the
large holes on a grater over a bowl to catch the pulp.

3. Heat the oil in a wok or large frying pan over a medium-high heat.
Add the mustard and cumin seeds and, as soon as they start to splutter
and 'pop', add the onion, green chillies, garam masala, turmeric, curry
leaves, and salt to taste. Reduce the heat and stir for about 2 minutes.

4. Stir in the prepared vegetables and continue stirring for 1 minute
longer. Add the tomato and continue stirring for 2–3 minutes.

5. Stir in the semolina and water, and increase the heat. Boil, stirring, for
a few minutes until the water is absorbed and the semolina is tender. If
the water is absorbed before the semolina becomes soft, add 150 ml water.

6. Remove from the heat and add extra salt, if necessary. Squeeze over
lime or lemon juice to taste and sprinkle with chopped fresh coriander.

Lentil Burgers

MAKES **4 SERVINGS**
PREP TIME: **ABOUT 10 MINUTES**
COOKING TIME: **UP TO 12 MINUTES**

THERE'S A LOT TO LIKE ABOUT LENTILS AND YOU SHOULD ALWAYS KEEP A GOOD SUPPLY
OF THEM (DRIED OR CANNED) IN YOUR CUPBOARD.

SERVE THESE ON HAMBURGER BUNS OR IN PITA BREADS WITH SLICES OF TOMATOES
AND LETTUCE. OR PUT THE BURGERS ON A PLATE AND SPOON TOMATO SAUCE AROUND.

1/4 onion
1 garlic clove
30 g shelled walnut pieces
6–8 sprigs fresh parsley
1 can (400 g) green lentils
1 teaspoon dried thyme
Pinch of dried sage
40 g fresh breadcrumbs (page 114)
115 g mature vegetarian Cheddar cheese
1 free-range egg, beaten
2 tablespoons plain wholemeal or white flour for dusting
Salt and pepper
Sunflower or canola oil for frying

1. Peel and finely chop the onion to make 2 tablespoons. Peel and finely
chop the garlic. Finely chop the walnuts. Finely chop enough parsley
leaves to make 2 tablespoons.

2. Tip the lentils into a sieve or colander over the sink and rinse with
cold water. Shake off the excess water.

3. Put the lentils, onion, garlic, walnuts, herbs and breadcrumbs into
a large bowl with salt and pepper to taste. Grate the cheese into the
bowl. Add half the egg and stir the ingredients together.

4. Put the ingredients in a blender and blitz until blended, but not so
smooth that they lose their texture. A stick blender is ideal for this, but
an upright blender will also work. Just be careful not to overblend.

5. Use your hands to shape the mixture into 4 balls, then press into
burger shapes. Put the remaining egg on a plate. Put the flour on a
separate plate and season lightly with salt and pepper. Put each burger
in the egg and then in the flour to coat on both sides.

6. Heat a thin layer of oil in a large frying pan, ideally non-stick, over
a medium-high heat. Add as many lentil burgers as will fit without
overcrowding and fry for about 5 minutes on one side until crisp. Use
a fish slice to turn the burgers over and continue frying for 5–6 minutes.

French Stewed Lentils

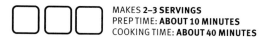

MAKES **2–3 SERVINGS**
PREP TIME: **ABOUT 10 MINUTES**
COOKING TIME: **ABOUT 40 MINUTES**

TINY GREEN LENTILS FROM PUY IN FRANCE ARE TOP OF THE POPS IN THE LENTIL WORLD, BUT THEY COME WITH A PRICE TAG, SO ANY GREEN LENTILS ARE SUITABLE FOR THIS DISH. DO NOT, HOWEVER, BE TEMPTED TO USE RED, ORANGE OR YELLOW LENTILS, BECAUSE THEY WILL JUST TURN TO MUSH.

GLAZED CARROTS (PAGE 81) ARE GOOD WITH THESE LENTILS, AS IS A SLICE OF SODA BREAD (PAGE 171).

1 onion, or 2 large shallots
1 celery stick
1 carrot
2 garlic cloves
6–8 sprigs fresh parsley
1 $^1/_2$ tablespoons olive oil
200 g green lentils
Vegetable stock, home-made (page 164) or from a cube, or water
1 bay leaf
Salt and pepper

1. Peel and finely chop the onion or shallots. Finely chop the celery. Scrub or peel the carrot and cut it into 0.5-cm dice. Finely chop the parsley leaves and stalks.

2. Heat the oil in a large frying pan with a tight-fitting lid over a medium-high heat. Add the onion or shallots, celery, carrot and garlic, and stir for 3–5 minutes until the onion is soft.

3. Stir in the lentils. Pour in enough stock or water to cover the lentils by 2.5 cm – the exact amount of liquid you will need depends on how wide your pan is.

4. Stir in the chopped parsley and bay leaf and bring the liquid to the boil. Reduce the heat to low, cover the pan and leave the lentils to simmer for about 35 minutes until they are tender. Taste and adjust the seasoning.

VARIATION
Leftover lentils make a good salad the next day. Toss the cool lentils with Vinaigrette Dressing (page 172), add extra chopped parsley, if you have any, and top with sliced free-range hard-boiled eggs. Garlic Bread(page 51) makes a good accompaniment.

Indian Lentils with Spinach

MAKES **2 SERVINGS**
PREP TIME: **ABOUT 10 MINUTES**
COOKING TIME: **ABOUT 45 MINUTES**

125 g split yellow lentils
About 600 ml water
1/2 teaspoon ground coriander
1/2 teaspoon ground cumin
Pinch of ground asafoetida (optional)
175 g fresh spinach leaves
2 spring onions
Large pinch of ground turmeric
Salt and pepper

FOR THE TEMPERING (OPTIONAL)
1 fresh green chilli
0.5-cm piece of fresh root ginger
1 1/2 tablespoons sunflower, rapeseed or groundnut oil
1/2 teaspoon mustard seeds

1. Put the lentils and 600 ml of water in a saucepan over a high heat
and bring to the boil. Reduce the heat to very low and leave the lentils
to simmer, skimming the surface as necessary, until the foam stops
forming on the surface.

2. Stir in the coriander, cumin and asafoetida, if using. Half cover the
pan and leave the lentils to continue simmering for a total of 40 minutes,
or until they are very tender and only a thin layer of water remains on
the surface. You don't have to stand and watch the whole time, but
check after about 20 minutes to make sure the pan isn't dry.

3. Meanwhile, rinse the spinach leaves in several changes of cold water
to remove any dirt, then remove thick stems. Chop the spring onions.
If you are going to add the extra spices for tempering, slice the chilli
lengthways and de-seed, then peel and finely chop the ginger.

4. When the lentils are tender and most of the liquid has evaporated,
uncover the pan and stir in the spinach and spring onions, and continue
simmering for about 5 minutes until the spinach wilts. Add salt to taste.

5. If any liquid remains, turn up the heat and stir until it evaporates.
You can eat the lentils as they are, or you can add extra spices. To do this,
heat the oil in a small pan over a high heat. Add the mustard seeds, chilli
and ginger and stir until the mustard seeds begin to pop. Pour the hot
spices and oil over the lentils.

Red Lentil Dahl

MAKES **2 SERVINGS**
PREP TIME: **ABOUT 10 MINUTES**
COOKING TIME: **20–30 MINUTES**

THE ESSENTIAL DISH FOR POST-PUB CURRIES.

125 g split red lentils
750 ml water
$^1/_2$ onion
1 green chilli
1 large garlic clove
1 $^1/_2$ tablespoons sunflower or groundnut oil
$^1/_2$ teaspoon turmeric
$^1/_2$ teaspoon garam masala
Salt
Chopped fresh coriander (optional)

FOR THE OPTIONAL TEMPERING
1 tablespoon sunflower, canola or groundnut oil
1 small clove garlic
$^1/_2$ teaspoon cumin seeds
1 dried red chilli

1. Peel and chop the onion. Peel and finely chop the garlic.

2. Put the lentils and water in a large saucepan over a high heat and bring to the boil, skimming the surface as necessary. Add the chilli and turmeric, reduce the heat to very low, cover the pan and leave the lentils to simmer for 20–30 minutes until the lentils are so tender, they have a mushy texture.

3. Meanwhile, heat the oil in a large wok or frying pan over a medium-high heat. Add the onion and fry, stirring frequently, for 3–5 minutes until soft but not brown. Add the garlic and stir for another minute or so – the onion will become golden brown; set aside.

4. When the lentils are tender, stir in the onion and garlic, garam masala and salt to taste. The dahl is now ready to eat but you can add extra flavourings, if you like.

5. Peel and thinly slice the garlic clove. For the tempering, heat the oil in a pan or wok over a high heat until it shimmers. Add the garlic, cumin seeds and chilli and fry until the garlic turns brown, but not black, and the seeds sizzle. Pour over the lentils.

Creamy Beans

MAKES **2–3 SERVINGS**
PREP TIME: **ABOUT 10 MINUTES**
COOKING TIME: **ABOUT 20 MINUTES**

THIS IS EXCELLENT SERVED WITH LONG-GRAIN BROWN RICE (PAGE 132), OR SPOONED OVER A HOT JACKET POTATO (PAGE 94). IT'S ALSO DELICIOUS ON ITS OWN WITH A CHUNK OF WHOLEMEAL BREAD.

1 can (400 g) flageolet beans
2 shallots
1 small carrot
2 sprigs fresh tarragon, or a pinch of dried tarragon
1 tablespoon olive, sunflower or canola oil
1 bay leaf
200 ml vegetable stock, home-made (page 164) or from a cube
2 tablespoons double cream
Salt and pepper

1. Rinse the beans in a sieve or colander in the sink, then shake dry and leave to drain.

2. Peel and finely chop the shallots. Peel or scrub the carrot and cut into 0.5-cm dice. Tear the leaves from the tarragon sprigs.

3. Heat the oil in a large frying pan or saucepan over a medium heat. Add the onion and stir for 3–5 minutes until soft.

4. Add the carrot to the pan and stir. Add the tarragon, bay leaf, vegetable stock and salt and pepper to taste, and bring to the boil. Reduce the heat, cover the pan and simmer for about 12 minutes until the carrots are tender.

5. Stir in the cream and return the mixture to the boil, stirring, until the sauce thickens. Taste and adjust the seasoning.

Bean Patties

MAKES **4 PATTIES**
PREP TIME: **ABOUT 10 MINUTES**
COOKING TIME: **UP TO 12 MINUTES**

TRY THESE HOT WITH A SALAD, SUCH AS GREEK SALAD (PAGE 60), ON THE SIDE.

1 can (400 g) mixed beans
$^1/_2$ carrot
2 spring onions
1 small fresh green chilli
$^1/_4$ teaspoon ground cumin
About 3 tablespoons sunflower or rapeseed oil
1 large free-range egg, beaten
About 2 tablespoons plain wholemeal flour
2 tablespoons grated vegetarian Parmesan-style cheese
Fresh fine breadcrumbs
Salt and pepper

1. Tip the beans into a sieve and rinse under cold water. Shake off the excess water, pat the beans dry and tip them into a large bowl.

2. Use a potato masher or large fork to break up and mash the beans. Peel or scrub the carrot and grate it into the beans.

3. Trim and finely chop the spring onions and add them to the beans. De-seed and slice the chilli, then add it to the beans, along with the cumin, 1 teaspoon of the oil and half the egg. Add salt and pepper to taste, then work all the ingredients together until a rough paste forms.

4. Put the remaining egg on a plate. Put the flour on a separate plate. Put the breadcrumbs on a third plate and stir in the grated Parmesan cheese.

5. Wet your hands and mould the bean mixture into 4 balls, then press into patties. Put each patty into the egg and then the flour to lightly coat on both sides; tap off the excess flour. Then press each patty into the breadcrumbs and cheese, and coat all over.

6. Heat a thin layer of oil in a large frying pan, ideally non-stick, over a medium-high heat. Fry the bean patties for 5 minutes on one side until crisp and brown. Use a fish slice to carefully turn the bean patties over and continue frying for a further 5–6 minutes. Avoid overcrowding the pan and fry in 2 batches, if necessary.

WEEKEND COOKING

When you've got a few hours to spare, making a big pot of something delicious can be relaxing. It will also be time well spent as you'll have food ready for reheating during the week. Cooking a big batch of food on the weekend is like making your own ready-meals – at a fraction of the cost. Its saves on washing-up time during the week as well.

Ideal dishes for this type of cooking include Essential Tomato Sauce (page 154), Fruit Spread (page 153) and Italian Beans & Tomatoes (page 159). Making a big bowl of Roast Vegetable Crisps (page 152) is so easy you can turn off the oven and leave them while you go to play.

Weekends, or whenever you have a free block of time, are the time to try new kitchen challenges. Practice baking a loaf of soda bread (page 171) or making a quiche (page 161).

Other recipes to stock up on when you aren't in a rush:
▸ Overnight Porridge (page 34)
▸ DIY Muesli (page 35)
▸ Spiced Winter Squash Stew (page 100)
▸ Cider-Barley Stew (page 142)
▸ All the dips on pages 174–179

Roast Vegetable Crisps

MAKES **4 SERVINGS**
PREP TIME: **ABOUT 10 MINUTES, PLUS OPTIONAL OVERNIGHT COOLING** / COOKING TIME: **ABOUT 40 MINUTES**

GRANTED, THESE DON'T HAVE THE SAME INSTANT GRATIFICATION AS OPENING A BAG OF CRISPS, BUT THEY AREN'T COOKED WITH ANY OIL, SO ARE MUCH HEALTHIER FOR YOU. THESE ARE ALSO HEALTHY FOR YOUR BANK BALANCE COMPARED TO THE PRICE OF SUPERMARKET VEGGIE CHIPS.

THIS RECIPE WOULD FIT JUST AS NATURALLY IN THE CHAPTERS ON GRAZING NOSH OR FEEDING YOUR FRIENDS. IT'S HERE, HOWEVER, BECAUSE IF YOU ARE GOING TO MAKE THESE YOU MIGHT AS WELL MAKE LOTS! THEY ARE VERY MORE-ISH AND A BIG BOWL CAN DISAPPEAR IN THE TIME IT TAKES TO WATCH A FOREIGN FLICK. IF YOU DO RESIST EATING THEM ALL AT ONCE, HOWEVER, THEY STAY FRESH IN AN AIR-TIGHT CONTAINER FOR A COUPLE OF DAYS.

USE THE WIDEST VEGETABLE PEELER YOU HAVE, AS THE NARROWER THE PEELER THE MORE LIKE FLOWER PETALS THE CRISPS LOOK. IF YOU DON'T HAVE SEVERAL BAKING SHEETS, BORROW A COUPLE. SET UP A PRODUCTION LINE AND DRY AS MANY BAKING SHEETS OF VEGETABLE STRIPS AS YOUR OVEN WILL HOLD AT ONE TIME.

2 large parsnips
2 carrots
2 raw beetroots
Salt and pepper – sea salt and coarsely ground pepper are best

1. Heat the oven to 110°C/225°F/Gas ¼.

2. Using a vegetable peeler, peel the parsnips, then cut long, very thin strips from the parsnips. Put the parsnip strips on a baking sheet in a single layer.

3. Repeat with the carrots and then the beetroots.

4. Put the baking sheets in the oven and bake for 45 minutes, turning all the vegetable strips over after 20 minutes. The vegetable strips should be dry and crisp.

5. Remove the vegetable crisps from the baking sheets and leave them to cool completely. Put them in a bowl and sprinkle with salt and pepper. Store any leftover crisps in an air-tight container.

Cook's Tip

If the vegetable strips aren't thin enough, they won't be crisp after 45 minutes in the oven. If this happens, turn off the oven and leave the crisps to dry overnight.

Fruit Spread

MAKES **4 SERVINGS**
PREP TIME: **ABOUT 5 MINUTES, PLUS BLENDING AND COOLING**
COOKING TIME: **30–40 MINUTES**

IT'S WORTH HAVING A BATCH OF THIS FLAVOURSOME FRESH APPLE AND DRIED FRUIT
PURÉE IN THE FRIDGE – SPREAD IT ON TOAST FOR A NON-FAT ALTERNATIVE TO BUTTER,
ADD A SPOONFUL TO A BOWL OF DIY MUESLI (PAGE 35) OR OVERNIGHT PORRIDGE
(PAGE 34), OR TEAM IT WITH A SLICE OF CHEESE FOR A SANDWICH.

WITHOUT PRESERVATIVES AND ADDITIVES THE FRUIT FLAVOURS REALLY
SHINE THROUGH.

2 large Bramley apples, about 500 g total
6 ready-to-eat dried pears
6 ready-to-eat dried peaches
300 ml apple juice
150 ml water
Pinch of ground mixed spice, or to taste
Lemon juice, to taste

1. Peel the apples, then cut them in half and remove the cores and chop
the flesh. Put the apple chunks, pears, peaches, apple juice and the
water in a heavy saucepan over a high heat and bring to the boil, stirring.

2. Reduce the heat to low and leave the mixture to simmer, uncovered,
for 30 minutes or so until no liquid remains on the surface. You have to
stir the mixture frequently or it will 'catch' on the bottom of the pan
and burn, so don't walk away and start watching TV.

3. Turn off the heat and leave the mixture to cool slightly. Taste and
add lemon juice to cut the sweetness.

4. Spoon the mixture into a blender and blend until a thick purée forms.
Leave the apple spread to cool completely, then put it in a jar and cover
tightly. It will keep in the fridge for up to 10 days, as long as you re-cover
the jar tightly each time you use the spread.

Essential Tomato Sauce

MAKES **2–3 SERVINGS**
PREP TIME: **ABOUT 5 MINUTES**
COOKING TIME: **20–25 MINUTES**

PASTA TOSSED WITH TOMATO SAUCE IS AS NATURAL A COMBINATION AS STUDENTS AND LATE MORNINGS. THIS BASIC SAUCE IS FOR SERVING WITH PASTA, BUT IT LIVENS SO MANY VEGGIE DISHES THAT IT IS WORTH HAVING A BOWL IN THE FRIDGE EVEN IF PASTA ISN'T ON THE MENU. JUST TRY IT WITH LENTIL BURGERS (PAGE 145), OR SPOONED OVER GRILLED POLENTA (PAGE 140), FOR EXAMPLE.

THIS SAUCE IS SO EASY THAT AFTER YOU'VE MADE IT ONCE YOU'LL COME BACK TO IT TIME AND TIME AGAIN.

SO MANY OTHER FLAVOURINGS AND INGREDIENTS CAN BE ADDED TO THIS RECIPE THAT YOU NEVER NEED TO TIRE OF IT. YOU CAN ALSO MAKE THIS SAUCE AS CHUNKY OR AS SMOOTH AS YOU LIKE.

1 onion
$^1/_2$ celery stick
1 or 2 large garlic cloves
1 tablespoon olive, sunflower or rapeseed oil
1 can (400 g) chopped tomatoes
Pinch of sugar
Vegetable stock, home-made (page 164) or from a cube, or water
  (optional)
Salt and pepper

1. Peel and finely chop the onion. Finely chop the celery. Peel and crush the garlic.

2. Heat the oil in a saucepan over a medium heat. Add the onion, celery and garlic and stir around until the garlic begins to colour: do not let it burn.

3. Tip in the tomatoes with the juices and add the sugar and salt and pepper to taste. Increase the heat and bring the sauce to the boil, stirring with a wooden spoon.

4. Reduce the heat to low, cover the pan and leave the sauce to simmer for 15 minutes. Uncover the pan occasionally to stir so the sauce doesn't 'catch' on the bottom. If it looks like it is drying out, stir in a little vegetable stock or water.

5. Uncover the pot and leave the sauce to simmer for a few minutes longer until it reaches a consistency you like. If it is too thick, it can be thinned with a little pasta cooking liquid, vegetable stock or water.

6. Taste the sauce and add extra salt or pepper, if necessary. The pasta can be used as it is, or for a smooth sauce blitz it in a blender or use the back of a wooden spoon to press it through a fine sieve. If you do purée the sauce, remember it will have to be reheated before tossing with the pasta.

7. Toss the sauce with hot, freshly boiled pasta. Sprinkle with grated cheese, if you like.

VARIATIONS
The possibilities are endless, but here are a few ideas:
► 'Some Like It Hot' Tomato Sauce: Add dried red chilli flakes or a chopped fresh red or green chilli to the sauce with the other flavourings in Step 3.
► Sprinkle the mixed sauce and pasta with freshly torn basil leaves. Tomatoes and basil are an Italian classic.
► Another Italian touch is to add about 150 ml of dry red wine to the onion, celery and garlic, leave it to bubble and let it reduce by half before adding the tomatoes with their juice.
► Add $1/2$ teaspoon dried mixed herbs with the other seasonings in Step 3. Or stir in a handful of freshly chopped herbs just before adding the sauce to pasta. Chives, oregano and parsley are good.
► For a Mediterranean flavour, stir in drained capers and pitted black olives while the sauce simmers.
► When you're really hungry, bulk this out with 200 g of drained and rinsed canned chickpeas or cannellini beans. Or add canned sweetcorn kernels.
► Add 100 ml of vegetable stock or water to tiny broccoli florets, to cook in the sauce with the tomatoes in Step 3.

Cook's Tip
Do not throw away any leftover sauce. Leave the sauce to cool completely, then put it in a bowl and pour a thin layer of olive oil over the surface. Cover the bowl with clingfilm and put in the fridge for up to 3 days. Just stir the oil into the sauce when you reheat it. Or freeze leftovers for up to a month.

Mediterranean Grilled Vegetables

MAKES **ANY NUMBER OF SERVINGS** / PREP TIME: **DEPENDS ON THE VEGETABLES YOU USE, BUT ALLOW 20–30 MINUTES** / COOKING TIME: **2–10 MINUTES, DEPENDING ON THE VEGGIES YOU CHOOSE**

ALL YOU HAVE TO DO IS SPEND ABOUT 45 MINUTES OR SO IN THE KITCHEN ONCE, AND YOU'LL BE SET UP WITH SEVERAL MEALS FOR THE NEXT COUPLE OF DAYS. CHOOSE WHATEVER VEGETABLES YOU LIKE FOR GRILLING AND THEN YOU'LL HAVE THE MAKING OF GREAT SANDWICH fiLLERS, SALADS AND QUICK SNACKS TO HAND. GRILLED VEGETABLES ARE FAST FOOD THE HEALTHY WAY.

THE SIMPLEST WAY TO EAT THESE IS STRAIGHT OFF THE GRILL SPOONED OVER GRILLED POLENTA (PAGE 140) OR ALONGSIDE SIMPLY BOILED RICE (PAGE 131) AND FRIED HALLOUMI (PAGE 54). OR TRY THE VEGETABLES AT ROOM TEMPERATURE, DRIZZLED WITH OLIVE OIL AND VINEGAR.

YOU NEED A PAIR OF TONGS TO TURN THE VEGETABLES AS THEY GRILL, AND A PASTRY BRUSH TO BRUSH THEM WITH OIL.

1–2 kg mixed vegetables, such as asparagus, chicory, courgettes, fennel bulbs, chestnut or Portobello mushrooms, red onions, thick spring onions, peppers, and radicchio – the choice is yours
Olive oil
Fresh oregano, thyme or marjoram (optional)
Salt and pepper

1. Heat the grill to its highest setting. Prepare each vegetable as necessary: hold asparagus spears at each end and bend until they snap, then cut off and discard the woody bottoms; cut chicory heads in half from top to bottom; cut the courgettes into long strips about 0.5 cm thick; slice each fennel bulb into several wedges, keeping them attached at the bases; leave mushroom caps whole, but remove the stalks; slice the red onions into 0.5-cm rings; trim the green parts off the spring onions, but leave the white parts attached at the root ends; cut each pepper half into 3 or 4 wedges and remove the cores and seeds; and cut each head of radicchio into wedges, leaving them attached at the bases.

2. Put the vegetables in a bowl, drizzle with olive oil and very gently use your hands to lightly coat all the pieces with oil. Put several tablespoons of olive oil in a small bowl to brush on the vegetables while they are grilling.

3. Lightly brush the grill rack with oil. Arrange vegetable pieces in a single layer on the grill rack and sprinkle with herbs if you have any. If your grill rack doesn't hold all the pieces in a single layer, grill them in batches.

4. Position the grill pan about 10 cm from the heat and grill the vegetables – you've got to stand and watch them as they cook. As each one starts to look charred, use a pair of tongs to turn it over and brush with more oil.

5. Continue grilling until all the pieces are tender when you pierce them with a knife. Transfer the vegetable pieces to a plate as they are tender.

6. Leave leftovers to cool completely, then put them in a bowl with olive oil to cover and chill for up to 3 days.

VARIATION
Char-grilled Mediterranean Vegetables: Follow the method above, but use a ridged cast-iron pan. (It is also easier to work with a smaller quantity of vegetables.) Heat a ridged cast-iron pan over the heat until a splash of water 'dances' when it hits the surface, then brush with olive oil.
▸ Be careful to use a pastry brush with natural bristles – if you use an inexpensive one with plastic bristles they will melt.
▸ Use a small amount of oil, because if it builds up between the ridges the vegetables will fry, rather than grill.

Caponata

MAKES **6–8 SERVINGS**
PREP TIME: **ABOUT 30 MINUTES**
COOKING TIME: **ABOUT 20 MINUTES**

KEEP A BOWL OF THIS IN THE FRIDGE AND YOU CAN EAT IT HOT OR COLD THROUGHOUT THE WEEK – IT TASTES GOOD AS IT IS FOR A VEGGIE SNACK, OR IT CAN BE REHEATED AND TOSSED WITH HOT PASTA, SPOONED OVER HOT COUSCOUS OR ADDED TO JACKET POTATOES.

2 aubergines, about 300 g each
1 red onion
125 g pitted green olives
2 tablespoons drained and rinsed capers
About 150 ml olive oil
2 teaspoons tomato purée
2 ¹/₂ tablespoons balsamic vinegar
1 tablespoon soft light-brown sugar
Salt and pepper

1. Remove the ends from the aubergines and chop into bite-sized pieces. Place the aubergine in a colander in the sink, sprinkle the aubergine pieces with salt and leave them for 20–30 minutes.

2. Meanwhile, finely chop the red onion. Slice the olives. Chop the capers.

3. Heat 2 tablespoons of the oil in a large frying pan with a lid, ideally non-stick, over a medium heat. Add the onion and fry, stirring occasionally, for 3–5 minutes until very soft. Add the tomato purée and stir for a minute or so.

4. Stir in the vinegar and sugar, stirring until the sugar dissolves. Add the tomatoes and their juices, the olives, capers and salt and pepper to taste, stirring. Slowly bring to the boil, then reduce the heat, cover the pan and simmer for 15 minutes.

5. Meanwhile, rinse the aubergines and pat them dry. Heat about 4 tablespoons of oil in another large frying pan or a wok over a medium-high heat. Add as many aubergine pieces as will fit and fry them until they are brown on each side. Use a fish slice to transfer them to kitchen paper to drain, letting the excess oil drip back into the pan. Use more kitchen paper to pat off the excess oil from the tops.

6. Continue until all the aubergine slices are fried, then simmer for 5 minutes longer.

7. Remove the pan from the heat and adjust the seasoning. If not eating at once, leave to cool completely, then place in a covered container in the fridge for up to 4 days.

Cook's Tip
If you are not reheating this, it tastes better at room temperature than straight from the fridge. It might need more seasoning, as flavours mellow when chilled.

Italian Beans & Tomatoes

MAKES **4 OR 5 SERVINGS**
PREP TIME: **ABOUT 12 MINUTES, PLUS OVERNIGHT SOAKING**
COOKING TIME: **UP TO 2 $^1/_4$ HOURS**

THE ITALIAN VERSION OF BAKED BEANS.
    THIS IS A BEAN DISH WORTH MAKING FROM SCRATCH WITH DRIED BEANS, AS THE COOKING LIQUID IS INCORPORATED INTO THE DELICIOUS TOMATO SAUCE. SERVE THIS HOT WITH FRESHLY COOKED POLENTA (PAGE 140) OR SPOONED OVER SEMOLINA GNOCCHI (PAGE 143). ANY LEFTOVERS ARE GOOD COLD MIXED WITH LEFTOVER RICE AND CHOPPED VEGETABLES. AND, OF COURSE, YOU CAN EAT THE HOT BEANS SPOONED OVER TOAST.

1 onion
1 carrot
1 celery stick
2 large garlic cloves
1 can (400 g) chopped tomatoes
1 teaspoon dried sage
3 tablespoons olive oil
250 g dried cannellini beans, soaked overnight and drained
$^1/_2$ tablespoon tomato purée
Pinch sugar
Salt and pepper

1. Heat the oven to 180°C/350°F/Gas 4. Peel and finely chop the onion. Scrub or peel and cut the carrot into very small dice. Cut the celery into very small dice. Peel and crush the garlic cloves.

2. Tip the tomatoes and dried sage into a blender and blitz until puréed. Alternatively, place a sieve over a bowl and work the tomatoes through the sieve, then add the sage.

3. Heat the oil in a large flameproof casserole or saucepan with a tight-fitting lid and ovenproof handle over a medium-high heat. Add the onion, carrot, celery and garlic, reduce the heat and stir for 3–5 minutes until the onion is tender. Stir in the beans, tomatoes and their juice, the tomato purée and the sugar. Add just enough water to cover the surface by 2.5 cm.

4. Bring the liquid to the boil. Cover the casserole and put it in the oven for 1–2 hours. Remove the casserole from the oven and begin testing the beans after 1 hour, because fresher beans cook quicker than older ones.

5. If the beans are not tender, re-cover the casserole and return it to the oven, then test again after 30 minutes. When they are tender, leave the lid off the casserole and return it to the oven for a further 15–20 minutes until the liquid has evaporated. Remove the casserole from the oven and give the beans a good stir.

Chilli sin Carne

MAKES **4–6 SERVINGS**
PREP TIME: **ABOUT 10 MINUTES**
COOKING TIME: **ABOUT 25 MINUTES**

2 onions
2 garlic cloves
1 can (400g) red kidney beans
1 can (400g) sweetcorn kernels
3 tablespoons sunflower or canola oil
1 tablespoon ground coriander
$^1/_2$ tablespoon ground cumin
1 teaspoon cayenne pepper, or to taste
1 teaspoon dried thyme
2 cans (400 g) chopped tomatoes
$^1/_2$ tablespoon tomato purée
$^1/_4$ teaspoon sugar
Salt and pepper

TO SERVE (OPTIONAL)
Garlic Bread (page 51)
Greek-style yoghurt

1. Peel and chop the onion. Peel and crush the garlic cloves. Tip the cans of beans and sweetcorn kernels into a sieve or colander over the sink and rinse. Shake off the excess water; set aside.

2. Heat the oil in a large frying pan or saucepan with a tight-fitting lid over a medium-high heat. Add the onions and fry, stirring occasionally, for 3 minutes. Add the garlic and continue stirring for 2–3 minutes until the onions are soft.

3. Reduce the heat a little, stir in the coriander, cumin, cayenne and thyme and stir for 2 minutes.

4. Stir in the tomatoes and their juice, tomato purée and sugar. Increase the heat to high and bring to the boil, stirring. Reduce the heat to its lowest setting, cover the pan and leave the tomato mixture to simmer for 15 minutes.

5. Tip the beans and sweetcorn kernels into the tomato sauce and increase the heat to high. Return to a light boil to heat through. Serve in a bowl with hot garlic bread, if you like. If you're not eating with a vegan, add a dollop of Greek-style yoghurt.

Make a Quiche

MAKES **6 SERVINGS** / PREP TIME: **ABOUT 15 MINUTES FOR THE PASTRY, PLUS CHILLING; 20 MINUTES FOR THE FILLING** COOKING TIME: **ABOUT 40 MINUTES**

REAL MEN DO EAT QUICHE! AND SO DOES EVERYONE – AS YOU WILL SOON DISCOVER IF YOU LEAVE A QUICHE IN THE FRIDGE FOR A DAY OR SO. CHANCES ARE YOUR FLATMATES WILL SLOWLY fiNISH IT OFF, SLICE BY SLICE. THIS IS GOOD HOT OR COLD AND AT ANY TIME OF THE DAY.

THE MAIN REASON FOR GOING TO THE EFFORT OF BAKING A QUICHE, RATHER THAN BUYING ONE, IS TO CONTROL THE QUALITY OF THE INGREDIENTS, ESPECIALLY IN THE PASTRY. YOU'LL fiND MOST SHOP-BOUGHT QUICHES CONTAIN LARD.

THIS IS A LONG-LOOKING RECIPE, BUT DON'T BE PUT OFF. IT'S BEEN DELIBERATELY WRITTEN WITH MANY SIMPLE STEPS SO YOU CAN LEARN HOW TO MAKE PASTRY. LIKE MANY fiRST EXPERIENCES, PASTRY-MAKING IS SOMETHING YOU DON'T WANT TO RUSH. READ THE RECIPE THROUGH CAREFULLY BEFORE STARTING.

SERVE QUICHE WITH A TOSSED GREEN SALAD ON THE SIDE.

FOR THE PASTRY

3 tablespoons water
75 g plain wholemeal flour
75 g plain white flour
Pinch of salt
50 g chilled butter
25 g soft vegetable fat

MAKING THE PASTRY

1. To make the pastry, begin by putting the water in a small bowl with an ice cube and set aside. Sift the flour and salt into a bowl.

2. Cut the butter into small dice and the vegetable fat into a couple of pieces. Add the butter and vegetable fat to the flour and use your fingertips to gently rub the fats into the flour: rub your fingers back and forth over a small amount of fat and flour until all the flour is incorporated and the mixture looks like fine breadcrumbs. Lifting your hands above the bowl and letting the flour fall back into the bowl will incorporate air, which makes the pastry lighter.

3. When all the fats are incorporated, sprinkle 2 tablespoons of the iced water over the flour. Use a fork to gently toss and mix the flour and water together.

4. Use your hands to press the dough into a soft ball. If the dough feels dry and crumbly, sprinkle over the remaining water. Wrap the dough in clingfilm and chill for at least 30 minutes, or up to 2 days.

ROLLING OUT THE PASTRY

5. After the pastry has chilled for at least 30 minutes, remove it from the fridge and leave it to stand for 10–15 minutes to come to room temperature.

6. In the meantime, heat the oven to 220°C/425°F/Gas 7 and cut out a 30-cm circle of greaseproof paper. Lightly flour the rolling pin and the work surface.

7. Place the pastry on the work surface and roll it into a circle about 25 cm across: roll the dough in one direction, then give it a quarter turn and roll it again in the same direction. Continue rolling and turning until a circle forms. Add a little extra flour to the surface or rolling pin if the pastry sticks, but don't be tempted to add too much, or the pastry will become tough.

8. Drape the pastry over the rolling pin, then ease it into a 20-cm ceramic quiche dish or loose-based tart tin with a removable base. Ease the pastry across the base and up the side, leaving a short overhang. If the pastry breaks, use your fingers to press any tears together.

BLIND BAKING

9. Place the dish or tin on a baking sheet. Trim the excess pastry hanging over the edge until there's just a 1-cm overhang. Prick the pastry on the base with a fork. Put the paper in the dish or tin and weight it down with dried beans or rice.

10. Bake the pastry case for 10 minutes, then remove it from the oven and carefully lift out the paper and beans or rice. Return the pastry to the oven for 5 minutes longer. When you take the pastry case out of the oven, reduce the temperature to 190°C/375°F/Gas 5.

11. Meanwhile, while the pastry case is baking, prepare the filling (see right).

BAKING

12. Spoon the filling into the pastry case. Place the quiche in the oven and bake for 25–30 minutes until the filling is golden brown and set.

13. Remove the quiche from the oven and roll the rolling pin over the top to cut off the overhanging pastry. Leave the quiche to stand on a wire rack for about 10 minutes before cutting.

FILLINGS

▸ Leek & Goat Cheese: Thinly slice and rinse 3 large leeks. Heat 1 $\frac{1}{2}$ tablespoons sunflower or rapeseed oil in a large frying pan, ideally non-stick, over a medium heat. Add 1 chopped garlic clove and stir for 2 minutes. Add the leeks and stir them around for a minute longer. Reduce the heat to low, cover the pan and leave the leeks to cook for 8 minutes.

Meanwhile, beat 3 large free-range eggs with 150 ml of milk and season with nutmeg, salt and pepper to taste.

Spoon the leeks over the pastry case and spread out. Pour the egg mixture over, then add 100 g diced vegetarian goat's cheese. Bake as in Steps 12 and 13.

▸ Courgette & Cheese: Slice 1 onion and 600 g courgettes. Heat 2 tablespoons of olive oil in a large frying pan, ideally non-stick, over a medium heat. Add the onions and stir for 3–5 minutes until soft. Add the courgettes to the pan and fry until golden on both sides. Remove the courgettes from the pan and drain well on crumpled kitchen paper. Beat 3 large free-range eggs with 150 ml milk and season with salt and pepper to taste. Coarsely grate 90 g vegetarian mature Cheddar or red Leicester cheese.

Arrange the courgettes on the base of the pastry case and sprinkle over half the cheese. Pour over the egg mixture and top with the remaining cheese. Bake as in Steps 12 and 13.

BIG BOWLS OF SOUP

Soup can be a meal in a mug or a snack on the run, and is very simple to make. In fact, making soup is a good first step for anyone new to cooking – a little too much of one ingredient or not quite enough of another is not going to ruin the result. Whatever you end up with will be comforting and nourishing. And who knows? You might 'invent' a new classic!

Once you've made a big pot of soup, you won't go hungry for a couple of days. The flavour of many soups actually improves over a day or two, and they are easy to reheat. Just don't leave them sitting in the fridge for more than three days or you'll have a feast of mould.

And if you want a big dose of self-satisfaction, make a loaf of Soda Bread (page 171) to eat with the soup. Your friends will think you're a veteran cook.

Vegetable Stock

MAKES **ABOUT 1.2 LITRES**
PREP TIME: **ABOUT 10 MINUTES**
COOKING TIME: **UP TO AN HOUR**

'STOCK' IS A FLAVOURED LIQUID THAT HELPS YOUR SOUPS, RISOTTOS AND VEGETABLE STEWS TASTE SO TEMPTING. THE QUICK OPTION IS JUST TO DISSOLVE A STOCK CUBE IN BOILING WATER, BUT CUBES ARE LOADED WITH SALT AND PRESERVATIVES. INSTEAD, MAKE UP A BATCH OF THIS AND SEE IF YOU CAN TASTE THE DIFFERENCE.

USING STOCK IN YOUR COOKING IS WHAT MAKES YOUR FOOD TASTE MORE LIKE JAMIE OLIVER'S THAN POT NOODLES! AND IF YOU'RE REALLY HUNG OVER, SIPPING A MUGFUL OF HOT STOCK WILL HELP YOU FEEL BETTER – IT'S PACKED WITH VITAMINS AND MINERALS.

3 large carrots
3 large onions
3 large celery sticks – include the leaves too, if you want
2 large leeks
1.8 litres water
10 black peppercorns
Bunch fresh parsley sprigs
1 large garlic clove – or a whole head
2 bay leaves
1/2 teaspoon salt

1. Scrub the carrot and cut it into large chunks. Cut each onion in half. Chop the celery sticks, including the leaves. Cut the leeks into thick slices. Put the leeks in a sieve and rinse under cold water to remove the grit and dirt between the layers, if necessary.

2. Put the chopped vegetables in a large saucepan with the water over a high heat. Bring to the boil, using a slotted spoon to remove the grey foam that comes to the surface. There isn't any getting away from this step – you just have to stand there and skim the surface.

3. Meanwhile, use a pestle and mortar or the back of a wooden spoon to slightly crack the peppercorns.

4. As soon as the water boils, turn the heat to the lowest setting. Add the peppercorns, parsley, garlic, bay leaves and the salt. Leave the stock to simmer for 45 minutes, uncovered. You don't have to stand over the stove at this point, but check occasionally to make sure the pot isn't boiling dry and to remove any foam that might develop.

5. Put a colander or large sieve over a large heatproof bowl in the sink. Strain the stock into the bowl, using the back of a wooden spoon to press down on the vegetables to extract as much flavour as possible.

6. The stock is now ready to use, or it can be left to cool completely and refrigerated or frozen until required. When it is cool, cover the bowl with clingfilm and chill for up to 3 days, or pack it in freezerproof bags and freeze for up to a month.

TAKE STOCK, THEN MAKE STOCK
Almost all vegetables can be used to make stock, so when you're considering making stock take a look at what vegetables you have before you go shopping. Treat the above recipe as a guide, and adapt it to what you have available.
▸ You get out of the stockpot what you put in, so you don't want to use rotting vegetables that belong in the bin. However, stock-making is a good way to make the most of vegetables slightly past their prime.
▸ Do not use potatoes – they make the stock cloudy.
▸ Beetroots, asparagus and broccoli have pronounced flavours and colour the stock, too.
▸ If you add onion skins to the simmering stock, it will develop a golden hue.
▸ Use carrot peelings, along with mushroom and stalk trimmings.
▸ Season lightly – you only need enough salt to draw flavour out of the vegetables. If you add too much salt, everything you later use the stock in will be too salty.

STAY COOL
It is vital to leave the stock to cool completely before you put it in the fridge or freezer. Otherwise you will create the perfect breeding ground for micro-organisms that can cause food poisoning.

Minestrone

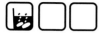

MAKES **4–6 SERVINGS**
PREP TIME: **ABOUT 15 MINUTES**
COOKING TIME: **ABOUT 15 MINUTES**

2 large tomatoes, such as beefsteak
1 large onion
1 large carrot
1 large celery stick
2 large garlic cloves
125 g Savoy cabbage
75 g thin French beans
8 sprigs fresh parsley
1 ^{1}/$_2$ tablespoons olive oil
1.25 litres vegetable stock, home-made (page 164) or from a cube
1 can (400 g) cannellini or white haricot beans
75 g shelled peas, fresh or frozen
75 g oz small pasta shapes for soup, or macaroni
Vegetarian Parmesan-style cheese
Salt and pepper

1. Skin the tomatoes (page 141), then cut the tomatoes into quarters and use a spoon to scoop out the cores and seeds. Dice the flesh; set aside.

2. Peel and finely chop the onion. Scrub or peel the carrot and finely dice. Trim and thinly slice the celery. Peel and crush the garlic cloves. Thinly slice the cabbage leaves. Top and tail the beans, then cut them into bite-sized pieces. Tie the parsley sprigs together.

3. Heat the oil in a large flameproof casserole or the largest saucepan you have over a medium-high heat. Add the onion, carrot and celery and stir for 3 minutes. Add the garlic cloves and continue stirring for a further 2 minutes. Add the stock and bring to the boil, skimming any foam from the surface.

4. Add the tomatoes, French beans, cabbage and fresh peas with salt and pepper to taste. Reduce the heat to low, partially cover the pan and simmer for 10 minutes.

5. Meanwhile, put a sieve in the sink. Tip the canned beans into the sieve and rinse them under cold water.

6. Stir the beans, cabbage and pasta into the soup. Bring to the boil, then reduce the heat and simmer for 10 minutes, or according to the packet directions, until the pasta is tender. Taste and adjust the seasoning. Ladle the soup into bowls then grate the cheese over each.

Creamy Cheese & Veg Soup

MAKES **4–5 SERVINGS**
PREP TIME: **ABOUT 10 MINUTES**
COOKING TIME: **ABOUT 25 MINUTES**

1 large waxy potato
1 carrot
1 onion
1 celery
1 red, green, orange or yellow pepper
2 tablespoons sunflower or canola oil
400 ml vegetable stock, home-made (page 164) or from a cube
4 tablespoons plain or wholemeal white flour
500 ml milk
Pinch of cayenne pepper
120 g vegetarian Cheddar cheese
Salt and pepper

1. Peel the potato and cut it into 0.5-cm dice. Peel and chop the onion. Scrub or peel and cut the carrot into 0.5-cm dice. De-seed and finely chop the pepper.

2. Heat the oil in a large saucepan over a medium heat. Add the vegetables and stir them for 5 minutes.

3. Pour in the stock and bring to the boil, stirring. Reduce the heat to low, cover the pan and simmer for 15 minutes, or until the potatoes are tender when you pierce them with a fork.

4. Meanwhile, put the flour, cayenne and salt and pepper to taste in a bowl and slowly stir in the milk, stirring until no lumps remain. Grate the cheese into the bowl and stir together.

5. Uncover the pan and increase the heat to medium, but do not let the soup boil. Stir several spoonfuls of the hot soup into the cheese mixture, then stir all the cheese mixture into the soup. Stir constantly for a few minutes until the soup thickens. Taste and adjust the seasoning.

Broccoli & Stilton Soup

MAKES **4 SERVINGS**
PREP TIME: **ABOUT 10 MINUTES**
COOKING TIME: **ABOUT 20 MINUTES**

$^1/_2$ head broccoli
1 floury potato, about 200 g
1 onion
2 garlic cloves
2 tablespoons sunflower or canola oil
900 ml vegetable stock, home-made (page 164) or from a cube
Salt and pepper
About 75 g vegetarian Stilton cheese

1. Cut the broccoli into small florets and the stalks into thin slices. Scrub or peel the potato and cut it into 0.5-cm dice. Peel and chop the onion. Peel and crush the garlic cloves.

2. Heat the oil in a saucepan over a medium heat. Add the potato, onion and garlic, and stir for 5 minutes.

3. Add the broccoli to the pan, then stir in the stock and $^1/_2$ teaspoon salt. Increase the heat and bring the stock to the boil, stirring.

4. Reduce the heat to low, cover the pan and leave the soup to simmer for 20 minutes, or until the potato is very tender. At this point the broccoli will be falling apart.

5. You can crumble over the Stilton and eat the soup as it is, or you can purée the soup and then add the cheese.

6. To purée the soup, put it in a blender and give it a blitz, or work it through a fine sieve, rubbing back and forth with a wooden spoon. Reheat the soup without boiling, then crumble over the cheese. Adjust the seasoning, if necessary, but remember, Stilton can be salty.

VARIATIONS
► As an alternative to the Stilton cheese, top the soup with lightly fried smoked tofu.
► Grated vegetarian Cheddar cheese is also a good alternative to the Stilton.
► Or top the soup with croûtons instead of the cheese.

Crisp Croûtons
► Croûtons are small pieces of toast that add extra crunch to soups and salads. Traditionally they are fried in oil and/or butter, but a healthier

method is to bake them. This is an excellent way to use bread that is starting to dry up. Make as many croûtons as you like (they keep fresh in an air-tight container for about a week) and in any size you like. Brush both sides of sliced bread with olive oil, then cut it into cubes. Place the cubes in a roasting tin and roast in a preheated oven at 200°C/400°F/Gas 6 for 10–12 minutes, stirring occasionally, until they are crisp on both sides.

▸ Sprinkle the bread with garlic salt or paprika before roasting.

Carrot & Orange Soup

MAKES **4 SERVINGS**
PREP TIME: **ABOUT 10 MINUTES**
COOKING TIME: **25–30 MINUTES**

TRY THIS WITH A WEDGE OF IRISH SODA BREAD (PAGE 171) – IT'S A FANTASTIC COMBINATION.

600 g carrots
1 celery stick
1 onion
1 ¹/₂ tablespoons sunflower or rapeseed oil
1 teaspoon ground coriander
Pinch of cayenne pepper
900 ml vegetable stock, home-made (page 164) or from a cube
1 large orange

1. Scrub or peel the carrots, as you like, then thinly slice. Finely chop the celery. Chop the onion.

2. Heat the oil in a large saucepan with a lid over a medium heat. Add the onion and celery and cook for 3–5 minutes until soft, stirring.

3. Add the carrot, coriander, cayenne and a pinch of salt, and continue simmering for about 5 minutes, stirring occasionally.

4. Pour in the stock, increase the heat and bring to the boil. Reduce the heat to low, cover the pan and simmer for 25 minutes, or until the carrots are very soft.

5. Pour the soup into a blender and blitz until it is smooth. Return it to the rinsed pan and reheat. Cut the orange in half and squeeze about 3 tablespoons of juice into the soup. Taste and add more juice or extra orange juice and salt and pepper, as you like.

See over for variations.

VARIATIONS

▸ The quantities can easily be doubled or tripled to serve for a dinner party. If you make the soup ahead, leave it to cool after it has been puréed and only add orange juice when you reheat.

▸ If you want a more filling meal, half fill your bowl with hot rice before you add the soup.

Curried Parsnip Soup

MAKES **4 SERVINGS**
PREP TIME: **ABOUT 15 MINUTES**
COOKING TIME: **ABOUT 35 MINUTES**

A GREAT BRITISH CLASSIC.

500 g parsnips
1 onion
1 sweet apple, such as Golden Delicious
15 g butter
1 1/2 tablespoons sunflower or rapeseed oil
2 1/2 teaspoons curry paste – you decide the strength of heat
900 ml vegetable stock, home-made (page 164) or from a cube
About 500 ml milk
Salt and pepper

1. Peel the parsnips and cut them in half lengthwise, then cut them again into long quarters and cut out the core; chop. Chop the onion. Peel the apple, cut it into quarters and remove the cores, then chop.

2. Melt the butter with the oil in a saucepan over a medium-high heat. Add the onion and stir for 3–5 minutes until tender.

3. Stir in the curry paste and continue stirring for 1–2 minutes. Stir in the apples and parsnips, then stir in the stock and slowly bring to the boil.

4. Reduce the heat to low, season with salt and pepper to taste and cover the pan. Leave the soup to simmer for 25–30 minutes until the parsnips are very soft.

5. Pour the soup into a blender and blitz until smooth. Wash and rinse the pan, then return the soup to it. Reheat the soup and slowly stir in the milk until you have a texture you like. Adjust the seasoning, if necessary.

Soda Bread

MAKES **1 LARGE LOAF**
PREP TIME: **ABOUT 10 MINUTES**
BAKING TIME: 30–40 MINUTES

NO, DO NOT FLIP PAST THIS RECIPE. DO YOU THINK BREAD-MAKING IS TOO DIFfiCULT? THINK AGAIN! AND THERE IS NO EASIER BREAD TO BEGIN WITH THAN TRADITIONAL IRISH SODA BREAD – IT IS MADE WITHOUT YEAST AND DOESN'T REQUIRE A LONG TIME TO RISE BEFORE IT IS BAKED.

ONCE YOU'VE TASTED YOUR OWN HOME-BAKED BREAD YOU'LL BE HOOKED.

280 g plain wholemeal flour, plus extra for the baking sheet
280 g self-raising white flour
1 teaspoon bicarbonate of soda
$^1/_4$ teaspoon salt
600–750 ml buttermilk
Butter or peanut butter, to serve

1. Preheat the oven to 190°C/375°F/Gas 5. Dust a baking sheet with flour: you don't need a lot, but enough to stop the bread sticking.

2. While the oven heats, sift the wholemeal and white flours with the bicarbonate of soda and salt into a large bowl, tipping in any of the bran left in the sieve.

3. Stir in 600 ml of buttermilk, then add as much extra as necessary to make a soft dough.

4. Lightly flour the counter and tip the dough on to it. Use your hands to push the dough around until it comes together and is smooth. Pat it into a ball about 20 cm across, then place it on the baking sheet.

5. Dip a cook's knife into the bag of flour, then cut an 'X' into the dough, cutting down about $^1/_3$ of the way. Use a pastry brush or scrunched kitchen paper to very lightly brush the top of the dough with water. Sprinkle very lightly with extra flour.

6. Put the bread in the oven and bake for 30–40 minutes: the loaf is baked through when you turn it over (use a folded tea towel to protect your hand) and it sounds 'hollow' as you tap it on the base. Leave the bread to stand for 10 minutes, then serve it hot, spread with butter or peanut butter.

Cook's Tip
Don't throw away leftover buttermilk. Stir it into Overnight Porridge (page 34), or use it in place of milk when making mashed potatoes. It can also be beaten with sunflower oil and crumbled blue cheese to make a creamy salad dressing.

Vinaigrette Dressing

MAKES **ABOUT 300 ML**
PREP TIME: **ABOUT 5 MINUTES**
NO COOKING

THERE CAN'T BE MANY SALADS THAT DON'T GO HAND IN HAND WITH THIS ALL-PURPOSE
FRENCH OIL-AND-VINEGAR DRESSING. IT'S EASY TO MAKE, KEEPS FRESH FOR AGES IN
THE FRIDGE AND SAVES YOU LOTS OF MONEY. ALL IN ALL, THIS IS AN IMPORTANT ADDITION
TO ANY VEGETARIAN KITCHEN.

FOLLOW THIS RECIPE ONCE, THEN FEEL FREE TO EXPERIMENT – ADD MORE OR LESS
VINEGAR, OIL, SUGAR OR MUSTARD UNTIL YOU GET A LEVEL OF SHARPNESS YOU LIKE.
EXPERIMENT WITH DIFFERENT FLAVOURS OF OIL AND VINEGAR AS WELL. WALNUT OIL,
FOR EXAMPLE, COMPLEMENTS MANY GREEN LEAVES.

250 ml extra-virgin olive or sunflower oil
6 tablespoons red- or white-wine vinegar
1 teaspoon soft light brown sugar
2 teaspoons Dijon mustard
Salt and pepper

1. Put the oil, vinegar, sugar, mustard and salt and pepper to taste
in a screw-top jar, screw on the lid and shake vigorously until blended.
Taste and add extra of any ingredient, if you like. Store in the fridge
and shake before you use each time.

VARIATIONS

‣ Balsamic Vinaigrette: Replace 2 tablespoons of the wine vinegar
with 2 tablespoons of balsamic vinegar.
‣ Creamy Vinaigrette: Add 2 tablespoons of single or double cream,
soured cream or yoghurt to the other ingredients before you shake.
This is particularly good for salads that include fruit. Use within 3 days.
‣ Garlic Vinaigrette: Add 2 crushed garlic cloves and leave the dressing
to stand for a couple of hours before serving.
‣ Honey Vinaigrette: Replace the sugar with 1 teaspoon of honey.
Use 3 tablespoons of red-wine vinegar and 3 tablespoons of raspberry-
flavoured vinegar.
‣ Mustard Vinaigrette: Increase the mustard to 1 1/2 tablespoons. Use
English, Dijon or wholegrain, each of which gives a different flavour.

FEEDING YOUR FRIENDS

Ready-meals might be all the rage, but in reality everyone loves home cooking. Your friends will too, but that doesn't mean you have to prepare a three-course meal every time you invite someone round. This chapter has ideas for party foods, one-course suppers to eat off your lap when you settle down with a video, and recipes for proper dinner parties. The recipes come with tips for getting most of the work out of the way before anyone arrives.

And if you have seduction on your mind, cooking will have a big pull. Booze might be easier, but a little kitchen magic is so much more stylish. When you have parties, you need lots of food so everyone doesn't drink on an empty stomach. The dips in this chapter aren't expensive and can be made to feed a lot of people. Put them out with a plate of vegetable sticks for everyone to nibble. They are cheap and will save the carpet so you don't lose your deposit.

Other recipes good for feeding a table full of friends:
- Baked Macaroni & 4 Cheeses (page 113)
- Couscous with Moroccan Vegetables (page 138)
- Spiced Winter Squash Stew (page 100)
- Thai Vegetable Laksa (page 126)

DIPS

Dips can be the ultimate party food – it doesn't cost a lot of money or take a lot of effort. Double or triple the following recipes to feed a house full.

But don't save dips just for feeding your friends. These recipes are ideal when you want a quick snack. Make up one and keep it covered in the fridge for snack attacks. All of these taste great served with toasted pita bread, Pita Crisps (page 179), breadsticks or big plates of raw vegetables – try broccoli and cauliflower florets, carrot slices, chicory leaves, courgette slices, pepper strips and radishes.

Beer & Cheese Dip

MAKES **4–6 SERVINGS**
PREP TIME: **ABOUT 8 MINUTES**
NO COOKING

YES, THERE ARE OTHER THINGS YOU CAN DO WITH BEER BESIDES GUZZLING IT.

400 g vegetarian Cheddar cheese
1 small garlic clove
225 ml lager
1 teaspoon dry mustard
Pinch of paprika
1 celery stick
$^1/_2$ grilled pepper (page 93), or Spanish pepper from a jar (page 180)

1. Coarsely grate the cheese into a bowl. Crush the garlic clove and add to the bowl.

2. Add about half the lager and use a wooden spoon to beat the cheese and lager together until a thick paste forms. Slowly beat in the remaining lager until the dip has a thick texture. Stir in the mustard and paprika to taste. Alternatively, put all the ingredients in a blender and blitz.

3. Very finely chop the celery and add it to the bowl. Cut the grilled pepper into very small pieces and add it to the bowl. Stir the veggies into the dip, then cover with cling film and chill until required.

Hummus

MAKES **4 SERVINGS**
PREP TIME: **ABOUT 8 MINUTES**
NO COOKING

THE UNIVERSALLY POPULAR MIDDLE EASTERN CHICKPEA DIP. WHEN FRIENDS COME
AROUND, IT IS WORTH MAKING DOUBLE AS IT DISAPPEARS SO FAST.

1 can (400 g) chickpeas
1 or 2 garlic cloves, to taste
125 g tahini paste
About 4 tablespoons lemon juice
Salt and pepper

TO SERVE
About 2 tablespoons extra-virgin olive oil
Cayenne pepper, to taste
Chopped fresh parsley
Black olives

1. Put a sieve or colander in the sink. Tip in the chickpeas and rinse
with cold water, then shake dry. Peel and crush the garlic cloves.

2. Put the chickpeas and garlic in a blender and quickly blend until the
chickpeas are chopped. Add the tahini paste, 3 tablespoons of the
lemon juice and salt and pepper to taste, and blend until creamy, but
not completely smooth. If the mixture seems too thick add more
lemon juice or a little water to thin.

3. Spoon into a bowl. Make an indentation in the centre with the back
of a spoon and drizzle in the olive oil. Sprinkle with cayenne, parsley
and olives.

Mezzo Magic
For a Middle Eastern mezzo platter, serve the hummus with toasted
pita bread, Fried Halloumi (page 54) and Greek Salad (page 60). Buy
some falafel balls from the deli counter to complete the platter.

Tahini-Yoghurt Dip

MAKES **4–6 SERVINGS**
PREP TIME: **ABOUT 5 MINUTES**
NO COOKING

THIS ALSO TASTES GREAT SPOONED OVER STEAMED BROCCOLI OR CAULIFLOWER FLORETS.

2 large garlic cloves
1 lemon
200 g natural yoghurt
75 g tahini sauce
1 tablespoon extra-virgin olive oil
2–3 tablespoons water
Salt and pepper
Chopped fresh parsley or coriander to garnish (optional)

1. Peel and crush the garlic cloves. Roll the lemon back and forth on the counter, pressing down firmly, then cut in half and squeeze the juice: you should have 2–3 tablespoons. Chop the parsley or coriander leaves.

2. Put the yoghurt in a bowl and beat in the tahini. Stir in the garlic cloves and 2 tablespoons of the lemon juice. Add 2 tablespoons of the water and continue stirring until the mixture is blended.

3. Season with salt and pepper, then taste the dip and add extra lemon juice, if you like. If the mixture is still too thick for dipping, slowly beat in a little more water to thin. Transfer to a bowl and sprinkle with the chopped herbs, if you have any. Leftovers will keep in a covered container in the fridge for up to 5 days.

VARIATION
Sprout Salad: Toss a selection of fresh sprouts, such as beansprouts or alfalfa sprouts, with chickpeas and grated radishes with enough of this dip to coat. Sprinkle with sunflower seeds and serve with chunky wholemeal rolls.

Other Quick Yoghurt Dips
▸ Pesto-Yoghurt Dip: Mix together equal quantities of Greek strained yoghurt and pesto sauce, home-made (page 171) or shop-bought. This is particularly good with courgette slices and red pepper strips.
▸ Mango-Yoghurt Dip: Spoon mango chutney into a bowl and stir in natural yoghurt. Serve this alongside curries, instead of raita (page 178), or for dipping vegetable samosas into.

Babaganoush

MAKES 2–3 SERVINGS
PREP TIME: **ABOUT 5 MINUTES, PLUS OPTIONAL CHILLING**
COOKING TIME: **30–35 MINUTES**

THE QUINTESSENTIAL MIDDLE EASTERN AUBERGINE DIP.

1 aubergine, about 500 g
1 garlic clove, large or small depending on your taste (see note below)
2 tablespoons lemon juice
2 tablespoons tahini sauce
About 1 ¹/₂ tablespoons extra-virgin olive oil, plus extra to serve
Salt and pepper

1. Preheat the oven to 230°C/450°F/Gas 8 or its highest setting. Use a fork to prick the aubergine all over. Put the aubergine directly on a grill rack and roast for 30–35 minutes, or until it is very soft and collapses.

2. Meanwhile, peel and coarsely chop the garlic. Remove the aubergine from the oven and set aside until it is cool enough to handle. Cut the aubergine in half and scoop the flesh into a blender and blend until it is smooth – it will only take a few seconds.

3. Add the garlic, lemon juice, tahini sauce and salt and pepper to taste, and blend together. Add the oil and blend again. Taste and adjust the seasoning.

4. The dip can be served straightaway, but it is best if you chill it for a couple of hours. Take it out of the fridge about 15 minutes in advance and drizzle with extra olive oil. If you have any leftovers, cover them with a thin layer of olive oil and chill for up to 3 days.

Great Roasted Garlic

If you're someone who can't get enough garlic, feel free to add more than one clove to this recipe, but roast it first so the raw garlic taste doesn't overpower the other flavours: roasting garlic mellows the flavour and takes away the harshness. Separate the cloves and rub off the papery outer skin, but leave the tight inner pink skin. Place the cloves on a piece of aluminium foil, drizzle with a small amount of olive oil, about 1 teaspoon for a whole head, and then squeeze the foil into a bundle. Roast the garlic at 200°C/400°F/Gas 6 for 25 minutes, or until it is very soft when poked with the tip of a knife. Store any leftover roasted garlic in an air-tight jar in the fridge – it's good spread on a slice of toast.

Raita

MAKES **4–6 SERVINGS**
PREP TIME: **ABOUT 10 MINUTES**
NO COOKING

CUCUMBERS AND YOGHURT ARE A WINNING COMBINATION – YOU'LL COME ACROSS IT TIME AND TIME AGAIN IN DIFFERENT CUISINES. THE GREEKS SERVE A VERSION, CALLED TZATZIKI (SEE BELOW), AS AN APPETISER WITH PITA BREAD OR SESAME-COATED BREADSTICKS; TURKS MAKE AN IDENTICAL VERSION CALLED CACIK.

INDIANS MAKE THIS RAITA TO COUNTER THE HEAT OF SPICY CURRIES, BUT IT IS ALSO A GOOD DIP TO SERVE WITH RAW VEGGIES.

1 cucumber, about 500 g
4–6 fresh coriander sprigs
300 g Greek-style yoghurt
1 teaspoon salt
1 teaspoon ground cumin
$^1/_4$ teaspoon ground pepper
Pinch of cayenne

1. Grate the cucumber by rubbing it up and down over the coarse holes on the grater directly on to a clean tea towel. Gather the towel up around the cucumber and squeeze to remove all the excess moisture. Tip the yoghurt into a bowl.

2. Finely chop the coriander leaves. Add the leaves to the bowl with the cucumber, then stir in the yoghurt.

3. Add the salt, cumin and pepper and stir together. Sprinkle with cayenne. Spoon the dip into a bowl and drizzle a little oil over the top, if you like.

VARIATIONS

▸ Potato Raita: Boil, drain and chop 225 g of new potatoes, then leave to cool and chill for 30 minutes. Fry $^1/_2$ teaspoon cumin seeds and $^1/_2$ teaspoon crushed coriander seeds in 1 tablespoon of sunflower or groundnut oil until the seeds jump. Add the cool potatoes with a pinch of cayenne pepper and $^1/_2$ teaspoon salt, and stir for 1 minute or so. Remove the pan from the heat and stir in about 200 g of Greek-style yoghurt. Cover and chill for 1 hour. If you have any fresh coriander sprinkle the surface with chopped leaves. Serve this as a dip or eat it with a wholemeal or plain pita for a light meal.
▸ Greek Mint Dip: Beat 300 g of Greek-style Yoghurt with 1 $^1/_2$ tablespoons olive oil, 1 crushed garlic clove, a large pinch of dried mint and salt and pepper. Stir in grated or diced cucumber. Add a crushed garlic clove, if you like. Put in a bowl and drizzle extra-virgin olive oil over the top and add a few black olives.

Smashed Cannellini Bean & Garlic Spread

MAKES **3–4 SERVINGS**
PREP TIME: **ABOUT 10 MINUTES**
NO COOKING

YOU DON'T NEED ANY COOKING SKILL OR SPECIAL EQUIPMENT TO MAKE THIS. JUST USE A FORK TO SMASH ALL THE INGREDIENTS TOGETHER. SO EVEN IF YOU'VE NEVER MADE ANYTHING TO EAT BEFORE, HAVE A GO WITH THIS. TRY THIS AS A DIP WITH CRISP VEGETABLES, OR SPREAD IT ON PITA CRISPS (BELOW).

1 can (400 g) cannellini beans
$^1/_2$ red onion
1 garlic clove, or to taste
Olive oil
1 lemon
$^1/_4$ teaspoon ground cumin
Pinch of paprika or cayenne pepper
Salt and pepper
Chopped fresh coriander or parsley

1. Put a sieve or colander in the sink, tip in the beans and rinse with cold water. Shake the beans to remove the excess liquid; set aside. Peel and finely chop the onion. Peel and finely chop the garlic.

2. Put the beans in a bowl and use a fork or potato masher to smash and break them up. Add 2 tablespoons of olive oil and beat together.

3. Add the onion and garlic to the bowl. Grate the lemon rind into the beans. Add the cumin, paprika or cayenne and salt and pepper to taste to the bowl, then stir until the ingredients are blended. Taste the spread and add lemon juice or extra salt and pepper.

VARIATION

▸ Use canned flageolet, butter or kidney beans instead.
▸ Try this with roasted garlic (page 177).

Pita Crisps

▸ Try these with the smashed bean spread or any of the dips on pages 174–179. Heat the oven to 180°C/350°F/Gas 4. Slice the pita breads in half through the pocket, then cut each half into 4 wedges. Lightly brush the rough side of the wedges with olive oil, then place on a baking sheet and toast for 15–18 minutes until golden brown and crisp. Leave to cool to room temperature, then store in an air-tight container.
▸ Sprinkle with garlic salt, paprika, garam masala or sea salt before toasting.

Spanish Pimientos

MAKES **8**
PREP TIME: **ABOUT 15 MINUTES, PLUS CHILLING**
NO COOKING

YOU'LL fiND JARS OF PIMIENTOS, LABELLED AS *PIMIENTOS DEL PIQUILLO*, IN THE SUPERMARKET. THESE ARE SHORT SWEET RED PEPPERS THAT HAVE BEEN CHAR-GRILLED AND SKINNED, AND ARE WELL WORTH STOCKING AS A CUPBOARD STAPLE. THEY ARE IDEAL FOR STUFfiNG, AS HERE, AND CAN BE SLICED OR CHOPPED FOR ADDING TO SALADS WHEN YOU DON'T HAVE TIME TO CHAR-GRILL PEPPERS.

GIVE YOUR FRIENDS A TASTE OF A BARCELONA TAPAS BAR AND SERVE THESE WITH TOMATO BREAD (PAGE 52).

1 garlic clove
1 lemon
4 sprigs fresh parsley
2 sprigs fresh mint
225 g vegetarian curd cheese
Pinch of dried oregano
8 bottled whole *pimientos del piquillo*
Pinch of paprika (optional)
Salt and pepper

1. Peel and crush the garlic clove. Finely grate the rind from the lemon. Very finely chop the parsley and mint leaves.

2. Put the curd cheese in a bowl and beat with a wooden spoon. Add the garlic, lemon rind, parsley, mint, oregano, paprika, if you are using, and salt and pepper to taste, and beat together.

3. Lift the pimientos from the jar, letting the extra oil drip back into the jar, then pat dry with kitchen paper. Use your fingers to open a pimiento, which will be hollow in the centre. Hold the pimiento in one hand and use a small spoon in the other hand to stuff the pimiento with 1/8 of the curd-cheese mixture.

4. Continue until all the pimientos are stuffed and the filling is used. Place the pimientos on a plate, cover and chill for at least 2 hours for the stuffing to firm.

VARIATIONS
▸ Other ingredients to use include sliced, pitted black or green olives, chopped spring onions, very finely shredded baby spinach leaves or rocket, or chopped toasted pine nuts.
▸ Use half curd cheese and half vegetarian Stilton cheese with 4 tablespoons of fresh snipped chives and 1 tablespoon of chopped fresh mint leaves.

Stuffed Peppers

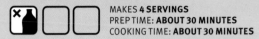

MAKES **4 SERVINGS**
PREP TIME: **ABOUT 30 MINUTES**
COOKING TIME: **ABOUT 30 MINUTES**

4 red, green, yellow or orange peppers
1 ½ quantities Essential Tomato Sauce (page 154), puréed in a blender,
   to serve (optional)

NUTTY RICE STUFFING
1 large onion
2 garlic cloves
Small bunch fresh parsley
40 g pine nuts
1 ½ tablespoons olive oil, plus extra for the peppers
200 g risotto or other medium-grain rice
¾ tablespoon tomato purée
400 ml vegetable stock, home-made (page 164) or from a cube,
   or water, boiling
75 g raisins or currants
Salt and pepper

1. To make the stuffing, peel and very finely chop the onion. Peel and crush the garlic cloves. Finely chop the parsley stalks and leaves until you have about 4 tablespoons.

2. Heat a large frying pan, ideally non-stick, with a tight-fitting lid, over a high heat. Add the pine nuts to the dry pan and stir them around for 20–30 seconds until golden brown. Immediately tip them out of the pan.

3. Heat the oil in the pan over a medium-high heat. Add the onion and stir for about 3 minutes. Add the garlic and continue stirring for a further 1–2 minutes.

4. Add the rice to the pan and stir until the grains are lightly coated in oil. Stir in the tomato purée and water with ¼ teaspoon salt and pepper to taste. Bring to the boil, then reduce to the lowest setting, stir once, cover and leave to simmer for 18 minutes until all the liquid is absorbed and the surface is covered with small indentations.

5. Re-cover the pan and leave the rice to stand for 5 minutes. Stir the raisins, currants and pine nuts into the rice. Taste and add salt and pepper to taste.

6. Meanwhile, heat the oven to 200°C/400°F/Gas 6. Slice off the tops of the peppers and set aside, then use a small knife to cut out the cores and seeds. Rub the outside of each pepper with olive oil.

7. Bring a kettle of water to the boil. Divide the stuffing between the peppers and press on the tops. Place the peppers in a roasting pan or ovenproof dish that will just hold them upright.

8. Pour about 2 ¹/₂ cm of water into the pan or dish and bake for 30 minutes, or until the peppers are tender.

9. If you are serving the peppers hot, they are good on a pool of puréed tomato sauce. Otherwise, leave the peppers to cool and serve with a salad.

Plan Ahead
Stuffed peppers are a good choice for a dinner party as they can be served hot, cold or just warm. You can make the rice stuffing through to Step 5 a day in advance.

Imam Bayildi

MAKES **4 SERVINGS** / PREP TIME: **ABOUT 10 MINUTES, PLUS SALTING THE AUBERGINES** / COOKING TIME: **20 MINUTES AND 30–40 MINUTES**

THIS TAKES TIME TO PREPARE, BUT IT IS VERSATILE ENOUGH TO fiT THE BILL WHEN FRIENDS POP ROUND TO WATCH A VIDEO OR DVD, OR IF YOU'RE PLANNING A SLAP-UP DP. SERVE IT WITH RICE (PAGE 131) OR CHUNKY BREAD AND A TOSSED GREEN SALAD AND EVERYONE WILL BE HAPPY.

2 large aubergines, about 400 g each
2 large onions
2 large garlic cloves
1 lemon
¹/₂ bunch fresh parsley, plus extra to garnish
4 tablespoons olive oil
2 tins (400 g) chopped tomatoes
3 tablespoons raisins or sultanas
1 teaspoon ground cinnamon
¹/₂ teaspoon ground coriander
¹/₂ teaspoon ground cumin
Pinch of sugar
Pinch of cayenne pepper, or to taste
Salt and pepper
Yoghurt, to serve (optional)

1. Cut each aubergine in half lengthways, then use the knife and a spoon to scoop out the flesh from all halves, leaving a 0.5-cm rim all round.

2. Meanwhile, finely chop the aubergine flesh, place it in a colander or sieve, sprinkle with salt and leave for 30 minutes. At the same time, sprinkle the inside of the hollowed aubergine halves with salt and leave upside down on a double thickness of kitchen paper for 30 minutes. Rinse the flesh shells with cold water and pat dry. Brush the edges with a little oil to prevent them drying out in the oven.

3. Meanwhile, peel and thinly slice the onions. Peel and finely chop the garlic. Finely grate the rind from the lemon and squeeze about 1 tablespoon juice.

4. Set aside some parsley leaves for a garnish, then finely chop the remaining leaves and stalks to make 4 tablespoons.

5. Heat the oil in a large saucepan or frying pan, ideally non-stick, over a medium heat. Add the onion and stir for 3–5 minutes until soft. Add the garlic and stir around for a minute or so longer: do not burn the garlic.

6. Add the aubergine flesh along with the tomatoes in their juice, parsley, raisins or sultanas, lemon rind and juice, the cinnamon, coriander, cumin, cayenne, sugar and salt and pepper to taste. Bring to the boil, stirring.

7. Reduce the heat and simmer, uncovered, for 20 minutes, or until the mixture is reduced and thickened. (If it starts to dry out, stir in a little vegetable stock or water and cover the pan.)

8. Meanwhile, preheat the oven to 190°C/375°F/Gas 5. Place the aubergine halves in a roasting tin or ovenproof dish that will hold them upright. Equally divide the filling between the aubergine halves, mounding it slightly in the centre.

9. Put the aubergines in the oven and bake for 25–30 minutes, or until the shells are very tender when you pierce them with the tip of a knife. Anyone who isn't a vegan can add a dollop of yoghurt.

Plan Ahead
This might not be quick cooking, but it doesn't have to be laborious. You can prepare the filling and stuff the aubergine halves through to Step 8 several hours in advance, ready for last-minute cooking.

Vegetable Bake

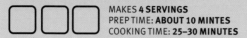

MAKES **4 SERVINGS**
PREP TIME: **ABOUT 10 MINTES**
COOKING TIME: **25–30 MINUTES**

WHEN IT'S YOUR TURN TO COOK FOR FLATMATES, THIS IS A GOOD DO-AHEAD DISH.
ALL YOU NEED TO SERVE WITH IT IS GARLIC BREAD (PAGE 51) AND A LARGE GREEN SALAD.

400 g chestnut, button or Portobello mushrooms, or a mixture
2 leeks
3 carrots
2 garlic cloves
3 tablespoons sunflower or canola oil
3 tablespoons plain wholemeal or white flour
1 teaspoon dried thyme
300 ml vegetable stock, home-made (page 164) or from a cube
Pinch of cayenne pepper, or to taste
Salt and pepper

FOR THE TOPPING:
2 large free-range eggs
300 ml Greek-style yoghurt
55 g vegetarian feta cheese, drained

1. Preheat the oven to 220°C/425°F/Gas 7.

2. Wipe the mushrooms with a damp cloth and trim the base of the stalks, then coarsely chop the caps and stalks. Cut the leeks in half lengthwise, then crosswise into thin slices. Rinse the leeks well and pat dry. Scrub or peel the carrots and cut into 0.5- cm slices. Peel and crush the garlic.

3. Heat the oil in a large saucepan or frying pan, ideally non-stick, over a medium heat. Add the leeks and stir for about 2 minutes. Add the mushrooms, courgettes and garlic and stir for about 5 minutes until the mushrooms give off their liquid.

4. Add the flour and stir for 2 minutes to remove the raw taste. Add the dried thyme and then stir in the vegetable stock, stirring until a thin sauce forms. Season with cayenne pepper, if you like, and salt and pepper to taste. Tip the vegetables into the prepared dish and spread out evenly.

5. To make the topping, put the eggs in a bowl and beat them together. Beat in the yoghurt and season to taste. Spoon the topping over the vegetables. Put the dish in the oven and bake for 40–45 minutes until the topping is golden brown.

Cook's Tip

Be very judicious with the amount of salt you add in Step 5 as the feta cheese in the topping will be salty.

Plan Ahead

The dish can be prepared through to Step 4, then left to cool and kept in the fridge for up to a day, covered with clingfilm. Take it out of the fridge while you heat the oven so it comes back to room temperature.

Vegan Note

If one of your flatmates or friends is a vegan, replace the cheese and cheese topping with crisp filo pastry. You will need about 115 g filo pastry, thawed, if necessary. Brush one sheet with sunflower or rapeseed oil and lay it over the vegetables, tucking in the edges. Brush the remaining sheets with oil and lay them over the top, scrunching them together to make a crisp 'ruffled' topping. Cover the dish with foil and bake for 10 minutes, then uncover and bake for a further 10–15 minutes until the top is golden brown and crisp (see Fab Filo Pastry, page 188).

Indian Spiced Pilaf

MAKES **4 SERVINGS**
PREP TIME: **ABOUT 10 MINUTES, PLUS SOAKING THE RICE**
COOKING TIME: **ABOUT 20 MINUTES**

SAVE THIS FOR A CELEBRATION MEAL – IT'S A FEAST OF FRUITY, NUTTY RICE FOR FRIENDS. THE LIST OF INGREDIENTS IS LONG, BUT THE COOKING IS EASY. PILAFS, FLAVOURED RICE DISHES COOKED IN A COVERED DISH AFTER THE RICE IS fiRST BRIEFLY COOKED IN OIL OR BUTTER, MAKE EXCELLENT ONE-POT MEALS. THIS IS A BASIC RECIPE AND, ONCE YOU'VE MADE IT A FEW TIMES, YOU'LL SOON SEE HOW EASY IT IS TO VARY THE INGREDIENTS AND FLAVOURINGS.

FOR A DINNER PARTY, SERVE WITH RAITA (PAGE 178) AND NAAN BREAD.

225 g basmati rice
1 onion
4 ready-to-eat dried apricots
4 ready-to-eat dried mangoes
2 tablespoons sunflower, rapeseed or groundnut oil
90 g blanched almonds
3 green cardamom pods, cracked
1 cinnamon stick
1 teaspoon cumin seeds
1 teaspoon black onion seeds
2 bay leaves, broken in half

450 ml water
1 teaspoon salt
$1/2$ teaspoon turmeric
40 g sultanas or raisins
Chopped fresh coriander (optional)

1. Put the rice in a sieve and rinse with cold running water until the water runs clear. Put it in a bowl, pour over enough water to cover and leave to soak for 30 minutes. Drain well, shaking off the excess water.

2. Meanwhile, peel and thinly slice the onion. Chop the apricots and mangoes into small pieces.

3. Heat the oil in a large flameproof casserole or saucepan with a tight-fitting lid over a medium heat. Add the almonds and stir them around until they become golden; immediately lift them out of the pan.

4. Add the onion and stir for 3–5 minutes until soft. Add the cardamom, cinnamon, cumin and black onion seeds and bay leaves, and stir for about 30 seconds.

5. Add the rice to the pan and stir until the grains turn translucent.

6. Stir in the water, salt and turmeric. Bring the liquid to the boil. Stir in the dried fruit, reduce the heat to low, cover the pan and leave to simmer for 15 minutes, or until all the liquid is absorbed and the surface is covered with small indentations.

7. Remove the pan from the heat, re-cover and leave to stand for 5 minutes. Use 2 forks to fluff the rice. Stir in the almonds and sprinkle with chopped coriander.

Spanokopitta

MAKES **6 SERVINGS**
PREP TIME: **ABOUT 25 MINUTES**
COOKING TIME: **ABOUT 40 MINUTES**

THIS GREEK FAVOURITE WITH ITS SPINACH AND CHEESE fiLLING AND CRISP fiLO PASTRY IS IDEAL FOR A DINNER PARTY – YOU CAN FEED A FULL TABLE OF FRIENDS WITHOUT BREAKING THE BANK, AND ALL THE WORK CAN BE DONE UP TO A DAY IN ADVANCE, READY FOR LAST-MINUTE COOKING WITHOUT A SINK OF WASHING-UP TO DO. AND – PERHAPS BEST OF ALL – THIS TASTES JUST AS GOOD AT ROOM TEMPERATURE AS IT DOES HOT, SO YOU CAN BE A COOL HOST OR HOSTESS.

IF SERVING HOT, THIS DOESN'T NEED AN ACCOMPANIMENT, BUT GREEK SALAD (PAGE 60) IS GOOD WITH A COLD PIE.

2 onions
1 kg fresh spinach
Fresh flat-leaf parsley
Several sprigs fresh dill
3 free-range eggs, beaten together in a small bowl
Freshly grated nutmeg
2 tablespoons sunflower or canola oil
200 g vegetarian feta cheese
About 100 g butter, cut into chunks
225 g filo pastry, thawed if frozen (see Fab Filo Pastry, page 188)
Pepper

1. Peel and chop the onions. Rinse the spinach in several changes of cold water to remove any dirt, then chop. Chop enough fresh parsley leaves to make 4 tablespoons, and enough fresh dill to make 2 tablespoons.

2. To make the filling, heat the oil in a large frying pan or saucepan over a medium heat. Add the onion and stir for 3–5 minutes until very tender.

3. Add the spinach with just the water clinging to its leaves to the pan and stir for 2–3 minutes until it wilts down. If your pan is small, only add one-third or half the spinach at a time, pushing it down with a wooden spoon – it will all eventually fit into the pan.

4. Remove the pan from the heat and tip the spinach into a sieve to drain. Press hard with the back of a wooden spoon.

5. Meanwhile, preheat the oven to 190°C/375°F/Gas 5. When the spinach is cool, use your hands to squeeze out all the excess liquid: this is an important step, or the filo pastry on the bottom of the pie will be soggy.

6. Put the spinach in a bowl. Stir in the parsley, dill and eggs, and beat together. Add several gratings of nutmeg and pepper to taste. Drain the feta cheese well, then crumble it into the spinach mixture.

7. Melt the butter in a small saucepan over a medium heat. Lightly grease the base and side of a 23 x 23-cm ovenproof dish or roasting pan with the butter.

8. Cut the filo to fit the size of your dish, if necessary. Place one sheet in the bottom of the dish and brush with butter. Repeat with half the pastry, brushing each sheet with butter before adding another.

9. Add the spinach-and-feta filling to the dish and smooth it out and into the corners with the back of a wooden spoon. Cover the top with the remaining filo pastry, brushing each sheet with melted butter and tucking in the edges. Brush the top layer with butter.

10. Use a sharp knife to score the top into 6 equal portions. Bake for 35–40 minutes until the top is golden brown. If serving hot, leave to stand for 2–3 minutes before cutting along the scored lines.

VARIATION

Spanakopitta Triangles: The same amount of filling makes about 60 individual triangle pastry shapes. These are ideal for parties. Make the filling above. Cut the filo pastry into long strips 5 cm wide. Work with one strip at a time and keep the others covered. Brush the filo strip with melted butter and put about 1 teaspoon of the spinach filling at one end. Fold one corner of the strip diagonally over the filling, so the short end from the base now lies along the bottom of a long side. This should make a triangle shape. Continue folding the pastry at right angles until you reach the top of the strip. Brush with butter and fold down the flap to seal. Continue until all the filo pastry is used. Place the filled pastries on a baking sheet and brush with more melted butter. Bake for 20–25 minutes until golden brown.

Cook's Tip

The spinach mixture has to be cool before you add the eggs in Step 3, or the eggs will scramble. If you are in a hurry, transfer the spinach to a bowl (otherwise leave it in the pan so you don't have extra washing-up).

Plan Ahead

If you want to make this in advance, complete the recipe through to Step 8, then cover and chill until 15 minutes before serving. Return the pie to room temperature while the oven heats.

Fab Filo Pastry

Filo pastry, sometime labelled as 'phyllo pastry' or 'strudel pastry', is ultra-thin pastry dough you will usually find frozen in supermarkets and Middle Eastern food shops. It is sold in sheets that become delicate and crisp when baked. Filo is dead easy to work with, but you need to observe a few rules:
► Thaw filo pastry overnight in the fridge, and do not unwrap it until just before you are ready to use it. It will stay frozen for up to a year.
► Keep any sheets of filo you aren't working with covered with a sheet of greaseproof paper under a damp tea towel to keep the pastry from drying out. Once the pastry dries it becomes brittle and unworkable.
► Do not unfold the pastry on to a damp work surface or let a damp cloth touch it – wet filo becomes soggy and unworkable.
► Different brands of filo are often different sizes. Use scissors or a knife to cut it to your required size.

Lentil Loaf

MAKES **4–6 SERVINGS** / PREP TIME: **ABOUT 45 MINUTES,
PLUS MAKING THE GARLIC MUSHROOMS (PAGE 87) AND
ESSENTIAL TOMATO SAUCE (PAGE 154)**
COOKING TIME: **ABOUT 45 MINUTES**

SO RETRO . . . SERVE THIS WITH CATALAN SPINACH (PAGE 98) AND GARLIC BREAD (PAGE 51)
OR TOMATO BREAD (PAGE 52).

1 garlic clove
1 fresh red chilli
300 g dried split red lentils
Sunflower or rapeseed oil for the tin
Several sprigs fresh parsley
100 g vegetarian Red Leicester or Cheddar cheese
1 quantity Garlic Mushrooms (page 87)
150 g fresh wholemeal or white breadcrumbs (page 114)
2 free-range eggs, beaten
Salt and pepper
1 quantity Essential Tomato Sauce (page 154), to serve

1. Bring a large saucepan of unheated water to the boil. Stir in the lentils
and return to the boil, skimming the surface as necessary. Reduce the
heat and when the scum stops rising, peel the garlic clove and stick it on
a wooden cocktail stick with the chilli, then add them to the pan. Leave
the lentils to simmer for 20–30 minutes until tender, but not falling apart.

2. Heat the oven to 180°C/350°F/Gas 4. Lightly grease the inside and
base of a 1-kg bread tin. Cut a piece of greaseproof paper to fit the base
of the tin. Put the paper in the tin and grease it. Very finely chop the
parsley leaves and sprigs. Grate the cheese.

3. Drain the lentils and remove the garlic and chilli. Shake off any excess
water from the lentils, then put them in a bowl. Stir in the chopped
parsley, cheese, breadcrumbs and salt and pepper to taste. Add enough
egg to bind the mixture together.

4. Spoon $^2/_3$ of the lentil mixture into the prepared tin and level the
surface. Use the back of a wooden spoon to make an indentation in
the lentil mixture, leaving a 1-cm border all around.

5. Spoon the Garlic Mushrooms into the indentation. Top with the
remaining lentil mixture and smooth the surface. Press on the sides
so both layers of lentils join.

6. Place the loaf in the oven and roast for 45 minutes, or until the top is
firm and crusty. Leave the loaf to stand for 5 minutes before turning out.

7. Use a pallete or table knife to loosen the loaf from the side of the tin. To turn out the loaf, place a plate large enough to hold the loaf on top, top-surface down. Using oven gloves, carefully invert the pan and plate, giving a shake halfway over. You should be able to hear a 'blop' as the lentil loaf drops on to the plate.

8. Lift off the tin and the lining paper. Cut into slices and serve with tomato sauce and steamed green vegetables.

Cook's Tips

► Be sure to grease the corners of the tin well. If you don't have a pastry brush, use a piece of crumpled kitchen paper.

► If you don't hear the loaf drop with a 'blop' in Step 7, it is stuck to the bottom of the pan. Fill the sink with enough hot water to come halfway up the side of the tin. Put the tin in the water for 10 seconds, then invert it and shake again.

Plan Ahead

This is a good do-ahead recipe for a dinner party. The Garlic Mushrooms and Essential Tomato Sauce can be prepared up to a day in advance, the lentils can be cooked earlier in the day and the whole dish can be assembled early in the day, ready for putting in the oven when your first guest walks through the door.

Make a Plate of Pancakes

MAKES **8–10 PANCAKES**
PREP TIME: **ABOUT 10 MINUTES**
COOKING TIME: **ABOUT 20 MINUTES**

DON'T JUST SAVE PANCAKES FOR SHROVE TUESDAY. IF YOU DECIDE YOU LIKE HAVING FRIENDS AROUND FOR MEALS, PANCAKES ARE FOR YOU. THEY COST VERY LITTLE TO MAKE AND CAN BE USED FOR STARTERS, MAIN COURSES AND DESSERTS. AND YOU CAN VARY THE FLAVOURINGS.

PRACTICE THESE ONCE OR TWICE AND YOU'LL GET THE KNACK OF TURNING OUT THE LIGHT, DELICATE PANCAKES THE FRENCH CALL CRÊPES. SPRINKLE YOUR TEST PANCAKES WITH SUGAR AND A SQUEEZE OF LEMON JUICE AS THEY COME OUT OF THE PAN FOR A TASTE OF PARISIAN STREET FOOD.

GOURMET COOKWARE SHOPS SELL PANS SPECIFICALLY SHAPED FOR MAKING PANCAKES, BUT A LARGE FRYING PAN IS FINE. AND A NON-STICK ONE HELPS MAKE THE LEARNING CURVE QUICKER.

125 g plain wholemeal or white flour
Pinch of salt
1 large free-range egg
About 300 ml milk
Knob of butter
Sunflower or canola oil or butter for cooking

1. Stir the flour and salt together in a large bowl. Make a well in the centre of the bowl and break the egg directly into the well. Add 150 ml of the milk.

2. Use a wooden spoon or a whisk to beat the egg and milk together, then gradually draw in the flour from the sides, beating constantly to avoid lumps forming. As all the liquid is absorbed, slowly pour in about 150 ml more milk and continue beating until a smooth, thin batter forms: it should be the consistency of single cream. Wholemeal flour might require a little extra liquid, depending on the pan. (At this point the batter can be left to stand for at least 30 minutes.)

3. Melt the knob of butter in a 25-cm frying pan, ideally non-stick, over a medium heat. Tilt the pan so the butter coats the base and sides, then tip the butter into the batter. Use a piece of crumpled kitchen paper or a pastry brush to rub a very thin layer of oil over the pan's surface.

4. Stir the batter. Tilt the pan and use a ladle to pour over 2 tablespoons of batter, then swirl the pan for the batter to form a thin 20–23-cm circle; pour any excess batter back into the bowl. Cook for about 1 minute until the batter looks dry on the surface and the base is set: use a pallete knife to lift the edge to check.

5. Use a spatula or a fish slice to lift and flip the pancake over. Continue cooking for 1 minute longer, or until the pancake is dry.

6. Slide the pancake on to a plate lined with greaseproof paper. The first pancake rarely turns out properly, so it is considered the cook's perk – go ahead and eat it.

7. Add a little more oil or butter to the pan, if necessary, then continue to make 7–9 more pancakes. As you remove the pancakes from the pan, layer each with a piece of greaseproof paper to prevent them sticking together.

VARIATONS
▸ Sweet Pancakes: Add 1 tablespoon of caster sugar to the batter and stir until it dissolves.
▸ Herb Pancakes: Add 4 tablespoons of chopped fresh herbs to the batter.

Plan Ahead

▸ If you aren't using the pancakes at once, they can be kept overnight in the fridge, with the pieces of greaseproof paper between each and wrapped in kitchen foil. Or you can put them in a freezerproof bag, seal the bag and freeze for up to 3 months. It only takes 30 minutes to thaw the pancakes at room temperature.

▸ You don't have to use all the batter at once. It will keep in a covered container in the fridge for up to 3 days. Stir well before using and add a little extra milk if it is too thick.

IDEA FOR PANCAKE STARTER OR SNACK

Mushroom & Goat's Cheese Parcels: Prepare Garlic Mushrooms (page 87). Divide the mushrooms between 8 pancakes. Top each with a slice of goat's cheese. Fold one side over the mushrooms and cheese, then fold over the other side. Fold up the bottom of the pancake, then fold down the top to make a square parcel. Flip the pancake parcel seam-side down on to a baking sheet and lightly brush with olive oil. Bake for 8–10 minutes until golden brown.

IDEAS FOR MAIN-COURSE PANCAKES

▸ Roll the pancakes around Roasted Asparagus spears (page 71) with crumbled vegetarian Wenslydale cheese and reheat as above.

▸ Roll the pancakes around Catalan Spinach (page 98). Place in a greased ovenproof dish and grate vegetarian Stilton or other vegetarian blue cheese over the top. Reheat as above.

IDEAS FOR DESSERT PANCAKES

▸ Crêpes Suzette (page 205).

▸ Chocolate Pancakes: Replace 1 tablespoon of the flour with unsweetened cocoa powder. Toss sliced bananas and toasted coconut or ground almonds (page 35) with crème fraîche and soft light brown sugar to taste. Roll the pancakes around the creamy mixture and chill until ready to serve. Dust with icing sugar just before serving.

▸ Spread a pancake with Fruit Spread (page 153), marmalade, jam or other fruit preserve, and roll up.

SWEET THINGS

For many people a meal won't be complete without a dessert, especially when you're entertaining. But that doesn't mean dessert has to always be rich, sweet and loaded with calories and fat. Think light. The easiest dessert that doesn't require any effort in the kitchen is, of course, fresh fruit. You can eat a bowl of fresh berries or pick at cherries while you get on with some reading.

But if you don't mind spending a little time and effort, fruity desserts such as Baked Spiced Pears (page 196) and Ginger Fruit Salad (page 194) hit the spot. Or take a look at the fruit and cheese combinations on page 206 for a sophisticated end to a meal.

When you're feeling broke, try either of the pasta recipes in this chapter. They will satisfy everyone's sweet tooth without you having to spend a lot of money.

Eating a healthy vegetarian diet doesn't mean you have to forego those rich, sweet concoctions that are always popular. Just save the Chocolate Slice (page 204) for occasional treats when you pass an exam or your family are visiting and you want to push the boat out.

Ice cream is another occasional treat. Premium brands are expensive, but you can save money with the recipes in this chapter – you don't need an ice-cream machine to be transported to couch-potato heaven.

Another sweet recipe to try:
► Overnight Dried Fruit Salad (page 36)

Ginger Fruit Salad

MAKES **4–6 SERVINGS**
PREP TIME: **ABOUT 20 MINUTES, PLUS MARINATING**
NO COOKING

TRY THIS WHEN YOU'VE COOKED AN INDIAN MEAL. IT'S SPICY BUT LIGHT AND REFRESHING. IF YOU'RE IN THE HABIT OF POURING LASHINGS OF DOUBLE CREAM OVER FRUIT SALADS, TRY A LITTLE GREEK-STYLE YOGHURT INSTEAD, BUT YOU MIGHT find THIS DOESN'T NEED ANYTHING EXTRA.

1 small cantaloupe melon
2 fresh apricots
1 orange
1 crisp apple, such as red delicious
250 ml ginger beer
60 g seedless white grapes
Handful of sliced almonds, toasted (page 35)

1. Cut the melon into quarters, then use a spoon to scoop out and discard the seeds. Cut each quarter into 2 long pieces, then use a small knife to cut off the peel. Cut the flesh into bite-sized pieces and put them in a large bowl.

2. Rinse the apricots, then cut them in half, cutting round the indentation. Twist the halves apart, then lift out the stone, or use the tip of a knife to prise it loose. Chop the apricots and add them to the melon.

3. Quarter, core and chop the apple. Add it to the other fruit. Pour over the ginger beer, stir, cover and chill for at least an hour, although you can leave the salad in the fridge for several hours.

4. When you're ready to serve, add the grapes to the other fruit and stir. Sprinkle the almonds over the top.

VARIATION
► Use ready-to-eat dried apricots in the winter.
► Include whatever fruits look good at the market. Bananas, kiwifruit, other melons, pears, pineapple and star fruit all go good with the ginger beer.

Caribbean Bananas

MAKES **2 SERVINGS**
PREP TIME: **2 MINUTES**
COOKING TIME: **15–20 MINUTES**

2 bananas
30 g butter, melted
1 $^1/_2$ tablespoons soft light-brown sugar
2 tablespoons orange juice
1 tablespoon lemon juice
1 tablespoon light rum

1. Heat the oven to 200°C/400°F/Gas 6. Peel the bananas and cut them in half lengthwise. Put the bananas in a small ovenproof dish.

2. Pour over the melted butter, then add remaining ingredients. Roll the bananas around so they are coated in the other ingredients.

3. Cover the dish with kitchen foil and bake for 15–20 minutes until the bananas are hot. Serve the banana halves with the juice from the dish spooned over.

VARIATIONS
► If you don't have any rum, use an extra tablespoon of orange juice.
► Sprinkle with fresh or desiccated coconut, if you like. Toasted coconut flakes from a health-food shop are good. Or use toasted and chopped hazelnuts (page 35).

Baked Spiced Pears

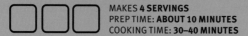

MAKES **4 SERVINGS**
PREP TIME: **ABOUT 10 MINUTES**
COOKING TIME: **30–40 MINUTES**

MAKE EXTRA, AS THESE TASTE JUST AS GOOD CHILLED AS THEY DO STRAIGHT FROM THE OVEN.

A little butter for the dish
4 black peppercorns
1 cinnamon stick
125 ml dry white vegetarian wine
4 tablespoons honey
2 star anise
2 cloves
4 dessert pears, such as Comice

1. Heat the oven to 190°C/375°F/Gas 5. Lightly grease an ovenproof dish with butter.

2. Use the back of a wooden spoon to lightly crush the peppercorns, and break the cinnamon stick in half. Put the spices in a small saucepan with the wine, honey, star anise and cloves, and stir to dissolve the honey. Slowly bring to the boil without stirring, then turn off the heat and cover the pan.

3. Cut the pears in half from top to bottom, then cut out the cores and stems. Peel the pears, then place them cut-side down in the dish. Pour over the spiced wine, including the spices.

4. Cover the dish with foil, shiny-side down, and bake for 30–40 minutes until the pears are tender when you pierce them with a knife. The exact time will depend on how ripe the pears are.

5. Use a small spoon to remove the spices, then serve the pears with the syrup spooned over.

VARIATION
If you don't have a selection of whole spices, use $1/2$ teaspoon ground mixed spice or ground cinnamon.

Yoghurt Mousse with Oranges

MAKES **2 SERVINGS**
PREP TIME: **ABOUT 15 MINUTES, PLUS AT LEAST 3 HOURS CHILLING / NO COOKING**

1 orange
5 green cardamom pods
1 medium free-range egg
2 tablespoons soft light-brown sugar
100 g Greek-style yoghurt
Piece of milk or dark chocolate, to serve

1. Finely grate the orange rind into a bowl. To segment the orange, work over the bowl to catch the juices. Use a small knife to cut off both ends and the peel and white pith underneath, which is very bitter. (A small serrated knife is best for this, but an ordinary knife will be fine.) Hold the orange in one cupped hand and slide the knife down one side of a segment, separating it from the membrane. Next, slide the knife down the other side of the segment, to release it from the other membrane. Let the segment drop into the bowl. Continue until all the segments have been removed.

2. Use the back of a wooden spoon to crush the cardamom pods, then remove the seeds. Add the seeds to the oranges.

3. Crack the egg and separate the white from the yolk, letting the white drop into a clean bowl. Put the yolk in a smaller bowl. Using a whisk or an electric hand-held mixer beat the egg white until it turns white and soft peaks begin to form. Add one-quarter of the sugar and continue beating until it is incorporated. Continue adding the sugar and beating until it is incorporated and the egg whites form still peaks when you lift the beaters.

4. Beat the egg yolk and yoghurt together. Spoon this mixture into the bowl with the stiff egg whites. Use a large metal spoon or rubber spatula to fold the two mixtures together, by lifting from the bottom of the bowl. Do not beat the mixtures or you will knock out all the air in the egg white.

5. Lightly stir in the orange segments and cardamom seeds. Spoon into bowls and leave to set for at least 3 hours in the fridge. When you're ready to serve, grate a little chocolate over the tops. (See note about uncooked eggs on page 42.)

Cook's Tip

The egg whites are stiff enough in Step 3 when you can hold the bowl upside down and they don't fall out.

Best Ever Lemon Ice Cream

MAKES **2–3 SERVINGS**
PREP TIME: **ABOUT 10 MINUTES**
NO COOKING

IF YOU'VE GOT AN ICE COMPARTMENT IN YOUR FRIDGE YOU CAN MAKE THIS LUSCIOUS
ICE CREAM. IT DOESN'T REQUIRE ANY FANCY EQUIPMENT OR THE REGULAR BEATING LIKE
TRADITIONAL ICE CREAM DOES. AND YOUR REWARD FOR THE EFFORT WILL BE AS GOOD
AS A PREMIUM BLEND AT A FRACTION OF THE COST.

1 lemon
70 g caster sugar
150 ml double cream

1. Finely grate the lemon rind into a bowl. Use your hand to roll the
lemon back and forth on the countertop, pressing down firmly. Cut
the lemon in half and squeeze out the juice. If you don't have a lemon
squeezer, squeeze each half with your hand and use a small knife
to pick out the seeds.

2. Add the lemon rind and sugar to the bowl and stir until the sugar
dissolves and the syrup becomes clear. Stir in the cream.

3. Spoon the lemon mixture into a freezerproof bowl. Cover with
kitchen foil and place in the ice compartment and leave for several
hours until frozen.

VARIATIONS
► For slightly fewer calories, replace the cream with Greek-style yoghurt.
► This recipe can be doubled or tripled as long as you keep the
proportions the same.

Mango Kulfi

MAKES **4–6 SERVINGS**
PREP TIME: **ABOUT 15 MINUTES, PLUS FREEZING**
COOKING TIME: **15–20 MINUTES**

TRY THIS RICH INDIAN ICE CREAM WHEN YOU'VE COOKED AN INDIAN MEAL. YOU MIGHT
JUST HAVE FRIENDS RINGING YOU, RATHER THAN THE LOCAL INDIAN RESTAURANT,
WHEN THEY WANT A TAKE-AWAY.

4 large free-range eggs
75 g caster sugar
450 ml milk
$1/2$ teaspoon vanilla essence
1 can (425 g) mangoes in light syrup
2 tablespoons lime juice

1. Separate the eggs and put the yolks in a large bowl with the sugar.
Beat together until the yolks become thick and creamy. An electric mixer
is the easiest to use, but you can still beat with a wooden spoon.

2. Stir in the milk and vanilla. Position a sieve over a saucepan, then
strain the egg mixture into it. Put the mixture over a low heat and simmer,
stirring constantly, until it becomes thick enough to coat the back of a
spoon. If you run your finger across the spoon, the mark should remain.
Transfer the custard to a bowl and set aside to cool for at least 1 hour.

3. Meanwhile, drain the mangoes. Put them in a blender and blitz until
puréed. Stir the mango purée into the cool custard. Pour into a shallow
freezerproof container and put in the ice compartment for about 2 $1/2$
hours until it is still mushy.

4. Tip the mango mixture into a bowl and use a fork to beat it. Return
it to the freezer for at least 4 hours. Remove it from the freezer about
20 minutes before serving.

Plan Ahead
If you want to make this for a dinner party, it can be made up to 10 days
in advance.

Jumbo Fruit & Nut Biscuits

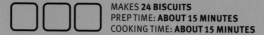

MAKES **24 BISCUITS**
PREP TIME: **ABOUT 15 MINUTES**
COOKING TIME: **ABOUT 15 MINUTES**

TRY THESE WHEN YOU'RE MISSING MUM'S BAKING. IF YOU AND YOUR FLATMATES DON'T DEVOUR THESE IN ONE SITTING, THEY WILL KEEP FOR UP TO 4 DAYS IN AN AIR-TIGHT CONTAINER. PUT ONE OR TWO IN YOUR BACKPACK AS YOU SET OFF FOR THE DAY.

175 g rolled oats
140 g plain wholemeal or white flour
2 teaspoons ground cinnamon
Pinch of salt
1 teaspoon baking powder
175 g butter, at room temperature
175 g caster sugar
175 g soft light-brown sugar
2 large free-range eggs
150 g coarsely chopped walnuts
150 g raisins

1. Heat the oven to 180°C/350°F/Gas 4. Lightly grease 2 or 3 baking sheets. If you only have 1 baking sheet, bake the biscuits in batches.

2. Put the oats in a blender and blitz until a fine powder forms. Sift the oats, flour, cinnamon and salt into a large bowl, tipping in any bran left in the sieve, if you have used wholemeal flour.

3. Beat the butter and both sugars together until soft and well blended. Crack the egg on the side of the bowl and beat until it is incorporated. Add the remaining egg and beat it in. A hand-held electric mixer makes this easy, but you can do it with a wooden spoon – it will just take longer.

4. Add the sifted dry ingredients and keep beating until incorporated. Place 24 heated tablespoons of the biscuit dough on the baking sheets. Leave plenty of space between each biscuit, because these spread to about 10 cm across while they bake.

5. Use the back of a wet wooden spoon to lightly press each biscuit. Bake the biscuits for 15 minutes or until light brown. Leave the biscuits to stand on the baking sheet for 5 minutes, then use a palette knife or fish slice to put them on a wire rack to finish cooling.

No-bake Boozy Chocolate Balls

☐ ☐ ☐ MAKES **ABOUT 20**
PREP TIME: **ABOUT 20 MINUTES**
NO COOKING

THE HARDEST CHALLENGE WHEN MAKING THESE IS NOT EATING THEM FOR AT LEAST
THREE DAYS – AND EVEN BETTER IF YOU CAN LEAVE THEM FOR AT LEAST TWO WEEKS!

150 g all-butter shortbread
85 g walnuts
55 g icing sugar, plus more for dusting
1 ^{1}/$_2$ tablespoons cocoa powder
2 tablespoons corn syrup
About 1 ^{1}/$_2$ tablespoons brandy, whiskey or bourbon, or whatever small
    amounts of booze you have in the bottom of bottles

1. Put the shortbread in a blender and blitz until fine crumbs form;
tip the crumbs into a bowl.

2. Add the walnuts to the blender and give a quick blitz to finely chop,
but do not turn to a powder. Add the nuts to the shortbread crumbs,
then stir in the icing sugar and cocoa powder.

3. Put the golden syrup in a small bowl with 1 tablespoon of the booze
and stir together until the syrup dissolves. Add it to the bowl and stir all
the ingredients together until a thick, grainy paste forms. If the mixture
doesn't come together, sprinkle over a little extra booze and stir again.

4. Using your hands, roll and press the mixture into about 20 smooth
balls, slightly smaller than walnuts in the shell. Put the chocolate balls
on a plate and sift over icing sugar to cover all over. Put the balls in an air-
tight container and leave for at least 3 days for the flavours to develop.
But the longer you leave them the better they will be.

Cook's Tip
If you don't have a blender, break up the shortbread, put it in a thick
plastic bag and use a rolling pin or the bottom of a heavy pan to crush
until fine crumbs form.

Spiced Noodle & Fruit Pudding

SERVES 4–6
PREP TIME: **ABOUT 15 MINUTES**
COOKING TIME: **40–50 MINUTES**

PASTA FOR DESSERT? IT MIGHT SEEM LIKE AN USUAL IDEA, BUT THIS MIDDLE EASTERN DESSERT IS REAL COMFORT FOOD. TRY THIS WHEN IT IS YOUR TURN TO COOK FOR YOUR FLATMATES.

450 ml milk
125 g dried tagliatelle or other noodle
1 lemon
1 orange
2 apples
2 large free-range eggs
³/₄ teaspoon ground mixed spice
4 tablespoons caster sugar
45 g ready-to-eat dried cherries
3 tablespoons raisins or sultanas
¹/₄ teaspoon salt
30 g butter, plus a little extra for the dish
Freshly grated nutmeg (optional)

1. Rinse a saucepan with water. Add the milk to the pan and bring to the boil over a medium-high heat. Add the noodles and cook for 15 minutes, or until the noodles are just tender and most of the liquid is absorbed.

2. Meanwhile, heat the oven to 180°C/350°F/Gas 4. Lightly grease a 900-ml ovenproof dish. Finely grate the orange and lemon rinds. Cut the apples into quarters, remove the cores, then chop into small pieces. Toss with a little of the lemon juice to prevent them from browning.

3. Break the eggs into a large bowl and beat together. Beat in the orange and lemon rinds, ground mixed spice and sugar. Add the apples, cherries, raisins or sultanas and salt.

4. Just before all the milk is absorbed by the pasta, add the butter to the pasta and leave it to melt.

5. Add the noodles to the bowl with the egg mixture. Stir together, taking care to distribute the fruit. Spoon into the greased dish and spread out evenly. Grate a little nutmeg over the surface, if you like.

6. Place the pudding in the oven and bake for 40–50 minutes until the top is set and a knife inserted in the middle comes out clean. Remove the pudding from the oven and leave to stand for 10 minutes before serving. This is equally good hot or at room temperature.

Indian Vermicelli Pudding

MAKES **2–3 SERVINGS**
PREP TIME: **ABOUT 5 MINUTES**
COOKING TIME: **35–40 MINUTES**

600 ml milk
1 tablespoon blanched almonds
40 g vermicelli or angel hair pasta
About 20 g butter
1 green cardamom pod
1 tablespoon golden raisins
About 60 g sugar

1. Rinse the widest saucepan you have with water. Add the milk and bring to the boil. Reduce the heat to low and leave the milk to simmer for about 25 minutes until it thickens and just starts to turn pale brown. Stir often to prevent it catching on the base.

2. Meanwhile, coarsely chop the nuts, and break the pasta into short pieces.

3. Melt the butter in a small saucepan over a medium heat. Add the nuts, cardamom and raisins, and stir around. Use a spoon to transfer the solid ingredients to the milk.

4. Add the vermicelli to the butter remaining in the pan and stir it around until it just starts to brown. Immediately tip it into the milk and add sugar to taste.

5. Bring the milk to the boil, then reduce the heat and leave it to simmer for about 5 minutes until the pasta is cooked. Eat at once or leave to cool completely and chill for up to a day.

Chocolate Slices with Cherries

MAKES **8 SLICES** / PREP TIME: **ABOUT 15 MINUTES, PLUS COOLING** / COOKING TIME: **1 HOUR, PLUS AN EXTRA 30 MINUTES IN THE OVEN**

150 g butter, at room temperature
150 g caster sugar
4 large free-range eggs
225 g drinking chocolate
75 g self-raising flour

FOR THE FILLING
1 can (400 g) cherries in light syrup
115 g fromage frais
40 g ground almonds
1 tablespoon caster sugar
1/4 teaspoon almond extract
Lemon juice

1. Bring a kettle of water to the boil. Heat the oven to 140°C/275°F/Gas 1. Fill a roasting tin with hot water and place it on the bottom shelf of the oven as it heats. Line the base and sides of a 30 x 20-cm Swiss roll tin with greaseproof paper.

2. Put the butter and sugar in a bowl and beat until pale and fluffy. Break the eggs into the bowl, one at a time, and continue beating until they are incorporated.

3. Add the drinking chocolate and flour and use a wooden spoon to stir all the ingredients together.

4. Pour the chocolate mixture into the prepared tin and smooth the surface. Put the tin in the oven and bake for 1 hour. Turn off the oven and leave the cake in the oven without opening the door for 30 minutes.

5. Remove the pan from the oven and invert the cake on to a wire rack. Peel off the lining paper and leave the cake to cool.

6. Meanwhile, make the filling. Tip the cherries into a strainer in the sink and leave them to drain, then stone and chop. Put the fromage frais, ground almonds, sugar and almond extract in a bowl, and beat together. Stir in the cherries.

7. Cut cake half into two 20 x 15-cm pieces. Place one piece on a plate. Spread the filling over the cake. Top with the second piece. Use a serrated knife to cut into 8 pieces.

Crêpes Suzette

MAKES **8**
PREP TIME: **ABOUT 5 MINUTES, PLUS MAKING THE CRÊPES**
COOKING TIME: **ABOUT 10 MINUTES**

THE ULTIMATE DINNER-PARTY DESSERT! WHEN YOU ARE OUT TO IMPRESS, THIS IS THE ONE
TO CHOOSE. HOWEVER, YOU HAVE TO BE SOBER WHEN IT COMES TO FLAMING THE CRÊPES,
OTHERWISE THE EVENING'S CLIMAX COULD BE A DISASTER. SO DO NOT ATTEMPT TO FLAME
THE CRÊPES IF YOU HAVE OVERINDULGED IN WINE DURING THE MEAL.

8 Sweet Pancakes (page 191)
1 large orange
90 g unsalted butter, diced
90 g caster sugar
90 ml orange-flavoured liqueur

1. The crêpes can be made earlier in the day and refrigerated with pieces
of greaseproof paper between each, or made several weeks in advance
and frozen. Finely grate the rind from the orange, then squeeze the juice
and set both aside separately.

2. Put the butter and sugar in a large frying pan, ideally with a long
handle, over a medium-high heat and stir until they both melt and form
a syrupy liquid. Stir in $^1/_3$ of the liqueur and the orange juice, and stir
around.

3. Fold the crêpes into triangle shapes and put them into the pan,
overlapping if necessary. Spoon the syrup over the crêpes.

4. Heat the remaining liqueur in a long-handled ladle over a gas
flame until it bursts into flame. Pour the liqueur over the crêpes and
immediately take the frying pan to the table. Let the flames die down,
then serve the crêpes with the orange sauce spooned over.

Plan Ahead
As well as making the crêpes in advance, you can prepare the dish
through to Step 3 a couple of hours in advance. Reheat the syrup
before you flame the liqueur.

Fruit & Cheese

Cheese can be served as dessert in place of a sweet dish. A cheese board can be as simple as one wedge of farmhouse mature vegetarian Cheddar cheese for mid-week supper, or a selection of vegetarian cheeses for a dinner party. Crisp celery sticks and juicy grapes are often served with cheese.

Another option is to serve fruit with a wedge of cheese. Here are some classic combinations using vegetarian cheeses:
- Apple with Cheddar
- Figs with ricotta – splash with a little rosewater
- Raisins, sultanas and/or currants with Lancastershire cheese
- Pear with Stilton or pecorino – add a few walnuts or pecans
- Or try pecorino-style cheese with a little honey drizzled over

COOKING WHEN U R BROKE

When the budget is shot, the bank balance is low and you can't go home to be fed for a couple of weeks yet, go back to basics. Start by using up everything fresh in the kitchen, then go to the back of the cupboard shelves and see what bags or cans have been forgotten since the beginning of term. As long as the cans don't have dents, they should be fine, but check the 'use by' dates. You might feel like you are metamorphosing into your parents, but plan your menus and shopping lists in advance. Make every penny count.

Head to the shops and stock up on bags of dried pasta and cans of tomatoes, baked beans and all sorts of pulses and veg. Can Cuisine (page 209) can get you through the lean times.

During most of the term the savings you make by soaking dried pulses doesn't compensate for the time, but when desperation hits stock up on dried beans and peas. Follow the soaking and cooking instructions on the packets and you'll have the foundation of several meals for very little money. (Just remember, adzuki, black-eyed, borlotti, kidney and soya beans require 10 minutes brisk boiling before simmering.)

A big pot of soup will last for several meals – and give you comfort when you're feeling sorry for yourself. There are several unusual ideas in this chapter, or try the recipes on pages 163–170.

This is definitely not the time for expensive ready-meals or take-aways. The money you will spend on getting a pizza delivered will be enough to feed you for a couple of days. The more effort you put into cooking and shopping, the more money you will have left for going out.

And forget about asparagus in December – local seasonal produce is the best buy. Don't forget fresh fruit either. There might just be words of wisdom in the old saying, 'an apple a day keeps the doctor away'. There are mega-bites of nutrition in apples and other fruit.

Other recipes for cheap eats:
- Curried Veg & Semolina (page 144)
- Fried-Egg Sandwich (page 41), or have an egg on toast
- Egg-fried Rice & Veg (page 135) – use any veg you have in the fridge
- Golden Lentils & Rice (page 134)
- Jacket Potatoes (page 94)
- Red Lentil Dahl (page 148)

There's More to a Can of Baked Beans Than Just Toast

Baked beans on toast is fine – it's a good, cheap source of protein – but you'll be very bored after a couple of meals, and your flatmates won't be happy either. You don't need a recipe for beans on toast, but try these ideas for variety:

► Baked Bean Stew: Empty the can of beans into a saucepan, along with a can of chopped tomatoes. Add hot-pepper sauce and mustard to taste, and bring to the boil, stirring until the mixture thickens. Spoon it over wholemeal rice or boiled new potatoes . . . or, of course, a couple of slices of wholemeal toast.

► Baked Bean Soup: Tip the beans into a saucepan, then add 2 canfuls of Vegetable Stock (page 164) or water and slowly bring to the boil. Add salt and pepper to taste. Eat with Tomato Bread (page 52) or Garlic Bread (page 51).

► Curried Baked Beans: Chop an onion and crush a garlic clove, then fry in 1 tablespoon sunflower or groundnut oil for 3–5 minutes until soft. Stir in $1/2$ tablespoon curry paste and stir for 2 minutes longer. Stir in the baked beans and simmer until hot. Spoon over rice (page 131) or a Jacket Potato (page 94).

► Smashed Bean Quesadillas: Fry 2 crushed garlic cloves in $1/2$ tablespoon olive oil in a saucepan. Add a chopped green or red pepper, if you have one, and fry for 5 minutes until soft. Add baked beans and leave to bubble until most of the liquid evaporates. Add salt and pepper and cayenne pepper to taste. (If you have any sweetcorn kernels, stir them in now.) Use a potato masher to smash the beans. Put a soft flour tortilla in a large frying pan without any oil. Spread the beans over half the tortilla, then fold over the other half. Leave to cook for about 1 minute until the tortilla is crisp, then flip the whole package over and continue toasting until the other side is crisp. Make as many as you like. Any leftover beans can be spooned over a Jacket Potato (page 94).

Can Cuisine

As long as you've got a can of pulses in the cupboard you can still
eat well.

▸ Chickpea Salad: Toss a drained can of chickpeas with chopped grilled
red pepper (page 93), soaked bulgar wheat (page XX), diced de-seeded
cucumber and chopped rocket leaves. Squeeze over half a lemon and
drizzle with olive oil. Add chilli flakes, if you like.

▸ Beans & Rice: Rinse a tin of kidney beans and reheat them with a
bowl of rice (page 131). If you have any parsley and/or chopped celery,
spoon those in.

▸ Refried Beans: Fry a chopped onion, crushed garlic clove and sliced
green chilli until soft in a large frying pan. Drain and rinse a can of kidney
beans, then use a potato masher to mash the beans. Add the beans
to the onion with 150 ml water, and stir together. Cook, uncovered, for
about 10 minutes until most of the liquid evaporates. Season. Roll up
in a soft flour tortilla, or grate vegetarian Cheddar cheese over the top
and eat with rice (page 131).

▸ Corn Fritters: Mix 75 g plain flour with a pinch of salt. Slowly stir in
6 tablespoons of water and 1 tablespoon sunflower oil, beating until
smooth. Put an egg white in a bowl and whisk until it becomes stiff, then
stir it into the batter. Add salt and pepper and any flavourings you have –
dried herbs, chilli flakes, fresh herbs or finely chopped garlic. Drain a can
(200 g sweetcorn kernels and stir them into the batter. Heat a thin layer
of oil in a large frying pan, ideally non-stick, and drop in spoonfuls of
the batter. Fry until golden and set, then flip over.

▸ Cabbage & Bean Soup: Fry a chopped onion and garlic clove. Add a can
of chopped tomatoes, a pinch of sugar and 2 cans of water in a saucepan
and bring to the boil, then lower the heat and simmer for 20 minutes,
using a wooden spoon to break down the tomatoes. Add finely shredded
Savoy cabbage and a rinsed can of cannellini or butter beans, and
simmer for 5 minutes until the cabbage is tender. Season to taste.

▸ Marmite Broth: Yes, it comes from a jar, not a can, but you get the idea.
You'll either love this or hate it. Put a spoonful of Marmite in a mug.
Add grated carrot or radish, or diced cooked potatoes, then pour
in boiling water, stirring until the Marmite dissolves.

Spanish Tortilla

MAKES **4–6 SERVINGS**
PREP TIME: **ABOUT 5 MINUTES, PLUS 10 MINUTE STANDING**
COOKING TIME: **ABOUT 30 MINUTES**

THERE ISN'T ANY PRETENDING THAT THIS IS QUICK COOKING, AND IT DOES DEMAND YOUR ATTENTION FOR JUST ABOUT THE WHOLE 35 MINUTES, BUT YOU CAN'T EAT MUCH BETTER FOR LESS. AND IF YOU EVEN CAN'T AFFORD AN ONION, THIS IS JUST AS SATISFYING WITH JUST A POTATO FOR THE fiLLING. ONCE YOU HAVE A TORTILLA IN THE FRIDGE YOU ARE SET UP FOR SOMETHING TO EAT AT JUST ABOUT ANY TIME OF THE DAY, EVEN BREAKFAST – IT TASTES EQUALLY GOOD COLD OR HOT, SO YOU CAN GRAB A SLICE AS YOU RUN OUT THE DOOR. (AT OTHER TIMES, WHEN YOU STILL HAVE MONEY FOR LONG PUB SESSIONS, A PIECE OF TORTILLA IS EQUALLY GOOD WHEN YOU STAGGER HOME LATE. IT SOAKS UP THE ALCOHOL QUICKLY.)

TORTILLA MAKES A GOOD SNACK – SPANIARDS SERVE IT IN SMALL WEDGES FOR TAPAS – BUT IT BECOMES A fiLLING MEAL WITH CHUNKY BREAD AND A LIGHTLY DRESSED TOSSED SALAD.

A HEAVY-BASED NON-STICK FRYING PAN REALLY MAKES EASY WORK OF THIS, BUT AN ORDINARY PAN WILL ALSO WORK, JUST REMEMBER TO HEAT IT WELL BEFORE ADDING THE OIL TO PREVENT THE INGREDIENTS STICKING.

200 g waxy potatoes
$^1/_2$ onion
1 garlic clove
$^1/_2$ red, green, yellow or orange pepper
Up to 125 ml olive oil
4 large free-range eggs
Salt and pepper

1. Scrub or peel the potatoes and cut them into thin slices. Peel and thinly slice the onion. Peel and crush the garlic. Remove the pepper core and seeds and cut the flesh into strips.

2. Heat a 20-cm frying pan, ideally non-stick, over a high heat. Add 3 tablespoons olive oil until you can feel the heat rising, then swirl it around the pan so it coats the sides as well as the base.

3. Reduce the heat to low, add the potatoes, onion, garlic and pepper, and fry, stirring occasionally, for 15–20 minutes until the potatoes are soft.

4. Meanwhile, crack the eggs into a bowl large enough to hold all the vegetables and beat them together with a fork. Season generously with salt and pepper; set aside.

5. Set a sieve over a large bowl and strain the potatoes, onion and pepper, reserving the oil that drips through the sieve. Stir the vegetables into the eggs and very gently stir together, taking care not to break up the potatoes.

6. Use a wooden spoon to remove any crusty bits that have stuck to the base of the pan. Reheat the pan over a medium-high heat. Add 4 tablespoons of oil and swirl it around to coat the sides again. Add the vegetable-egg mixture and spread out the vegetables into a single layer.

7. Cook for 7–10 minutes, shaking the pan back and forth occasionally, until the base of the tortilla is set and golden. Use a palette knife or round-bladed knife to loosen the side of the tortilla.

8. Cover the pan with a large plate and invert the tortilla on to it. Carefully slide the tortilla back into the pan. Use the palette knife to 'tuck in' the edge, then continue cooking until the base is golden and set.

9. Leave the tortilla to stand for 5 minutes before cutting into wedges and serving straight from the pan.

Pasta Soup

MAKES **2 SERVINGS**
PREP TIME: **ABOUT 5 MINUTES**
COOKING TIME: **10 MINUTES**

ITALIANS SERVE THIS AS A fiRST COURSE OF A HEAVY MEAL, BUT IT WILL fiLL YOU UP CHEAPLY. AND IF YOU'VE GOT SOME ALMOST-TOO-DRY BREAD IN THE BREAD BIN, MAKE SOME GARLIC BREAD (PAGE 51).

450 ml vegetable stock, home-made (page 164) or from a cube
200 g small dried pasta shapes
Salt and pepper
Vegetarian Parmesan-style cheese (optional)

1. Bring the stock and a pinch of salt to the boil in a saucepan over a high heat. Add the pasta shapes and continue boiling for 10 minutes, or according to the packet instructions, until the pasta is al dente.

2. Add salt and pepper to taste. Ladle the soup into a bowl and grate over cheese, if you have any.

Peanut Butter Soup

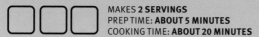

MAKES **2 SERVINGS**
PREP TIME: **ABOUT 5 MINUTES**
COOKING TIME: **ABOUT 20 MINUTES**

IT MIGHT SOUND LIKE A TRULY DESPERATE SITUATION TO BE MAKING SOUP OUT OF PEANUT
BUTTER, BUT THIS IS DELICIOUS. IN FACT, IT'S GOOD ENOUGH TO SERVE TO FRIENDS.
AND WHAT'S MORE, IF YOU EAT IT WITH SOME CHUNKY BREAD IT WILL fiLL YOU UP.

1 celery stick
1 small onion
1 tablespoon sunflower or rapeseed oil
2 teaspoons plain white or wholemeal flour
450 ml vegetable stock, home-made (page 164) or from a cube –
    or water if things really are desperate
125 g crunchy peanut butter
Pinch of cayenne pepper (optional)
Single cream (optional)
Salt

1. Cut the leaves from the celery stick and set aside. Finely chop the
celery stick. Peel and chop the onion.

2. Heat the oil in a saucepan over a medium-high heat. Add the celery
and onion and stir for 3–5 minutes until the onion is soft, but not brown.

3. Stir in the flour and reduce the heat to low. Stir the flour for a minute
or two to remove the raw flavour.

4. Add the stock and peanut butter, and stir together. Increase the heat
to high and bring the soup to the boil. Reduce the heat, partially cover
the pan and leave to simmer for 10 minutes.

5. Season to taste with cayenne, if you have any, and salt and pepper
to taste. If your budget runs to a small pot of cream, stir a little in.
Finely chop the reserved celery leaves and sprinkle them over the top,
if you like.

Oatmeal Broth

MAKES **2 SERVINGS**
PREP TIME: **ABOUT 5 MINUTES**
COOKING TIME: **ABOUT 20 MINUTES**

STICK-TO-YOUR-RIB ENERGY FOR PENNIES.

1 onion
1 tablespoon sunflower or rapeseed oil
1 $^1/_2$ tablespoons medium pin-head oatmeal
300 ml vegetable stock, home-made (page 164) or from a cube, or water
300 ml milk
Salt and pepper

1. Peel and chop the onion. Heat the oil in a saucepan over a medium-high heat. Add the onion and stir for 3 minutes. Add the oatmeal and continue stirring for 2 minutes or until the onion is soft and the oatmeal is toasted.

2. Add the stock and bring to the boil, stirring. Reduce the heat to low, cover the pan and leave to simmer for 30 minutes, until the oatmeal is tender.

3. Pour the soup into a blender and blitz. Return the soup to the saucepan and stir in the milk. Heat until just below boiling, then season with salt and pepper to taste.

VARIATION

If you have any cooked veggies in the fridge, finely chop them and add them in Step 3. If you have any uncooked carrots, leeks, parsnip, swede or turnips, peel and cut them into fine dice and add them in Step 2.

PARTY TIME

Nobody would believe you if you even attempted to claim student life is all work and no play. Everyone knows student days are a balancing act between work and play, and sometimes the balance tips in favour of play.

Of course, it's easy to open a few bottles of beer or wine, but occasionally you're likely to hear the call of the cocktail shaker. So don't fight it – get shaking. Instead of binging down at the pub, set up a cocktail bar at home and invite your friends round – move over Tom Cruise!

You don't need to go out and buy new glasses, and you don't need a degree in mixology. Just get a bottle of your favourite spirit, mixers and lots of ice, and start shaking. The sound of a cocktail shaker lifts the spirit, but if you don't have one, improvise with a glass jug and give all the ingredients a good stir. Pro bartenders use special measures called jiggers (1 ¹/₂ oz) and ponies (1 oz), but you can use tablespoons – two tablespoons equal one ounce. And there's a good reason why bartenders use measures. The drinks actually taste better when the flavours are blended in proportion.

When you're having a big party, mix big jugs of everything before the party starts. That way you can avoid a long line of people waiting for a drink. And make sure you have lots of nibbles so nobody drinks on an empty stomach.

And for anyone who doesn't want to overindulge, there are a selection of mocktails at the end of the chapter. Cheers!

You could just put out bowls of crisps, or you could try:
- Babaganoush (page 177)
- Beer & Cheese Dip (page 174)
- Garlic Bread (page 51)
- Lettuce Rolls (page 62) – let everyone assemble and roll their own
- Hummus (page 175) with lots of veggies
- Pita Crisps (page 179)
- Roast Vegetable Crisps (page 152)
- Spiced Nuts & Seeds (page 57)
- Tandoori Paneer (page 55)
- Tomato Bread (page 52)

More substantial food that acts like blotting paper (without breaking the bank):
- Artichoke & Pepper Frittata (page 70)
- Baked Jacket Potatoes (page 94)
- Baked Macaroni & 4 Cheeses (page 113)
- Chilli sin Carne (page 160)
- Cheese & Leek Quiche (page 161) – or a couple quiches
- Spanokopitta (page 186)

VODKA

Bloody Mary

THE ULTIMATE 'HAIR OF THE DOG' FOR THE MORNING AFTER, BUT JOLLY GOOD, TOO, WHEN YOU AREN'T HUNG OVER. ESSENTIAL FOR WEEKEND BRUNCHES.

MAKES 1 COCKTAIL
1 tall glass of tomato juice
2 oz vodka
1 teaspoon lemon juice
Salt and pepper
Hot-pepper sauce

Pour the tomato juice into a tall glass over ice. Add the vodka, lemon juice, salt and pepper and hot-pepper sauce to taste. Give the drink a good stir. Add a celery stick, if you like.

Black Russian

A WINTER WARMER.
MAKES 1 COCKTAIL
1 $^1/_2$ oz vodka
$^1/_2$ oz Kahlúa

Put both ingredients into a cocktail shaker with ice cubes, and shake. Strain into a cocktail glass.

Moscow Mule

MAKES 1 COCKTAIL
2 oz vodka
Juice of $^1/_2$ lime
Ginger beer

Pour the vodka over ice in a tall glass, then squeeze in the lime juice. Top up with ginger beer and stir.

Sea Breeze

WHEN EXAMS ARE OVER, THIS WILL HIT THE SPOT. MULTIPLY THE QUANTITIES
AND USE FOR ALL SUMMER PARTIES.
MAKES **1 COCKTAIL**
2 oz cranberry juice
1 oz vodka
1 oz grapefruit juice

Put all ingredients in a cocktail shaker with ice, and shake.
Strain into a cocktail glass. Add a lime slice, if you like.

Cape Codder

MAKES **1 COCKTAIL**
150 ml cranberry juice
1 $^1/_2$ oz vodka

Put the cranberry juice in a tall glass with ice. Pour in the vodka
and give the drink a good stir. Add a lime slice, if you like.

WHISKY

Rob Roy

A TASTE OF WILD SCOTLAND.
MAKES **1 COCKTAIL**
1 $^1/_2$ oz whisky
$^1/_2$ oz sweet vermouth

Stir the whisky and vermouth around with ice, then strain into a glass.

BRANDY

Between the Sheets

WHO KNOWS WHERE YOU WILL END UP AFTER A COUPLE OF THESE!
MAKES **2 COCKTAILS** – WELL, YOU DON'T WANT TO END UP BETWEEN
THE SHEETS BY YOURSELF, DO YOU?

2 oz brandy
2 oz Cointreau, or other orange-flavoured liqueur
2 oz white rum
2 oz lime juice

Put all the ingredients into a cocktail shaker with cracked ice, and shake. Strain into a cocktail glass. If you're really in bartending mode, add a lemon twist to each glass.

GIN

Gin Fizz

MAKES **1 COCKTAIL**
2 oz gin
2 tablespoons lemon juice
1 teaspoon icing sugar
Soda water

Put the gin, lemon juice and icing sugar in a cocktail shaker with ice, and shake. Strain over ice cubes in a glass and top up with soda water.

RUM

Blue Hawaiian

DRINK LOTS OF WATER BEFORE YOU GO TO BED AFTER THESE, OR YOU'LL
FEEL BLUE AROUND THE GILLS IN THE MORNING. (TAKE A LOOK AT POSSIBLE
HANGOVER CURES ON PAGE 30.)
MAKES **1 COCKTAIL**
2 oz Bacardi
1 oz pineapple juice
$^1/_2$ oz blue curaçao
1 teaspoon coconut cream

Put all the ingredients into a cocktail shaker with cracked ice, and shake.
Strain into a cocktail glass.

TEQUILA

Brave Bull

JUST BE CAREFUL NOT TO ACT LIKE A BULL IN A CHINA SHOP AFTER A COUPLE OF THESE.
MAKES **1 COCKTAIL**
1 $^1/_2$ oz Kahlúa or Tia Maria
1 oz tequila

Stir the ingredients together in a short glass, then add ice cubes.

Eldorado

WITH THE FRUIT JUICE AND HONEY YOU COULD ALMOST BE EXCUSED FOR THINKING OF
THIS AS A HEALTH DRINK. BUT IT ISN'T – THIS DOES NOT COUNT TOWARDS THE 5-A-DAY!
MAKES **1 COCKTAIL**
2 oz tequila
1 tablespoon honey
1 $^1/_2$ oz lemon juice
1 orange slice

Put all the ingredients into a cocktail shaker with cracked ice, and shake.
Strain into a tall glass.

Icebreaker

MAKES **1 COCKTAIL** – JUST MULTIPLY UP SO EVERYBODY CAN TOAST
NEW FRIENDSHIPS AT ONCE.
JUST WHAT YOU NEED FOR MEETING THE PEOPLE IN THE NEXT-DOOR FLAT OR HOUSE
AT BEGINNING OF TERM. MIGHT AS WELL START THE WAY YOU INTEND TO GO ON.

2 oz tequila
2 oz grapefruit juice
1 tablespoon grenadine
2 teaspoons Cointreau, or other orange-flavoured liqueur
Crushed ice

Put everything in a blender and blitz for 10–15 seconds. Strain into
a glass and chat to the person standing next to you.

WINE DRINKS

Kir

IF YOU WANT TO BE AUTHENTIC, LOOK FOR WHITE ALIGOTÉ WINE FROM BURGUNDY
FOR THIS, OTHERWISE CHOOSE A DRY WHITE.
MAKES **1 COCKTAIL**

1 glass white wine
Splash of crème de cassis

Pour the crème de cassis into the white wine and stir. Add a twist
of lemon, if you like.
‣ Kir Royale: Use sparking wine.

Champagne Cocktail

THIS IS FOR A REAL CELEBRATION – DID ANYONE MENTION A 2.1?
MAKES **1 COCKTAIL**

1 small sugar cube
2 dashes of bitters
Chilled champagne or sparkling wine

Sprinkle the sugar with the bitters in the bottom of a champagne flute,
then top up with champagne or sparking wine.

MOCKTAILS

These are the drinks for the drivers. And believe it or not, there are some people who prefer not to overindulge.

Safe Sex on the Beach

BETTER SAFE THAN SORRY . . . MAKES **1 COCKTAIL**
125 ml cranberry juice
125 ml pineapple juice
Soda water

Pour the cranberry and pineapple juices together into a glass with ice cubes, then top up with soda water. Give it a good stir . . . you just have to add an umbrella, don't you think?

Chocolate Orgasm

A REAL SEDUCTION FOR CHOCOHOLICS. MAYBE THE ONE THING BETTER THAN CHOCOLATE!
MAKES **1 COCKTAIL**

125 g vanilla ice cream
125 ml milk
1 tablespoon chocolate syrup
Crushed peppermint sweet or grated dark chocolate

Put all the ingredients in a blender and blitz. Pour into a glass and sprinkle peppermint sweet or chocolate over the top.

Cinderella

AT LEAST WITH THIS MOCKTAIL, YOU'LL BE SOBER ENOUGH TO KNOW
IF YOU'RE KISSING A FROG.
MAKES **1 COCKTAIL**
100 ml orange juice
100 ml pineapple juice
Dash of grenadine syrup
Soda water

Pour the cranberry and pineapple juices and grenadine syrup together into a glass with ice cubes, then top up with soda water. Give it a good stir.

Virgin Mary

MAY BE ONE FOR THE MORNING AFTER A FEW TOO MANY COCKTAILS!
MAKES **1 COCKTAIL**
225 ml tomato juice
2 teaspoons lemon juice
Salt and pepper – try celery salt
Hot-pepper sauce

Pour the tomato juice into a tall glass with lots of ice. Stir in the lemon juice, then add more lemon juice and salt and pepper to taste. Add hot-pepper sauce to taste, and stir with a stick of celery.

Shirley Temple

MAKES **1 COCKTAIL**
1 dash of grenadine
Ginger ale

Add the grenadine to a glass filled with ice cubes, then top up with ginger ale and stir.

INDEX